Journey To
A Dream

Craig Briggs

For Dad – Donald Briggs
(1932 – 2007)

And for my wife, Melanie.
Without whose patience,
tolerance, help and support,
this endeavour would not
have been possible.

CONTENTS

Acknowledgments

Special thanks go to Peter Hinchliffe of
openwriting.com for his encouragement,
guidance, and mentoring; and to Elizabeth 'Mitty'
Varadan, for her infectious energy and sound
advice.

I would also like to thank Janet and Bob
Braithwaite for reading every word before
publication and their help and advice on a range
of issues. Thanks also to Terri Anderson for her
forthright introduction to the art of editing and
Jennifer Kidd for her astute observations.
Thanks also to Helen Stothard and Jane Todd
for their invaluable advice

But most of all I wish to thank my wife Melanie,
for those endless cups of coffee, acute editing
skills, and unwavering support.

1

Inception

The afternoon sun warmed my face as I wandered around the garden of our temporary Spanish home. I paused for a moment, staring into a cloudless, blue sky. An airliner cruised overhead, marking its progress with a long, wispy vapour-trail: Just one more carrier heading home with its cargo of introspective holidaymakers. All too soon, lazy-day memories will be replaced by a predictable routine. For many it's a daily trudge along the treadmill of life. This year; however, I wouldn't be joining them. My wife Melanie and I have chosen a different path.

Living abroad was a dream I'd nurtured for many years. It all began on the Greek Island of Corfu. I was 17 at the time. A fun-packed holiday with my best friend Mark was drawing to a close. During our last night on the island I found myself alone, sitting on the beach. Waves lapped gently onto the sandy shore as I stared out across the moonlit Mediterranean. I longed to stay and not return home, but lacked the confidence to follow my impulse.

More than 20 years have passed since that fleeting, rebellious moment, but now the wait is over.

My journey from dreamland, to mainland Spain began some months earlier. A casual remark about the future of our small printing business, developed into serious negotiations over its sale. Within weeks we had received a formal takeover offer. This modest windfall could open the door to a new life abroad. What seemed like an easy decision became a very difficult choice. After weeks of soul searching, we decided to sell-up and chase our dream.

Most of our evenings and weekends were now spent on the internet, trawling through foreign property sites. We focused our search on two areas, the Costa Blanca on Spain's Mediterranean coast and the Canary Isle of Lanzarote. We'd almost decided on Lanzarote when purely by chance I discovered a website promoting properties in a place called Galicia.

The advertised listings radiated rustic charm. There were quaint little cottages, romantic ruined farmhouses, and majestic manors; all at unbelievably low prices. Night after night I scoured the internet, desperate for information on this little known region of Spain.

Galicia is situated in the northwest corner of the Iberian Peninsula. To the east it's bordered by the regions of Asturias, and Castile and Leon; and in the south by the country of Portugal. To the north and west it borders the Atlantic Ocean. Its rugged coastline is aptly named, *Costa del Muerte* (Coast of Death). For centuries, ships and their crews have met a watery grave along this treacherous stretch of coastline. The interior is characterised by high mountains and deep river valleys. It's an unspoilt rural landscape where man and wildlife live in harmony.

Cleverly worded marketing is one thing, but to satisfy our curiosity we needed to fly out and take a look.

At the end of February that's exactly what we did. We flew with British Airways from London Gatwick to Porto in Northern Portugal, having planned a three night break to explore Galicia and view some properties.

After collecting the hire-car we headed north. The scenery through Portugal was stunning. We drove through high mountain ranges covered in deep-scented eucalyptus forests. Wide valleys and rolling hills meander their way through the forested peaks. Small hamlets speckle the landscape as the main highway carves its way through the lush, green valleys on tall concrete stilts. Within an hour we had drifted over the border and into Spain.

Our destination in Galicia was a small village called Caldelas de Tui. Hours of internet surfing had led to the discovery of a restored manor house, reincarnated as a rural hotel. Within its grounds, several outbuildings had been converted into small self-catering cottages. One of which would provide a countryside retreat for the duration of our stay.

Once across the border we headed for the cathedral city of Tui. After leaving the main highway we trundled along winding local roads and into the city centre. The streets were deserted. There was no sign of activity anywhere. The pavements were empty and the shops closed. Unbeknown to us, we'd arrived during lunchtime siesta. Previous holidays on the Mediterranean coast had not prepared us for this type of urban abandonment.

'It must be around here somewhere,' I said, as we drove through the empty streets, 'Why is there never a signpost when you want one?' I added.

'Where is everybody?' asked Melanie.

'I've no idea.'

Up to this point, the trip had run like clockwork. It hadn't occurred to me that we wouldn't be able to find the hotel. We drove around the city aimlessly, looking for any signs of life. Even the petrol station was closed. After an anxious 15 minutes Melanie spotted an old man sitting on a doorstep.

'There's someone!' she shouted, waving frantically to the right.

I jumped on the brakes and we ground to a halt. A narrow pavement separated the road from a row of small cottages. An old man was sitting on his doorstep bathing in the wintry sunshine. Melanie lowered her window and asked for directions. Her enquiry met with silence. A curious expression spread across the old man's weathered face. Holiday Spanish had not equipped us for such native encounters. Fortunately, I'd printed off the hotel details from the computer.

'Show him the printout,' I said, urging Melanie to make a more direct approach.

Surely he'll recognise a picture, I thought to myself.

She leapt from the car, thrust the printed sheet at him, and repeated the question. He squinted at the paper, studying it carefully. Time drifted on and still he stared.

'*Es un hotel* (It's a hotel),' said Melanie, urging a reply.

She glanced across at me, looking for inspiration. I thought that he might have dozed off in the warm sunshine. I was just about to tell her to get back in the car when the old man slowly lifted his head. He looked at Melanie and then at me, shrugged his shoulders and handed her back the printout. Without speaking a single word, he made it perfectly clear that he had no idea where we might find the hotel. We thanked him politely and continued on our quest.

A deserted city and a clueless local had done nothing

for our confidence. I began to fear that we were nowhere near our intended destination. Another 10 minutes passed before we spotted our next would-be-guides: two young men walking along the street. I pulled alongside and Melanie shouted out of the window. Both men approached the car and looked carefully at the printout.

'Yes, I know where this is,' said one of the young men.

An enormous sense of relief flooded the car. He wasn't sure of the hotel's exact location but pointed us in the right direction.

'Ask again when you get a bit closer,' he added.

We sped off into the countryside, leaving the historic centre of Tui far behind. Narrow country lanes wound their way through picturesque villages and quaint hamlets. The scenery was beautiful, but we'd been driving for over 10 minutes and still hadn't come across our elusive hotel.

'Do you think we've missed it?'

No sooner had I asked the question than we spotted the village sign – Caldelas de Tui.

'Can you see a hotel anywhere?' I asked eagerly.

'No,' snapped Melanie in frustration. 'There must be a sign somewhere,' she added.

Spotting a young man, walking towards his car, I darted across the road and pulled up alongside.

'Do you know where this hotel is?' asked Melanie showing him the printout.

'Yes, follow me. I'm going that way.'

He jumped into his car and headed off up the road. Finally, we'd stumbled upon someone who knew its location. With a flash of his lights and a toot on the horn, he guided us right to the main entrance.

The printed photos failed to portray the romantic beauty and charming character of this restored manor house. Entry into the grounds was through a pair of grand wooden gates, guarding an imposing stone entrance. We walked through the gateway into a flagged courtyard. A well dressed woman stepped out of a small office opposite the entrance. With a beaming smile she introduced herself as the housekeeper, and welcomed us to the hotel. Politely, and without fuss, she led us through the courtyard and along a gravel path to a delightful stone cottage.

A roaring fire welcomed our arrival. The warm air was filled with the intoxicating aroma of wood smoke. Large pine logs crackled and hissed as they flamed in the open hearth. In the lounge, a long bay-window framed a landscape of distant snow capped mountains fringed with dark-green forests. A combination of exposed natural granite, and polished plaster lined the interior of our weekend retreat. The roof space was open: exposed, wooden ceiling joists lay on thick oak rafters. The cottage was idyllic: a quiet and peaceful location set amongst pine forests and orchards.

The following morning, after a good night's sleep, we set off to meet the estate agent. He had arranged to meet us in the nearby coastal resort of Baiona. We arrived in good time and waited outside the tourist information office as agreed. Waiting in the bright, warm sunshine was pleasant enough, despite a stiff sea breeze; but as time drifted on I began to feel a little uneasy. Arranging to meet potential clients on the promenade of a seaside town in the depths of winter hardly seemed the most appropriate meeting place.

Surely, a bona fide estate agent would have an office we could meet at, I thought to myself.

Hanging around in the middle of the street only served to fuel my suspicions. Our only contact with him was through the internet. Everything seemed real enough on screen but how could we know for sure. After waiting for over half an hour I decided to give him a ring. The agent, a man called Ramon, answered.

'Hello, this is Mr Briggs. My wife and I have been waiting for you for over half an hour,' I said abruptly.

His response was unconvincing, 'I waited for almost an hour but couldn't see you anywhere,' he pleaded.

Having checked that we were waiting in the right place, we agreed to meet again later that afternoon.

'What did he have to say for himself?' asked Melanie bluntly.

'He said that he'd waited for nearly an hour and then left, thinking that we weren't coming.'

'That can't be true,' barked Melanie, 'We would have seen him. Is he coming now?' she added.

'He wants us to meet him back here at three.'

'Well that's been a waste of a morning,' she said, as we marched back to the car.

Determined not to miss our mystery estate agent, we returned in good time for our three o'clock appointment. In contrast to this morning, the area around the tourist information office was alive with people. Smartly dressed Spaniards gathered along the sweeping promenade directly in front of the tourist office. Elegant ladies, wearing thick, fur-collared coats, were accompanied by chic gents in stylish overcoats. Young children, in their Sunday-best, played excitedly in the wintry sunshine. Conscious of missing the agent, but curious to know the reason for this impromptu assembly, we strolled over to the seafront to take a look.

Standing at one end of the beach was a young man. He was fumbling with the cables of a personal address system.

Above the beach, on the promenade, was a large garden shed that doubled as a tourist information office. A series of electrical cables ran from the office, across the promenade, underfoot of the assembled crowd, and along the beach to a small amplifier. I couldn't help but wonder what a UK Health and Safety official might make of such an arrangement.

We stood and watched for a while, constantly looking around to make sure we didn't miss Ramon. The swelling crowd made it increasingly difficult to see who was coming and going so we decided to step back a few metres from the front. No sooner had we done so than a group of players, dressed in medieval costume, began congregating on the beach.

The central character of this rehearsed performance was a noble looking gentleman astride a jet-black stallion. He wore a brightly coloured *Jacqueta* or jacket. This close tailored jacket had a quilted appearance with many buttons and an exaggerated collar. Tied around his neck was a *Mantanilla,* or cape, which lay across the horse's hind quarters. The finishing touch to his flamboyant appearance was a *bonetilla:* a dark coloured, brimless hat sporting a single colourful feather.

With the ensemble complete the Master of Ceremonies began. The combination of a strengthening sea breeze, inadequate amplification, and a seemingly unpunctuated Spanish narrative, left us none the wiser. However, a plastic banner flapping in the wind gave the game away. Emblazoned across its length were the words *Cristóbal Colón* (Christopher Columbus). By pure chance, our arrival in Baiona had coincided with an annual fiesta to celebrate Columbus' return to Spain after discovering the Americas.

Leading the performance were three priests, walking in a triangular formation from the water's edge. Cloaked in ceremonial white robes, the lead priest carried a two metre high processional cross. The other two carried colourfully embroidered standards. They were followed by Columbus, mounted on his stallion. Trouping behind the horseman was a small company of soldiers: young men who had left their Spanish homeland as *reconquistas* and returned as *conquistadores*. A disorderly group of sailors, carrying the spoils of discovery, followed the soldiers. Their treasures included pineapples, turkeys, tobacco, and even a few scantily-clad native slaves.

The colourful performance lasted about 10 minutes and provided a pleasant distraction from our tedious wait. Within a few minutes the watching crowd had dispersed and we were alone once again.

'Where the hell is he?' I snarled.

'I don't know,' replied Melanie, stating the obvious.

My earlier concerns flooded back: why can't we meet at his office; what kind of an estate agent arranges to meet his clients on a seaside promenade. Question upon question raced through my mind.

'Give him another ring,' snapped Melanie in annoyance.

I tapped out his number and waited patiently for a response. After a few rings he picked it up.

'Hello, this is Mr Briggs again,' without pausing I continued, 'we've been waiting here for nearly an hour. Where are you?'

'I waited outside the tourist information office for almost an hour, and didn't see anyone,' he replied.

His assertive tone seemed quite genuine.

'But we've been waiting since before the performance.'

'What performance.' he asked.

His assured tone might have sounded sincere, but if he hadn't seen the medieval theatre, had he actually been here!

'The arrival of Christopher Columbus: didn't you see it?' I asked.

The line fell silent.

I've got him now, I thought to myself.

After a short paused he replied. 'What time do you make it now?' he asked.

'It's almost four o'clock, and as I said, 'we've been waiting here for almost an hour''.

'Now I see the problem,' said Ramon, 'your watch is wrong, it's almost five o'clock.'

I couldn't believe this idiot, and was just about to tell him so when he added, 'Your watch is set to English time.'

'That can't be right,' I insisted, 'I checked my watch when we landed in Porto yesterday.'

'Ah, now I see,' added Ramon

"Now I see", "now I see"! Who does he think he is: an estate agent or a bloody clairvoyant!

'Portugal is the same time as England but Spain is an hour in front,' he added.

All of a sudden the penny dropped: It wasn't Ramon who was the idiot, it was me.

What we had failed to realise when flying into Porto the previous day, was that Spain is an hour in front of both Portugal and the UK. On crossing the border I should have advanced my watch the required hour. Even after waiting for us for almost an hour, Ramon was leaving the meeting place minutes before we were arriving. He appeared to take the confusion in good heart and agreed to drive out and introduce himself.

Five minutes later he arrived, driving a very old 7 series BMW with Dutch registration plates. Its shabby appearance took me by surprise and did nothing to ease my concerns about his credibility as an estate agent. The bodywork sat low on the road as though parts of the suspension had collapsed and the lustre of its metallic, olive-green paintwork had long since faded. A plume of thick, black smoke rose from the exhaust pipe as it shuddered to a halt. By the time he'd introduced himself, the sun was setting over the town. House viewing would have to wait until tomorrow. We synchronised watches and arranged to meet early the following morning.

Time difference aside, I still had my concerns over this so called estate agent; however, at this stage our suspicions about Ramon were inconsequential. We were here on a fact finding mission; an exploration of this picturesque and little-known corner of northwest Spain.

For our rendezvous the following morning, Ramon had chosen another unusual place: Junction 287 on the main inland motorway. With the previous day's events still fresh in our minds, we arrived promptly. His clapped-out BMW was nowhere to be seen.

'It's definitely the right time, isn't it?' I asked, as we pulled up the slip road.

'Yes,' replied Melanie, categorically.

We would just have to be patient and wait for him to arrive. Another half an hour passed before his jaded, green machine trundled up the slip road in a cloud of black smoke. I was furious, but after yesterday's events I was hardly in a position to complain about his timekeeping.

There were two other people in the car with Ramon: a young man sitting alongside him and a woman in the back. Moments later another car exited the motorway and pulled up behind the BMW. One by one, the occupants of both vehicles stepped out onto the road.

'What's going on now?' I asked, impatiently.

'We're going to have to go and say hello,' said Melanie.

Reluctantly, we marched down the road to meet

Ramon who introduced us to everyone. Travelling with him was his son, and his wife; the driver of the second vehicle turned out to be the owner of the house we were waiting to view. After lengthy introductions, we eventually got underway.

On his website, Ramon described the property we were about to view as, 'A typical Galician farmhouse: habitable but needing reform'. Included in the asking price were two watermills, both of which required restoration, and 40,000 square metres of land. We were about to be taught our first lesson in Galician estate agent speak.

Access to the house was down an unmade track, about 500 metres long. Over the passage of time and the action of rainwater, it had become deeply rutted and barely passable. We crept down the lane, trying to avoid the deepest ruts. After about 300 metres our three vehicle convoy, led by Ramon, came to a halt. The passenger door opened and his son stepped out into the lane.

'What the hell's going on now?' I moaned. All we wanted to do was get to the house.

'That's one of the watermills!' he shouted, pointing into the dense undergrowth.

Melanie and I stared into the bramble infested forest at a pile of stones. We glanced back at each other trying desperately not to laugh. This so called watermill looked more like a pile of builder's rubble than any mill I'd ever seen. Ramon's son slipped back into the car and we continued on. Moments later the convoy ground to a halt again, and once again Ramon's son stepped from the car. Before he could utter a word, I lowered my window and shouted, 'Don't tell me, that pile of rubble is the second watermill!'

He nodded his head in recognition before slouching back into the car.

Eventually, we reached the end of the track. On the right was the farmhouse we had come to view. To the left, and literally within touching distance, was a semi-derelict building occupied by gypsies. According to the key-holder the gypsies had squatted there for as long as he could remember.

Scattered around the grounds were several dilapidated outbuildings. A rag-tag assortment of livestock wandered in and out of the ruins, they included; a small flock of dirty and diseased sheep, several flea-bitten goats, and numerous scrawny looking chickens. The place was an absolute shit-hole. Opposite the farmhouse, in one corner of the grounds were several single-storey cattle sheds with potential for conversion; but we were interested in the farmhouse. Described in the information as 'habitable', we were keen to get inside.

To describe the place as 'habitable' was the most inappropriate description I could think of. I wouldn't have asked one of the diseased sheep to live in such appalling conditions. The floors were rotten, plaster was crumbling from the walls, windows were smashed, and parts of the wooden ceilings had collapsed. The house had no redeeming features whatsoever. The access was atrocious, the rooms were too small with badly positioned windows; and the less said about the neighbours the better. The only plus-point of the entire property was the view: a panoramic landscape of deep-green coniferous forests and snow-capped mountains, for as far as the eye could see. Even with an outstanding view, this place definitely wasn't for us: after this experience, perhaps Galicia wasn't for us.

Time was short, by tomorrow afternoon we would be heading back to Porto for our flight home. We were desperate to get at least one more house viewing in before we left. I asked Ramon if he had any other properties to show us, somewhere fit for human rather than insect habitation. Eagerly, perhaps too eagerly, he assured us that he had.

The drive back to the hotel passed in silence. Neither of us expected to find our dream home at the first time of asking, but this morning's experience was far worse than either of us had imagined. We arrived back just in time for lunch.

Outside the cottage was a wooden table and chairs. We sat in the warm sunshine amidst the aromas of pine trees and wood smoke. After lunch we went for a stroll through the surrounding country lanes. Creamy-white calla lilies grew wild along the roadside verges and sheep grazed in open fields to the sound of birdsong. Set within walled gardens were granite stone cottages with small vegetable plots and tiny vineyards. Absent from this rural bliss was the constant drone of motor vehicles. We decided to stop at a local bar and have a drink.

In my best holiday Spanish I order two beers. *'Dos cervezas por favor.'*

We sat near the window looking out at half a dozen chickens, pecking at the earth.

'What do you think of Galicia?' I asked, as we sipped our cold beer.

Despite the unmitigated disaster of this morning's house viewing, Galicia had surprised us both. The area was beautiful and the idea of living a peaceful, rural lifestyle was very appealing.

'Do you think we can live here?' I asked.

Neither of us was sure: the weather was much better than we'd expected, the people were warm and welcoming; and the landscape had more than a passing resemblance to our native Yorkshire.

The following morning Ramon turned up at the hotel as agreed. We were soon on our way; time was of the essence. Wintry sunlight flickered into the car as we sped down narrow country lanes lined with leafless trees. Ten minutes into the journey we stopped on the outskirts of a large village. Before we could get out of the car Ramon was at the window.

'Just wait here for a moment,' he said, before heading off across the street and disappearing into a bar.

'I don't believe this guy,' I muttered under my breath.

After a few minutes he reappeared, accompanied by a tall, slim man. They chatted on the pavement for a while before Ramon returned to his car.

'What on earth was that all about?' I mumbled to Melanie.

A cloud of black smoke, billowing from Ramon's exhaust pipe, signalled his readiness to depart. At the top of the street we turned right. Parked at the roadside was Ramon's mystery man: leaning out of the driver's side window of a fairly new 4x4. Once again we were part of a three car convoy led by some guy from the local bar, but not for long. Two minutes later we ground to a halt outside a modern chalet-style house.

'Surely he hasn't brought us to see this monstrosity,' I snarled, increasingly frustrated by Ramon's inept performance.

The man from the bar headed towards the house. Moments later he returned, accompanied by a stocky looking chap with greying hair and a dark moustache. An old, rusting box-van became the new leader of our convoy. Before long we were zipping along country lanes and heading into the mountains. The higher we climbed, the narrower the lane became. Eventually we stopped, outside a driveway. Tall metal gates guarded the entrance, hiding whatever lay beyond. After fumbling around in his trouser pockets for the key, the van driver unlocked the gates. One by one we pulled off the lane and into the field beyond.

To our surprise, and delight, we were greeted with a recently restored farmhouse. All the exterior walls were clean and had recently been pointed. The roof was covered with bright, new, red-terracotta tiles. At one side of the property was an old mill-stone. The living area was on the first floor, a traditional feature of houses in the area. On the ground floor were several old animal stalls, and two *bodegas* (Wine cellars). To access the living accommodation we climbed up several stone steps. These led to a covered balcony with planked flooring and a wooden balustrade.

This is more like it, I thought to myself.

At the end of this charming covered balcony was a door which led into the main accommodation. This marked the point where the restoration ended and the work in progress began.

I thought things were going too well.

With time, effort, and money, this could be a fabulous home. Not the home for us, but it had reignited our passion for Galicia and shown us what could be achieved.

Back at the hotel, we just had time for lunch before setting off to Porto and our flight back to England. We sat outside, enjoying the wintry sunshine and chatting about the weekend's events. Seeing the house this morning had given us the confidence to follow our dream. Galicia had seduced us with its peace and tranquillity, the friendliness of the locals, and the appeal of a rural lifestyle. We had a few reservations, who wouldn't; but our decision was made. Galicia would be the starting point for our Spanish adventure. All we needed to do now was finalise the sale of our business.

2

A Nervous Farewell

Back in England, I focused all my efforts on selling the business. We were aiming to tie everything up by the 6th of April to coincide with the financial year-end. The actual mechanics of selling were proving far more difficult than I'd expected. The two prospective buyers were struggling to secure the financial backing they needed. Staying aloof from that problem, while focusing on managing the business, was becoming increasingly difficult. As the managing director and majority share holder, I was used to being in control of events. If things weren't happening, I would make them happen. Waiting for others to act was alien to me and I was struggling to cope with this unfamiliar situation.

The financial year-end came and went; a new deadline was set – the end of April. Every hour of every day brought a roller-coaster of emotions. Time was galloping by, we were approaching the end of April and still hadn't heard anything. The last four weeks had been the longest and most stressful of my entire life. Our dream of moving to Galicia seemed as far away as ever.

On Saturday, our home had been packed with family and friends: a congregation of well-wishers giving us a loving send-off. The party had been planned for weeks but the uncertainty surrounding the negotiations had put all our plans in jeopardy. We couldn't call it off; everything was prepared. The drinks had been bought and the furniture rearranged. There were pork pies warming in the oven and mushy-peas bubbling on the hob: a last supper of good-old Yorkshire fare

Everyone had wished us well, tears were shed and gifts presented; but for me, despite a glass or two of wine, the whole day was a rather sobering event. I couldn't shake off the notion that in the not too distant future, all these generous gifts would have to be returned to their rightful owners: what a depressing thought.

On returning to work the following Monday, I was greeted by the first piece of positive news in several weeks. The buyers had secured the necessary finance and were in a position to complete the deal. At long last a piece of good news. Arrangements were made to meet at the solicitors on Thursday afternoon. The contract had been gathering dust for several months. Finally, we were going to sign it. Promises had been made before but this felt different. For the first time since negotiations had started, we were about to make it as far as the solicitors. Surely, nothing could go wrong now.

One couple missing from our sending-off party were our good friends Ann and Dave. They'd been unable to attend but were eager to meet before we headed off to

Spain. We arranged to have a pub lunch together on Wednesday, the day before the proposed completion.

That morning I received some devastating news. One of the buyers rang me at work to say that the agreed finance had not materialised but hoped for better news tomorrow. This crushing message threw the buy-out into question. A sale now seemed extremely unlikely. My heart sank; I was overcome with a sense of emptiness and nausea. My emotional roller-coaster ride had finally left the tracks, crashed and burned, leaving our Spanish dream in tatters. The last thing I needed right now was a light-hearted lunch with friends, but plans had been made.

By the time I arrived at the pub, everyone else was there. Before I could speak, Ann threw her arms around me, squeezed tightly and kissed me on both cheeks. Despite all the ups and downs of the last four weeks, I'd managed for the most part to stay calm and in control. Ann's warm embrace shattered my fragile emotions, momentarily tipping me over the edge. Struggling to hold back tears of disappointment, I blurted out my demoralizing news. Throughout lunch, Ann and Dave did their utmost to lift our spirits but no words of comfort could raise our morale.

My mind and soul were in a state of limbo. Hoping something will happen does not make it so, a fact I was constantly impressing on my staff. Conceding that the sale had collapsed meant acknowledging our dream was over; I was desperate to hang on to it. As long as the chance remained, I would cling on to that hope. Tomorrow, one way or another, the axe would fall.

The following morning I arrived at work unsure what the day would bring. Melanie was at home, waiting for my call. Try as I might, I found it impossible to focus on anything other than the sale. The phone rang; I glanced at the clock, 9:30 a.m.

Somehow I knew that this was the call, the call that would decide our future.

Nervously, I picked up the receiver. 'Hello.'

'Hello Craig, this is Phil.'

Was this the upbeat response I was longing for.

'Good news. The backers have finally agreed to lend us the money.'

My sense of relief was overwhelming. The exchange of contracts could take place at the solicitors as planned, later that afternoon. No sooner had I finished the call than I lifted the receiver again, this time to give Melanie the news we'd been waiting for.

Just before lunch I left work and sped off home to collect Melanie. Without delay, we headed straight to the solicitors. We hardly spoke a word on the way, choosing instead to keep our own counsel. Before long we were driving through the grubby streets of Bradford. This once proud textile city has been in decline since the late '60s. The solicitor's offices were housed in an imposing Victorian building, just one of many lasting legacies of this once thriving industrial city. Being lunchtime, the street outside was quiet. We parked at the kerbside and climbed the half-dozen stone steps to reception. After introducing ourselves, the receptionist asked us to take a seat. An anxious hour passed before we were finally shown to our solicitor's office.

Susan, the solicitor, apologised for the delay; and explained that the other parties had not yet arrived. Melanie was furious; I was concerned. This unplanned delay afforded Susan the opportunity to explain the sale process to us and get a head start signing the paperwork.

For the sale of such a small company, the amount of paperwork was remarkable. By the time we'd signed everything, our arms were aching and another hour had slipped by. The passing of a third hour initiated an uncompromising phone call from Susan to their legal representative. He claimed to be completely oblivious to the agreed meeting. As far as he knew, his clients were still waiting for confirmation of funding. He would contact them immediately and ring her straight back.

We were dumbfounded by this latest revelation. It seemed as though we were trapped in a continuous cycle of false hope and depressing disappointment. It felt like an extreme form of psychological torture from which we had no escape. Another half an hour passed before he returned the call. After a brief exchange, Susan replaced the receiver and turned to us.

'He said that his clients will be in a position to exchange contracts tomorrow. I've rescheduled the appointment for 11:00 a.m.'

We were unconvinced; Susan could tell from our lack of response that we were sceptical about the news. She suggested that we remain at home tomorrow morning and if, or when, the other party arrived, she would ring us.

'This time we'll make them wait,' she added purposefully.

We thanked her for her time before setting off home. All we could do now was wait and hope.

That night, sleep was a luxury neither of us quite managed to achieve. My mind was a continuous merry-go-round of conflicting thoughts and emotions. Eventually the morning arrived. Time was passing slowly: seconds seemed like minutes and minutes like hours. Nine o'clock came and went: ten o'clock came and went but still no phone call. The morning drifted by in quiet contemplation. We hardly spoke a word to each other, neither of us had anything to say. By 11 o'clock, Melanie had had enough.

'I can't wait around here listening to time tick away,' she said quietly. 'I'm going down to see granny.'

Melanie had always been very close to her granny. Hopefully, she could find the words to ease the pain of waiting.

'That's fine,' I replied. 'If there's any news I'll let you know.'

By now I was pacing up and down, desperately trying to organise my thoughts. The clock reached 11:30 and still no call. The tension was unbearable.

Enough is enough, I thought to myself.

If I haven't received the call by 12 noon, then the deal is off. I'll ring the solicitor and tell her to forget the whole thing.

For the first time in two months I'd taken control. The sense of relief was unbelievable. It felt like an enormous weight had been lifted off my shoulders. I was still pacing up and down but now I was planning my business strategy for the next three years. Positive thoughts rushed into my head like a tidal wave of ideas. Before long, these random concepts began forming into a structured framework for the future.

Without warning, my quiet contemplation was shattered by the high pitched ringing of the phone. Quickly, I glanced across at the clock. Incredibly it read five minutes to twelve. If our move to Spain was meant to be, this would be the solicitor, if not, then the future was set. I lifted the receiver and calmly answered the call.

'Hello.'

'Mr Briggs' enquired the caller.

'Yes' I replied.

'Hello Craig this is Susan, I didn't call earlier as the buyers have only just arrived. Would you be so kind as to make your way to the office?'

'Certainly' I replied.

Broken promises and contradictory statements had been a feature of the last seven days. I should have been excited by Susan's news but felt nothing. I rang Melanie and asked her to return. I could tell from her response that she was as numb as I was.

Arriving outside the solicitors we found the road much busier than yesterday. Eventually we found a parking space and made the short walk to the offices. We entered the familiar reception area, announced our arrival and took a seat. Before long we were being escorted from reception, up a flight of stairs, along a corridor and into Susan's office. I expected to see the buyers, anxiously waiting to exchange contracts but this wasn't the case. Susan explained that they, and their solicitor, were waiting in an office along the corridor.

No sooner had we sat down than Susan was once again asking for our signatures. Paper after paper landed on the desk, one after the other. As quickly as we could sign them, another would instantly appear. A young office junior hurried along the corridor ferrying a seemingly endless stream of neatly typed papers from one office to the other.

'That's it,' remarked Susan, as I slid another printed sheet across the desk for Melanie to sign. 'Would you like to meet the other party to shake hands?' she added.

We were stunned. Was that it. I don't know what we were expecting but this wasn't it.

'Err… Yes, yes that would be fine.'

I couldn't help thinking, what an anticlimax.

Was it really over? Had we actually sold the business?

Seconds later the two buyers appeared. They seemed very satisfied with this morning's proceedings, laughing and joking as if they hadn't a care in the world. We wished them both the best of luck, handed them the factory keys and left.

On the pavement outside the offices we paused for a moment. The street was lined on both sides with a continuous row of tall, dark, Victorian buildings. The clouds overhead were thick and grey and the stiff breeze had a chilling bite. The day's events had developed into a surreal experience. We were struggling to comprehend what had actually happened and found it difficult to believe that the business was really sold.

'Is that it?' asked Melanie in disbelief

'Yes. That's it,' I replied.

We'd done it, we'd finally done it. The business was sold and our Spanish adventure was about to begin.

As a consequence of all the delays, Jazz's export licence had expired. Jazz is our beautiful collie-cross. More cross than collie but a much loved member of the family. We rescued her from the RSPCA 4 years ago. Earlier in the week we'd considered renewing the licence, but at that time the sale seemed unlikely. By the time we arrived home from the solicitors, it was too late. To make matters worse, the vets was closed over the weekend and Monday was a public holiday. We had no alternative but to delay our departure until Tuesday.

We spent the weekend trying to unwind from the stresses and strains of the previous week. It still hadn't sunk in that we'd actually sold up. I checked the car in readiness for the coming journey: tyre pressures, water levels, and a spare set of bulbs, a legal requirement for European travel. Melanie finished the last few bits of packing; most of it had been done weeks ago. The only thing left to do was load the car on Tuesday morning.

We had arranged to rent a house in Galicia through Ramon, in a place called Ferreira. Earlier in the year, in a moment of excited enthusiasm, I'd bought a European road atlas. Over the weekend I used this, and a well thumbed collection of old road maps, to write out an ordered sequence of road numbers. This would see us through to our destination. To make doubly sure, I checked my research against Microsoft Route Planner and printed out detailed driving instructions.

The first leg of our journey would see us leave Huddersfield and spend a night with my sister Julie, in London. After a good night's sleep, I was confident of completing the 1200 mile journey in a single day.

Over the last few weeks, we had carefully packed and labelled all our worldly goods. Everything deemed non-essential was ferried to my dad's to find a new home in his loft. With a combination of architectural-style precision, and sheer brute force, the remainder was squeezed into our trusty Rover saloon.

The luggage space was packed to capacity and the cabin, loaded to the gunnels. On the back seat, Jazz had just enough room to curl up in a ball; and secured to the rear cycle carrier were our two mountain bikes. Tentatively I pressed down on the rear of the car to test the suspension. To my surprise there was at least an inch of travel.

With the three of us sitting as comfortably as commuters on a rush-hour train, we cautiously set off on the first leg of our journey – an overnight stop at Julie's, before catching the Eurotunnel train from Folkestone, England, to Calais, France.

The journey to London proved uneventful; what greeted us on arrival was alarming. Stuck in the middle of her secure driveway was a bright-yellow skip, half full of building rubble. I couldn't believe it. We had no alternative but to park on the public road outside her house. As a consequence, we had to unload everything of value and reload the car first thing in the morning. With a 6:00 a.m. train reservation and an hour's drive to Folkestone, repacking the car would mean a very early start: to say nothing of the inconvenience. That night we set the alarm for 3:45 a.m. Our Spanish adventure hadn't got off to the best of starts.

The following morning was dark and damp. In the dim glimmer of a nearby streetlight, we repacked the car. By 5:00 a.m. we resumed our adventure – destination, Folkestone. Our first brush with disaster came just half an hour into the journey. In the early morning darkness, I failed to properly secure the mountain bikes to the carrier. A glance in my rear-view mirror revealed one of them swinging uncontrollably from side-to-side. Quickly, I pulled onto the hard shoulder to inspect. In the rhythmic flashing of the hazard warning lights, I re-tightened the holding straps and cautiously continued.

Time was now against us, and that wasn't the only thing. A few miles further on, a bright-red glow pierced the darkness of the dashboard. The fuel-fill light had illuminated, alerting us to our last gallon of petrol. We'd hoped to reach France before needing to fill up as fuel is cheaper there but we couldn't take the risk. Having just passed a petrol station, I decided to leave the motorway at the next exit, turn around and head back in the direction of

London. After refuelling, we rejoined the carriageway heading to Folkestone and onward to the train.

We arrived at Folkestone passenger terminal with five minutes to spare, drew up to the check-in booth and handed over our tickets and passports. The check-in clerk carefully studied our documentation.

'Boarding for the six o'clock train has finished,' announced the clerk.

Panic flooded the car. What if we have to wait ages for another train, or worse still have to return another day.

'You'll have to take the 6:20 now,' said the clerk, after a mischievously long pause.

Panic over.

'Are you aware that it's a public holiday in France today?' she enquired.

I wasn't aware of that, and couldn't imagine why she was asking, but thought it best to sound positive.

'Yes,' I said confidently.

While queuing to board the train, Melanie suggested the question might be related to our ticket purchase. Because of a hugely disproportionate price difference between a one-way ticket and a cheap day return, we opted for the latter. Why this should have any bearing on whether France was on holiday or not, was anyone's guess. After all, anyone with half an ounce of wit could see from the overloaded car that we had no plans to return anytime soon. Moments later we were boarding the train and heading for France.

The train emerged from deep below the English Channel, local time 8:00 a.m. Within seconds of it grinding to a halt, the carriages' large steel doors slid open. Conscious of our reduced ground clearance, I carefully drove off.

Before long we were on the main road, heading for Paris. On silky smooth tarmac the powerful V6 engine ate up the kilometres. After an incident-filled start to the day, things finally seemed to be going our way; even the weather was improving.

By 10 o'clock the sun had burnt through the clouds, revealing a beautiful spring day. Quiet, free-flowing country highways had brought us to within 10 kilometres of the French capital. The traffic was noticeably heavier and became busier with each passing kilometre. With the road sign reading Paris 5 km, all three carriageways ground to a virtual standstill.

Repeating in my mind, over and over again like a stuck record, were the words of the Eurotunnel check-in clerk. 'Are you aware that it's a public holiday in France today'?

Like the allure of a Siren from Greek mythology, the beautiful spring weather had enticed every Parisian car owner onto the roads. Over the next five hours, under the blazing heat of the midday sun, we covered just 10 kilometres. Once through this giant Parisian car park we continued south, with our travel schedule in tatters and daylight fading fast.

With less than half our journey covered we decided to take a break for dinner. By 10 p.m. we were back on the road. The weather had worsened significantly; a light drizzle accompanied the dark, moonless night. The wet, greasy windscreen fragmented the glaring lights of oncoming vehicles. A long day behind the steering wheel was starting to effect my concentration. As if stitched to my cheeks with elastic bands, my eyelids ached to close. I needed to stop and get some sleep. We pulled off the main road into a public service area. The car was so tightly packed that reclining the seats was impossible. For almost an hour we sat upright, like crash test dummies, listening to the pit-a-pat of rain on the car's roof. With sleep seemingly impossible we decided to drive on.

Before long, the spectre of tiredness crept over me once again. Falling asleep at the wheel is like freeze-frame photography in reverse. The bend up ahead is 200 metres away, in the blink on an eye it's within 100 metres; a second later I'm tugging at the steering wheel to avoid a catastrophe. As the car swerved sharply to the left, the carefully packed contents on the back seat slipped onto Jazz. Startled and confused she clambered over the fallen items. Melanie tried to calm her down but Jazz was intent on sitting on my lap.

We stopped again but once more, sleep eluded us. We drove on, crossing the Spanish border at two in the morning. A third stop, an hour later, finally gave our exhausted minds and bodies the brief interlude they craved.

After a short sleep, even the darkness of the early hours seemed a shade lighter. The computer-aided directions had proved invaluable, not a single wrong turn throughout our mammoth journey, but even these had a sting in the tail.

We arrived at our Spanish destination at noon. The signpost into the village read Ferreira but after just 200 metres and having passed only two houses, a similar sign informed us that we were leaving the village. This couldn't possibly be the Ferreira we were seeking.

Two hours later, after driving up and down mountain tracks in the middle of the Spanish wilderness with the car running on petrol fumes, we rejoined a main road. I pulled over and dug out the road atlas. By a miraculous piece of good fortune, we found ourselves less than 50 kilometres away from our real destination, Ferreira de Panton. The journey had been tiring, arduous and at times dangerous but, after 35 hours on the road, we were almost there.

3

Hello Elo

The road sign read Ferreira de Panton. We turned off the main carriageway onto the slip road and followed the signs for the village centre. Ramon had arranged to meet us in a bar on the high street called Bar Castilla.

During our marathon drive through France and Spain, we had observed countless romantically appealing villages with picture-postcard charm. Ferreira was not one of them. The approach road was wide and dusty; crudely constructed apartment blocks blighted the skyline. These modern built monoliths cast menacing shadows over the more picturesque buildings. Driving slowly, we continued down the main street. Faded, sun-bleached blinds hung in shop windows. The street was deserted, not a soul in sight. Once again, we'd arrived in an urban centre during lunchtime siesta. Halfway down the main street we spotted the bar.

'There it is,' chirped Melanie, trying her best to seem enthusiastic.

At least parking wouldn't be a problem. I pulled up next to the kerb, directly opposite the tired looking bar.

'You wait here with everything and I'll go and find Ramon,' I said confidently.

Jazz was asleep, curled up in a tiny space on the back seat as she had been for most of the journey. As a guard dog, her skills are limited to barking at men carrying ladders. If anyone tried to break into the car, she was more likely to lick them than bite.

I flung open the car door and heaved myself out onto the pavement. The air was warm and heavy, a stark contrast to the cool air-conditioned cabin. It made me feel light-headed as I walked stiffly across the road: my body felt hunched and contorted after hours behind the steering wheel.

Earlier in the day, during one of our many fuel stops, I called Ramon. I thought it wise to keep him updated on our progress, particularly given the confusion earlier in the year. Give-or-take half an hour, we had arrived pretty much as expected.

Hesitantly, I pushed open the door and walked into the bar. All eyes focused on the alien intruder. Purposefully, but without engaging direct eye-contact, I surveyed the bar's clientele, Ramon was nowhere to be seen. A sense of nervous dread filtered through my mind. Three and a half years at night school, attempting to grasp the basics of the Spanish language, were about to be put to the test. Racking my brain for the correct words, I stepped up to the bar. A broad smile from a motherly looking barmaid calmed my nerves. In my best holiday Spanish I asked, '*¿Hay una telefono aqui?*' (Is there a telephone here?)

'*Si,*' she replied.

This short, reassuring response was closely followed by an outburst of narrative, none of which sounded remotely like Spanish. Fortunately, her dramatic hand gestures were far more informative.

She walked to the end of the bar and pointed at a door in the corner. It led into a dimly lit but refreshingly cool hallway.

'There,' she said, pointing at a pay-phone mounted on the wall.

I smiled back at the barmaid and added, *'Gracias.'*

She reciprocated my expression, turned and left. I'd written Ramon's telephone number on a piece of paper and stuffed it into my trouser pocket. I slipped it out and carefully unfolded the flimsy note. From my other trouser pocket I took out a fist-full of euro coins, inserted one into the stainless steel slot and stacked the remainder on top of the phone like a pile of casino chips. With my preparations complete, I gingerly lifted the receiver and raised it to my ear. The tone was unfamiliar: one continuous high pitched sound.

Should it sound like this? I asked myself, or is it broken?

Taking great care, I punched out Ramon's nine digit number on the square metal keys. After the third number in the sequence the continuous tone stopped. With the final digit entered I waited, hoping for a response: the silence was deafening. A quick check on the liquid-crystal display confirmed that I had dialled the correct number. With no response I decided to replaced the receiver and try again. This time I punched the numbered keys with greater deliberation, and slightly more force; as if that would make the slightest bit of difference. Completing the sequence delivered exactly the same silent response.

It must be broken, I thought to myself.

It seemed highly unlikely that the well mannered and helpful barmaid would lead me to a broken telephone.

Perhaps she wasn't aware that the phone was out of order. All I needed to do was ask; the mere thought of it filled me with dread. Asking if the establishment had a phone was one thing, entering into a conversation about the workings of a public telephone was quite another. After considering my dilemma, attempting to communicate with a Spanish barmaid seemed preferable to explaining the situation to Melanie. After all, she hadn't slept or bathed properly for almost two days; and was currently sitting in the car in the middle of a deserted Spanish village, with the midday sun attempting to microwave her exhausted frame.

Stepping from the dark hallway into the brightness of the bar was like leaving the cinema after an afternoon matinee. Like the appearance of *The Creature from the Black Lagoon* all eyes focused on me, the strange foreigner. As I moved towards the bar, the barmaid moved towards me. With a sharp intake of breath I let out an apprehensive, '*Errrm…*'

To my great relief, the barmaid interrupted my stutter and asked me a question. The only two words I could decipher were, Ramon, and telephone. It seemed prudent to answer yes, '*Si,*' I replied.

In a crude attempt at further communication, I pointed to the piece of paper containing Ramon's telephone number and held out the euro coins I was clutching. I stared forlornly at the barmaid and shrugged my shoulders in a gesture of clueless naivety.

Taking pity on a weary traveller, she spoke again. The speed of her narrative left me wide-eyed and open mouthed. Fortunately for me, her gestures were far easier to interpret. She was obviously asking me if I would like her to try ringing Ramon. What a marvellous idea; quickly I replied, '*Si.*'

I handed her the phone number and a fist full of

change. The paper she gratefully accepted, the change she refused. I followed her through into the hallway.

After several failed attempts, we walked back into the bar.

'Espera, espera' (Wait, wait) she urged.

I assumed that Ramon's telephone was temporarily unavailable; at least that's what I hoped. In an effort to appear less conspicuous I casually leant against the bar. This delay gave me the opportunity to acquaint myself with these unfamiliar surroundings.

My initial impression was of a quiet reading room. Standing at the bar were three men of various ages. One was reading a newspaper while the other two stared aimlessly into the room. All three had a tiny cup of thick, black coffee. The air had a mixed aroma of stale alcohol, strong coffee, and cigarette smoke. The bar was topped with a slab of thick dark marble, flecked with small paler coloured crystals; and featured two tall beer pumps. The first, *Estrella*, was made from white china and looked more like an ornate vase than a beer pump. The second was made from highly polished stainless steel. Cool droplets of condensation dribbled down the shiny surface. Mounted on the back wall, were several smoked-glass shelves laden with a comprehensive collection of bottled spirits. By far the most prominent feature was a large, multi-cup coffee maker which stood proudly on a counter behind the bar. The place was spotlessly clean, with one exception. The terrazzo tiled floor was littered with discarded rubbish. I'd never seen such a mess, there were stubbed out cigarettes, empty sugar packets, toothpicks, burnt-out matchsticks, and torn bits of paper, anything and everything had been dropped on the floor.

I was just starting to feel a little uncomfortable when the barmaid slipped back out into the hall. Moments later she returned, a cheeky grin confirmed her positive news.

Ramon was on his way, and should be here in about five minutes. Delighted by the news, I responded with a melodic *'Muchas gracias.'*

Before leaving I made one final attempt to give her the handful of change I'd been clutching, but once again she politely refused.

The bright sunlight briefly blinded me as I stepped from the subdued lighting of the bar into the street. Squinting through half closed eyelids, I walked across the deserted street to the car. Melanie had waited patiently: if truth be known I think she was too exhausted to come looking for me. I explained what had happened and that Ramon would be here in a few minutes.

'Is there time to get a few essentials?' she asked.

Two doors up from the bar was a mini-supermarket. If Ramon turned up he would just have to wait.

'Yes, I'm sure there is. You get what we need and I'll wait here.'

Other than a few snacks we had bought in France after negotiating our way around Paris, we hadn't eaten anything since our meal the previous evening. Melanie trudged off up the street to the supermarket, and I waited in the car. I slumped into my grey, velour seat and ached for our nightmare journey to come to an end. The trials and tribulations of the last three days were starting to take their toll.

Melanie's reappearance from the supermarket coincided perfectly with Ramon's arrival. He pulled up on the opposite side of the street. From our dealings three months earlier, I recognised him immediately; despite the fact that he had changed his dilapidated BMW for a less prestigious Citroën. He on the other hand had forgotten all about us. Fortunately, our English registered car was a bit of a giveaway. He walked across the road and greeted me with a limp handshake. He explained that the house we were renting was nearby.

'Follow me,' he said, before marching back to his car and driving off up the street.

Quickly, I turned in the deserted street and drove off in pursuit of his little, red Citroën. Moments later we pulled off the road and onto a grassy open space. The rental property was situated on the village green, in a quiet and peaceful location. The house was known locally as, *Casa de Elo*, after its owner, Elo Gonzalez. A pair of imposing wrought-iron gates guarded the driveway entrance. By the time we'd pulled up behind Ramon's Citroën, he was standing outside the gates chatting to a middle-aged woman. We dragged our tired frames out of the car and sauntered over to meet them.

'This is Elo,' announced Ramon, 'the owner of the house.'

'Hello Elo,' I said, to a muted response.

Elo looked exactly how I imagined all Spanish women of her age would. She was quite short and slim, with deep brown eyes and jet-black, shoulder-length hair. She was very pretty, without being beautiful, and had an air of elegant nobility. Her warm, genuine greeting took me by surprise. She pulled me close until our cheeks touched; first the right and then the left, with the whisper of a kiss floating away on the breeze.

With the introductions over, Elo unlocked the gates. The house stood in about an acre of walled grounds, an ideal garden for Jazz to run free. The property was a modern, Swiss-style chalet of enormous proportions. Any sense of anticipation, or excitement, had long since waned. All we wanted to do was pay the rental money, wish our two guides well, and relax over a glass of something cool. Unfortunately, Elo had other plans.

Elo lived and worked in Santiago de Compostela, about an hour and a half from Ferreira. She rented the house to supplement her income. This grand property had once been her marital home. It now served as a shrine to her late husband whom, after a short and unexpected illness, passed away just after the birth of their second child. It also stood as a testament to her personal struggle to raise two children on her own. To Elo, we were merely transient occupiers charged with the care and preservation of her family memorial.

Elo's most memorable trait, and the most annoying, was her use of the Spanish language and the speed of her delivery. She refused to simplify her diction to help our understanding; this kind of linguistic arrogance is usually associated with Brits abroad. She began by asking if we understood Spanish.

'A little,' replied Melanie.

Thankfully, I'd kept quiet. Melanie's confession was the only encouragement Elo needed to direct all the instructions at her. After virtually no sleep and feeling physically and mentally exhausted, I simply couldn't have coped with Elo's ramblings.

Her incomprehensible Spanish tutorial began in the kitchen. Every electrical appliance had its own unique operating procedure. Quite literally, nothing worked as it should.

'And don't use the dishwasher; it's broken,' she said emphatically, pulling open the door and peering inside.

Despite appearances, we quickly discovered that this was a common theme running throughout the property. The narrative droned on and on. By the time she had finished describing the white-goods we were desperate for her to leave, but Elo had just begun.

She marched from the kitchen into the *galleria*. Like a

37

well trained lap-dog, Ramon scampered after her: Melanie and I brought up the rear. The *galleria* is a long, narrow sitting-room with floor to ceiling windows running along two sides.

'Do not try and use the *persianas*,' she instructed, 'They're broken,' she added.

Well there's a surprise, I thought to myself.

Persianas are a common feature in many Spanish homes. They're a type of roller blind made from a series of interlocking plastic lats. When lowered over the window, they form a solid plastic curtain that completely blocks out daylight.

'Instead of using the *persianas* you must draw all the curtains during the day,' our bemusement was clear to see but Elo continued on regardless, 'if you don't draw the curtains the sunlight will damage the furniture.'

Melanie and I stared at the furniture and then glanced at each other in disbelief. The faded fabric on the sofa was threadbare. I hardly think the sun could inflict any more damage on such a tired stick of furniture. Brushing past us she marched back into the hallway.

How much longer is this going to take?

Elo opened a door opposite the kitchen. A terrazzo tiled staircase led down to a partially subterranean basement. At the foot of the stairs a long, tiled corridor ran the length of the house. To the left, a door led into an enormous garage with space for at least four cars. To the right of the stairs, another door led into a large dining room.

'This room is lovely and cool in the summer,' remarked Elo, 'very nice for dining.'

When it's hot and sunny we want to be outside, not stuck down here in the basement, I thought to myself.

At the end of the corridor was a shower-room,

complete with toilet, bidet, and washing machine. Surprisingly, this was the only room without a door.

The basement was also home to the boiler-room. This fact gave Elo the opportunity to introduce her friend Antoniño into the conversation.

'If you stumble across an old, silver-haired, distinguished-looking gentleman wandering around the basement after dark, don't be alarmed,' she said, 'that will be Antoniño.'

Although we were paying the agreed rental rate, Elo clearly didn't trust us to use the heating responsibly. To this end, Antoniño was charged with the duty of igniting the central heating boiler, if and when he deemed it necessary.

How thoughtful, I thought sarcastically.

Having completed the basement tutorial, we marched back upstairs into the main hallway. From here, two flights of creaking wooden stairs led to the first-floor landing. There were three bedrooms and two bathrooms on this floor, including the en-suite master bedroom. We trooped in and out of each one in turn, interrupted by Elo's ritual raising and lowering of the window *persiana*. Why she couldn't switch the light on to illuminate the room was anyone's guess.

We were beginning to think that this tortuous tour would never end. Every minor instruction was accompanied by a plethora of rapid and unintelligible narrative. By now, neither of us was paying a blind bit of notice. Our brains were frazzled and our heads felt as if they could explode at any time. We kept glancing at each other, trying vainly to synchronise our nodding heads and forced smiles to coincide with a momentary pause in the diction. Having for the third time explained how to remove and replace a gas regulator, on this occasion for a

SuperSer gas fire located in the upstairs bathroom, she finally asked, 'Any questions?'

Any questions, any questions! Not-on-your-Nellie, I thought to myself.

Without hesitation Melanie quickly replied 'No.'

The only outstanding issue separating Melanie and me from some much needed peace and quiet, was the small matter of the rental payment.

'There's just the payment to sort out now,' I chimed, in an effort to keep matters moving along.

'Let's go through to the kitchen,' replied Elo.

She led the way and we dutifully followed.

We had chosen to bring travellers cheques rather than cash, it seemed the safest thing to do. We were carrying more funds than normal, and didn't know how long it might take to open a bank account or transfer funds.

Back in the kitchen I signed the required number of cheques and handed them to Elo. I could tell from her cautious acceptance that she wasn't happy. She held one out at arms length and stared at it long and hard, firstly the front and then the back. Her facial expression made it perfectly clear that travellers cheques were not her preferred payment method.

Having suffered a very long and extremely boring guided tour of *Casa de Elo*, I refused to even consider that American Express travellers cheques, which are accepted at thousands of locations worldwide, would not be accepted here. Elo began whispering to Ramon.

'Is there a problem?' I asked.

For the first time since meeting Elo, I had reduced her noisy chatter to a faint mumble.

'Do you have any cash?' asked Ramon.

'You can pay them into the bank just like cash,' I added.

That's when the penny dropped: even in my mentally drained condition I realised that the key part of my last sentence was, 'pay them into the bank'. That would mean declaring the income, something neither of them was keen to do. It didn't matter to us; we'd already paid our taxes. Fearing that they would never leave, I promised to replace the cheques with cash if Elo had a problem banking them. Seeing that she had no alternative, she begrudgingly agreed. With the deal concluded they wished us a happy stay and left.

'Thank heavens for that. I thought they were never going to go,' said Melanie, relieved that we could finally relax and unwind.

I waited a few minutes to make sure the coast was clear before pulling the car into the garage and Melanie made a few sandwiches. Unpacking the car could wait until tomorrow. We quickly devoured the sandwiches, washing them down with a bottle of lukewarm beer. Now we had a new challenge, how to stay awake when every fibre of our body's was demanding otherwise. If we went to bed now we would probably end up waking in the middle of the night. With the evening sunlight casting lengthening shadows, we conceded defeat and at 7 o'clock retired to bed.

4

The Dash for Cash

The bed felt warm and cosy. I could have stayed there forever, but it must be time to get up by now. I rolled over and opened my eyes.

Oh my God! I've gone blind.

The room was in complete darkness: not a hint of light or the faintest outline anywhere.

Unlike curtains, *persianas* form a solid plastic blind. Once closed, they completely smother any hint of daylight.

'I can't see a thing,' said Melanie as she fumbled in the blackness searching for her slippers. 'Here they are.'

She slid along the smooth parquet floor, arms outstretched, feeling for the windows. By touch alone she found the *persiana* draw-cord and tugged. Gradually the thick plastic shield rose; needle-like beams of sunlight radiated into the room through small holes in the interlocking plastic slats. Eventually the whole room was bathed in warm sunlight.

'You'll never believe it!' I exclaimed. 'It's 9:30.'

Thirteen and a half hours after collapsing into bed exhausted, we had finally woken from our unbroken sleep.

We spent the rest of the morning relaxing, familiarising ourselves with our temporary new home. Melanie began unpacking a few items of clothing while I went in search of the phone.

'I don't believe it.' I snarled at Melanie. 'There's no bloody telephone!'

Ramon had a number of properties for rent in this area but for us, access to a telephone was the most important criteria. For a relatively short-term rental, this request was quite unusual. Before booking I'd checked, and later rechecked to make doubly sure that this property had a phone. Ramon had told us not to worry and assured us that this house definitely had a telephone.

Undeterred by my lack of success, I broadened the search to include telephone sockets.

'I've managed to find two sockets, but I still can't find a phone,' I said, after wandering around the entire property for what seemed like hours.

'There's a telephone table in the hall with cupboard doors on the front,' chirped Melanie. 'Have you checked in there?'

'That was the first place I looked,' I snapped back, with more than a hint of sarcasm.

Melanie's response was to push past me, march down the hall, and tug open the doors of the table in annoyance. Silently, I was praying that she wouldn't find anything; I would never hear the last of it.

'See, I told you,' I said, after waiting for a few seconds to make absolutely sure that she hadn't found anything.

'Well I don't know then. Where else have you looked?' replied Melanie, in an increasingly agitated manner.

'I've looked everywhere.'

'Well there mustn't be one then. You'll have to ring Ramon and get him to sort it out. I'm sure I remember seeing a call-box at the end of the street,' she added.

Leaving Melanie to calm down, I walked to the end of the street in search of the call-box. To my amazement, I found it, exactly where she had suggested.

How does she do that? I thought to myself.

In contrast to yesterday, my call connected at the first attempt. I explained the situation to Ramon and waited for his response.

'There's definitely a phone line into the house,' insisted Ramon.

'I know there's a line, but where is the actual telephone?' I demanded.

'I don't know where that is,' replied Ramon. 'Only Elo will know where the telephone is,' he added.

I could hardly believe the incompetence of this character.

'Can you ring her and find out where it is? It's very important to us.'

He agreed to ring Elo. As soon as he knew anything, he would call at the house and let us know.

Later that afternoon, Ramon rang the doorbell. He had spoken with Elo; she had confirmed the presence of an incoming line and would explain fully when she returned to Ferreira next weekend. No amount of persuasion or coercion would change this situation: we would just have to wait.

I'm sure we can survive for a week without one, I thought to myself.

'There's one other thing,' said Ramon sheepishly. 'Elo said that the bank wouldn't accept the travellers cheques. She would like to swap them for cash.'

I found it difficult to believe that Elo had even been to the bank, never mind had the cheques refused; however, I had promised to swap them and felt duty bound to do so.

'That's fine,' I replied begrudgingly. 'I'll have the cash ready for her next weekend,' I added.

It seemed ironic that Ramon drove away with a smile on his face, while we were left without a phone, and obligated to replace the rental payment with cash.

The following week passed quickly, we found it difficult not to think of ourselves as being on holiday. We spent the time relaxing in the garden, soaking up the warm spring sunshine and familiarising ourselves with our new surroundings. The days passed quickly and by Friday morning we still hadn't been to the bank to get Elo's cash.

'We'd better go and get the rental money today,' I said to Melanie over breakfast. 'Elo will be here tomorrow.'

'Time flies when you're having fun,' added Melanie.

For a small village, Ferreira has a remarkable number of banks. Finding one to exchange some travellers cheques shouldn't be a problem.

Later that morning we strolled the short distance into the village. The first bank we entered was Caixa Galicia. We waited patiently in the queue. Melanie was deathly quiet, absorbed in concentration: mentally rehearsing her encounter with the teller. Conscious of the required effort, I kept quiet. Conversing with the locals was proving far more difficult than either of us had anticipated.

She slid the cheques across the counter, along with my passport.

'We would like to exchange these cheques please,' she said, in her accented Spanish.

'¿Que?' responded the teller in a brusque manner.

Nervously, Melanie repeated her prepared statement. The teller picked one of the cheques off the counter and held it at arms length. He examined it carefully, in the same suspicious manner that Elo had.

'I can't exchange these,' announced the teller after a lengthy delay.

The limitations of our night-school Spanish were becoming increasingly apparent with every passing encounter. With neither the will nor the linguistic skill to enquire further, we left and walked to the next bank. One after the other, each bank on the high street gave us the same response. Perhaps Elo was right after all. I preferred to think that these small satellite branches were not authorised to undertake foreign exchange transactions.

'We'll have to go into Monforte de Lemos after lunch,' I said, as we exited the last of Ferreira's banks. 'There's bound to be one there that can exhange them.'

Monforte de Lemos is the nearest town to Ferreira. It's quite a small place with a population of just over 20,000 but it has all the amenities associated with a modern 21st century town. Despite its size, Monforte is a city, a title bestowed on the town in 1885 by King Alfonso XII. Its most prominent historic buildings are the monastery of San Vicente do Pino, and the Torre da Homenaxe: both of which are perched high on a hill in the centre of the town, dominating the surrounding area.

The monastery, which dates from the 17th century, has been converted into a luxurious Parador hotel. The Torre da Homenaxe, or Homage Tower, dates from the 14th century and was part of a castle which once stood on the site.

Another building of historic interest is the convent of the Franciscanas Descalzas. This is situated in the heart of the town close to the river Cabe. The convent's church, which is still in regular use today, is extremely modest. Within the convent is the Nais Clarisas museum which contains some of the highest quality religious artefacts in the whole of Spain.

But perhaps the most impressive of all Monforte's historic buildings, is the college of Nuestra Señora la Antigua. Designed by Jesuit architects in the Herrera-style, it features a long Renaissance-style frontage and provides a focal point for most of the town's activities.

After a lazy lunch, we made the short drive into Monforte. To our dismay, all the banks were closed: I couldn't believe it.

'What are the opening hours?' I asked, pointing at a notice stuck on the door of one of the banks.

It turned out that from May, right through until the end of September, all the banks closed at lunchtime. Our amble along the incline of local knowledge was becoming a sprint up a steep learning-curve. Leaving things to the last minute in our new environment was a definite no no. Everything now rested on wrestling some cash out of the Spanish banking system tomorrow morning, before our meeting with Elo. Conscious of our tightening schedule, we made sure to set the alarm clock before retiring.

By 8:30 the following morning we were up, washed, dressed and halfway to Monforte. The town was quiet when we arrived, not a soul in sight. Slowly we drove through the abandoned streets looking for any signs of life.

'They're all closed,' said Melanie as she stared into another empty bank.

'They can't be,' I replied anxiously.

The thought of Elo turning up at the house with the

Guardia Civil, demanding our eviction, filled me with a sense of dread. What would she think of us if we weren't able to swap her travellers cheques for hard cash! Given our limited Spanish, it wasn't as if we could adequately explain our dilemma. I parked the car and we headed off to the nearest bank. Carefully, we re-read the opening-times notice.

Open Saturday: 8:00 – 13:30 (October – April only)

How could we have missed it? what were we thinking?

I racked my brains for a solution. What on earth are we going to do? The only thing I could think of was, 'The Dash for Cash'. The idea was a long shot but we'd run out of options.

'The Dash for Cash' calls for split second timing and lightening speed, both of which are better suited to a younger man. The idea is to withdraw as much cash as possible from one ATM and then hot-foot it to another and repeat the process. The 'Dash' ends when the computerised international banking system catches up and prevents further withdrawals. Inserting my cash-card into an ATM, entering the pin number and withdrawing my cash limit, would signal the start of 'The Dash'. From that moment on, speed was of the essence. I had to sprint to the next ATM and repeat the process as quickly as possible. At some point the system would catch up and refuse further transactions. The last time I'd attempted this desperate act, I was in my teens. I could only hope that things hadn't changed over the last twenty years.

From the ATM outside the Banesto bank, I could clearly see another two cash dispensers. Unfortunately, both of these were on the opposite side of the street. This meant running the gauntlet of traffic, a risk I had to take. Ideally, I wanted cash from all three ATM's, but to get enough money to exchange Elo's travellers cheques, I had to make the first two.

'Be careful,' pleaded Melanie, 'and watch out for the traffic.'

After several deep breaths, 'The Dash' commenced. From now on, timing was everything: I needed to synchronise my cash withdrawal with a break in the traffic. I inserted my bank card and typed in the PIN number, once I'd selected cash there was no turning back. I looked behind me, left and then right. The traffic lights were changing from green to red; now was the time. I span around, hit select cash and punched in 600 euros. The transaction seemed to take forever: eventually the machine spat out my bank card, all I needed now was the cash. I stared longingly at the slit in the machine, trying desperately to stay calm. Suddenly the notes appeared, squeezed out like wet clothes through an old mangle. I stripped them out, sprinted between two waiting cars and ran across the road.

Panting heavily I repeated the sequence at the next ATM.

Insert bank-card – type in PIN number – select cash – 600 euros.

Hallelujah! The cash had been dispensed and I was on my way to the third and final machine.

There's life in the old dog yet, I thought to myself, as I gasped for a lungful of oxygen.

A withdrawal from the third ATM would be the icing on the cake. In breathless desperation I began the process again.

Insert bank-card – type in PIN number – select cash – 600 euros – No funds available.

My luck, and my time, had run out. Maybe 20 years ago I might have made it, but not today. In part, my desperate scheme had worked and the threat of eviction, real or imaginary, had passed. We returned home, pleased with our morning's pursuit.

Later that morning the doorbell rang. Jazz started barking at this unfamiliar sound. She dashed to the front door, slipping and sliding on the hard tiled surface of the hall. I pulled it open and she darted out. She ran up the driveway to the gates, barking ferociously. Ramon had rung the bell; as Jazz bounded towards him he took a step back.

'Come in,' I shouted, to a nervous looking Ramon. 'She makes a lot of noise but wouldn't harm a fly,' I added as I headed up the drive.

Deciding that discretion is the better part of valor, he waited for me to open the gates. Ramon was a strange character, with an air of indiscernible falseness. Nothing I could put my finger on, more a feeling than anything else, even Jazz wasn't her normal, affable self around him.

'We have to meet Elo in the village, to find out about the phone,' he said as I opened the gates.

'OK,' I replied. 'I'll just get Melanie.'

Moments later we were following Ramon on the short drive to the village. We pulled up outside a row of tired-looking terraced houses. The outside rendering was weathered and cracked and the once white paintwork had faded to a flaky brown. Ramon knocked on one of the doors; it opened instantly, and Elo stepped out. I suspect she'd been waiting some time for our arrival. Once again she was stylishly dressed, as if she was about to attend a church mass. After a brief exchange with Elo, Ramon approached us.

'She's had the phone line disconnected,' said Ramon, crouching at the car window.

I looked at him sternly and was just about to speak when he added, 'But don't worry, it's a simple matter to get it reconnected in your name.'

The first step was to contact Telefonica, the Spanish phone provider, which Elo was happy to do on our behalf. It all sounded very straightforward; we were about to find out that nothing in Spain is ever straightforward.

'We must go to Bar Castilla,' said Ramon.

'Bar Castilla.' I enquired.

'Yes. Elo can use the public phone to make the arrangements with Telefonica.'

In the time it took Ramon to explain, a new character had arrived on the scene, Antoniño.

Antoniño is a tall, slim, distinguished looking gentleman and, given his age, dashingly handsome, with a full head of grey-white hair and a deep tan. He was the man, charged by Elo, with the responsibility of lighting our central heating boiler should the temperature dictate. He used to be the village headmaster, now retired, and is a lifelong friend of Elo.

The five of us strolled across the road and into the bar. In stark contrast to my last visit, the bar was busy and very noisy. Elo told us to take a seat and order some drinks. She clearly relished her role as commander in chief. While we ordered drinks, Elo, Antoniño and Ramon went to call Telefonica.

After about fifteen minutes the three of them returned. Elo and Antoniño were huddled together in conversation. Ramon stood on the fringes looking like a little boy lost. I suspected that things had not gone as planned. Eventually, Ramon shuffled over to us

'Before Telefonica will reconnect the phone line, you'll need to open a bank account,' explained Ramon.

'Open a bank account,' I enquired.

'Yes. Telefonica only accept payments from a Spanish bank account,' he added.

Perhaps we can finally get rid of these troublesome travellers cheques, I thought to myself.

'But you can't open a bank account without an NIE.'

'Without what?' I asked.

Ramon explained; an NIE is a national identity number for foreigners, roughly equivalent to a UK national insurance number. The issuing authority is the local police. As soon as we had a number, we could open a bank account; once we had opened a bank account, we could ask Telefonica to reconnect the telephone. What could be simpler?

Elo was busy bending Antoniño's ear: she could really go on when she put her mind to it. I couldn't help but feel sorry for the guy, particularly as his instructions were for our benefit.

Elo was the only one to have spoken with Telefonica and Ramon was the only competent bilingual member of the group. Both of them were heading off home tomorrow, Elo to Santiago and Ramon to his home on the coast. That left me, Melanie and Antoniño to sort the situation out on Monday.

'Antoniño will call at the house on Monday morning at 11,' said Ramon, translating Elo's instructions. 'He'll take you to the police station in Monforte to get your NIE number and then on to the bank to open an account.'

With that sorted, all that remained was to exchange Elo's travellers cheques. For a moment, I thought she'd forgotten. Mind you, given the trouble we had getting the cash, I was pleased she hadn't. With the day's business concluded we thanked all concerned and headed off home.

Antoniño arrived promptly on Monday morning. He

drove a Rover 75, a car befitting his status as the former headmaster. I sat alongside him in the front and Melanie reclined in the back. Ten minutes later we were pulling up outside the police station in Monforte.

Spain has three main police forces, the *Policia Locales*, the *Policia Municipales* and the *Guardia Civil*. The three forces seem to overlap in many areas of responsibility but not when it comes to issuing NIE certificates, this is the responsibility of the *Policia Locales*.

Antoniño's presence in the police station brought a chorus of greetings from all the officers we met. He was obviously well known, and thankfully for all the right reasons. We were guided to a desk where a well spoken clerk asked us a series of personal questions. Using a dictionary, we struggled our way through the short question and answer session. All our responses were carefully entered into the computer, our passports were photocopied and the NIE certificate printed off. The signature of a ranking officer, and the thump of a rubber stamp, completed the process. Within 10 minutes of entering we were off, certificate in hand.

Next stop the bank. For reasons best known to her, Elo had insisted that Antoniño take us to the Banesto bank to open an account. Our entry provoked a similar response to that at the police station. All of the bank staff appeared to know Antoniño and most of the customers acknowledged him as well. The bank's décor looked shabby and dated. At one side of the room, behind a glass security screen, sat a single teller. There were three desks on the opposite side, two of which were occupied by staff members. At the far end of the room was a fourth, piled high with folders and paperwork. In front of each desk were two comfortable looking chairs, as customers vacated them, others would quickly take their place. Without an orderly queue, or concertina-style guide rope, I had no idea how anyone knew who was next. Surprisingly, no one seemed the slightest bit bothered by this chaotic free-for-all.

We had hardly walked through the doorway when Antoniño was warmly greeted by the bank manager. Brazenly, he marched over to a vacant desk and took a seat. Sheepishly we followed, shuffling past waiting customers. Antoniño explained our dilemma; a few forms later the account was open. We even managed to get rid of our troublesome travellers cheques. What happened next was unbelievable.

After years of being in business I had developed a very low opinion of banks and their managers. Imagine my surprise when, having completed the paperwork, the manager picked up the phone, and on our behalf rang Telefonica. Galicia and its people were proving to be full of surprises.

Unfortunately, his helpful gesture was not reciprocated by the national phone company; a long wait followed. Conscious of neglecting other customers, but eager to help, he handed the phone to Antoniño. He relished the chance to sit in the manager's chair. Holding the phone to his ear, he rocked back-and-forth on its sprung spindle and swung from side-to-side. Images of a naughty schoolboy, wearing short trousers and a peaked cap, flashed through my mind.

'*Musica*' he exclaimed, holding the phone towards us at arms length.

Unable to think of an appropriate response we smiled back. A further 10 minutes passed before he tired of his temporary role. We thanked the manager for his help and returned to Ferreira to try again.

Back at Antoniño's house, he tried again; this time the

response was much swifter. The operator was unable to commit to an exact date for their engineer to call but they would contact Antoniño within the week with an exact time and date.

The morning's events had run much smoother than we'd anticipated. Before long we should be reconnected with family, friends and perhaps most importantly, the internet.

5

The Search Begins

The following weekend, Ramon turned up at the house unannounced.

'I've got some houses to show you,' he shouted, from the top of the drive.

'Come in,' I called. 'Wait in the garden while we get ready.'

Faced with the prospect of being alone in the garden with Jazz, he declined, preferring instead to wait in his car. Although his visit was unexpected, he couldn't have chosen a better day for viewing houses. The late-spring sunshine was bright and warm with hardly a cloud in the sky and not a breath of wind: perfect.

I pulled the car out of the garage and onto the village green.

'Follow me,' shouted Ramon, leaning from his open window.

With that we were off, zipping along narrow country lanes in pursuit of Ramon's little red Citroën. After a short drive we turned off the tarmac lane and parked in a clearing.

'The house I'm going to show you is a *Pazo*,' announced Ramon, as we strolled along a leafy track.

A *Pazo* is a Galician manor house, built between the 17th and 19th centuries. They were grand houses for the local nobility. The track leading to the house was overgrown with tangled weeds. Dappled sunlight filtered through the leafy shade creating a cool, dark corridor.

Following Ramon, we made our way carefully to the entrance. Huge granite blocks formed an impressive archway. The keystone featured an intricately chiselled coat of arms. Through the passage of time, once proud, hardwood gates had been reduced to nothing more than rotting timber panels, held slightly ajar by the unkempt undergrowth. Despite its ruinous appearance we entered with a sense of excitement as, one after the other, we squeezed through the narrow opening.

We found ourselves in an L-shaped courtyard. Snaking brambles snared the unsuspecting visitor. To the right, a flight of weather-worn, stone steps climbed to the first floor entrance. Ramon led the way, clearing a path by stamping flat the tallest weeds. To my surprise, the door into the house was slightly ajar. Violently, he pushed it open, almost as if he expected something to come rushing out. I started to feel a bit uneasy; we were practically breaking and entering.

Does Ramon have permission to be here? I thought to myself.

Barging open the door revealed the sheer enormity of the place. A central hallway ran the length of the house with doorways leading off from both sides. Initially, an internal viewing seemed questionable; all that remained of a once welcoming threshold was a gaping hole in the floorboards. Undeterred, Ramon stepped cautiously over the hole and onto the exposed wooden boards beyond.

'Be careful there,' said Ramon, stating the obvious.

With more than a little apprehension, I planted my best foot forward and stepped across. Having steadied myself, I turned to Melanie.

'This part seems fine,' I said, tapping gently on the boards around me. 'Here, give me your hand.'

Holding out an outstretched arm, I guided Melanie to the relative safety of the long hallway.

To the front of the house, an open wooden gallery connected all the rooms. The floors throughout were riddled with woodworm: tiny volcanoes of wood-dust littered the floors. Carefully we moved along the hall, peering through open doorways into neglected rooms. Towards the end of the hallway our passage was interrupted by a cavernous hole. Both the floor and the ceiling above had been destroyed by rainwater leaking through the roof. A concentrated beam of sunlight arrowed through the gaping fissure, illuminating the ancient roof joists. A solitary floorboard remained on the edge of the void. Without hesitation, Ramon confidently stepped on it and bridged the gap. My reluctance to follow was patently obvious.

'Don't worry,' said Ramon, 'it's perfectly safe.'

That was easy for him to say. He had clearly been here before.

'Look,' he said, stamping his foot on the floor and barking, 'Gud wud! Gud wud!'

The man was an idiot.

Filled with trepidation, but not wanting to seem like a wuss, I took a deep breath and followed.

'I'll wait here,' said Melanie. 'And *do* be careful.'

My leap of faith had its reward. At the end of the hall,

an open doorway led into a large room running the width of the house. With an air of childlike excitement, Ramon beckoned me to enter.

'This is a very important artefact,' said Ramon, in a hushed voice, 'very old and very rare.'

Spanning the length of one wall, and running from floor to ceiling, was an ornately carved wooden altar. Both water damage and woodworm infestation had taken their toll, but the original lustre of this vibrantly painted artefact could still be appreciated – Wow!

'Melanie, you've got to see this,' I called from the open doorway.

'What is it?' she asked.

'It's unbelievable. You've just got to come and see.'

Eventually I managed to cajole her across the gaping chasm. We stood in reverent silence for a while, admiring this unexpected, ancient treasure. With the viewing over, we carefully retraced our steps and returned to the courtyard.

'How much is it?' I asked Ramon.

'Ten million.'

'Ten million!' I blurted out in surprise.

'That's pesetas, ten million pesetas,' He added quickly, aware of our confusion.

Although Spain has been using the Euro since January 1999, any items of value are still quoted in pesetas.

'And how much is that in euros?' I asked, frustrated that I could never remember.

'That's 60,000 euros,' he said instantly.

I could have forgiven him for reverting to an obsolete currency if he was struggling to convert old to new, but he wasn't; he knew the conversion instantly.

Why didn't he just tell us in euros to begin with?

We ambled back along the lane to the waiting cars. My

mind was racing with the endless possibilities for this enormous property.

'The next house is quite close. Follow me,' said Ramon as he slammed shut his car door and started the engine.

Once again we were speeding down quiet country lanes pursuing Ramon.

'What did you think?' I asked Melanie as we sped along.

'It needs a hell of a lot of work,' she replied.

'I know but it could be magnificent,' I added.

'It could be,' repeated Melanie, with an air of scepticism.

Within a few minutes we had slowed to a crawl and entered a sleepy village. We crept down a narrow, winding lane, lined both sides with quaint looking cottages. The lane opened up into a small square. We parked the cars on a grassy verge in the shadow of a stone farmhouse.

'Wait here,' said Ramon. 'I'll just get the keys.'

We watched as Ramon wandered up the lane and disappeared from sight. A few minutes later he reappeared, accompanied by the key holder. She was a beaming old lady with a weathered and wrinkled face. She greeted us warmly before waddling off up the lane with the three of us following like ducklings.

After the majestic dereliction of the previous house, this property was something of a disappointment: far less majestic and far more derelict. We entered with a sense of trepidation. Amazingly, the interior appeared as though the owners had nipped out for a pint of milk, more than 20 years ago, and failed to return.

The sink was overflowing with dirty dishes; the kitchen cupboards were stocked with unopened packets and tins. Every room was fully furnished. Family photos hung on the walls and sentimental bric-a-brac filled cabinets and shelves. In the bedrooms, the beds were made-up and clothes were hanging neatly in the wardrobes. With the exception of a thick layer of dust, and peeling wallpaper, the house looked like it hadn't altered in decades.

It felt as if we were surveying the Spanish equivalent of the *Mary Celeste*. Was I about to befall a similar fate to that of my namesake, Captain Briggs and his family?

Leaving unexplained mysteries aside, my biggest concern with this house was the condition of the walls. At least one wall in every room was severely cracked. Like forks of black lightening on a white-washed backdrop, the cracks ran floor to ceiling.

'What do you think?' asked Ramon.

'I'm not a surveyor but there seems to be a structural problem,' I replied, pointing at another fracture.

'That's just the plaster,' insisted Ramon. 'Long, hot summers followed by damp cold winters commonly cause this kind of problem,' he added.

Unconvinced by Ramon's knowledge of structural engineering, we moved into the lounge.

'And what about this one?' I asked, pointing at a crack in the outer wall wide enough to put my arm through and shake hands with passing villagers. Even he had to concede the stupidity of his argument here.

This house was not for us, it had no redeeming features whatsoever. With our minds made up, we brought the viewing to a rapid conclusion.

We strolled slowly back to the car, conscious not to rush the elderly key holder. It wasn't her fault that Ramon had brought us to see this unsuitable building. All she wanted was some new neighbours. With Ramon acting as our interpreter, she pleaded the virtues of life in a rural village.

'It would make a lovely family home,' she insisted.

Having mentioned the phrase, 'family home', I had a good idea what was coming next.

'Do you have any children?' she asked.

Spaniards of all ages have an overwhelming affection for children. Whenever we're introduced to someone new, it's only a matter of time before they get around to asking about children; this lovable old lady was no exception.

'No, no children,' replied Melanie.

'We have a dog,' I chirped. 'They're far less trouble and much cheaper to keep.'

The old lady chuckled to herself before adding, 'You're still young enough.'

Young we might be; parental we certainly aren't.

'Before you leave you must take a glass of wine with me,' she said.

A surprise invitation we were delighted to accept.

We wandered back across the village square and down a narrow cobbled track. A short distance down, the old lady stopped and gestured Melanie and me towards a shabby wooden door. She pushed open the unlocked door and stepped inside, flicking a light switch on as she entered. The room was dimly lit, a solitary light bulb hung from a length of thin electrical cable. The floor was nothing more than compacted damp earth, firm yet cushioned underfoot. The walls were bare granite stone and the ceiling was made up of irregular wooden planks laid on thick wooden joists. The air was cool and musty, quite refreshing after the humid heat of early afternoon. We'd entered our host's *bodega*: a traditional wine store. At one end of the room were two oak casks resting on wooden plinths which raised them off the damp floor.

'This is my *bodega*,' she announced proudly. 'My son makes the wine from our grapes. Would you prefer red, or white?' she enquired.

On such a warm, sunny day we decided a cool glass of white would be the most refreshing.

At one side of the barrels stood a curious collection of dirty bottles, perched precariously on a warped shelf. She leant across, snatched the first bottle that came to hand, and placed it carefully under the wooden tap protruding from the smallest cask. A gentle but swift twist of the tap released a small amount of wine into the dirty bottle. She swilled it round a couple of times and tipped the contents onto the floor. I glanced across at Melanie; her facial expression mirrored my thoughts.

'I think that means it's clean,' I whispered to Melanie.

Had we made the right choice, accepting this apparently generous invitation, or might we live to regret it?

After filling the bottle with wine, she ushered us outside. Squinting in the bright sunshine, we followed her across the cobbled lane and through another unlocked door. To our surprise, we entered a bright, clean and modern kitchen.

'Come sit here,' she said, ushering us towards a farmhouse-style table with bench seating either side.

Like a typical granny, the old lady busied herself in the kitchen.

'Here you go,' she said, setting three clean tumblers down in the centre of the table. Quickly, Ramon snatched one.

'Is she not having a drink?' I asked Ramon.

He turned to the old dear and after a short exchange said, 'Her doctor has told her not to drink alcohol.'

As she began to pour I could see why, for a white wine it certainly had an unusual hue. Its colour had more in common with fluids leaving the body than anything I might normally drink. Our host scuttled back into the kitchen leaving the three of us to reflect on this curious brew. Undeterred, Ramon lifted his glass and guzzled a good mouthful.

'It's gud,' he remarked.

Who were we to argue?

Melanie and I raised our glasses and proposed a toast, *salud!* And cautiously took a sip. A fair appraisal of its palate might well have read, 'Tastes better than it looks, but looks bloody awful'. The old lady returned from the kitchen, laden with goodies. Tucked under one arm was a large crusty loaf and under the other a wooden chopping board. In one hand she carried two plastic food containers and in the other a long, menacing-looking carving knife and several small chorizo sausages. Clumsily she placed all the items on the table.

'Good wine, isn't it?' she enquired.

Through a grimaced smile we politely agreed. Like a doting granny she marched back into the kitchen, returning with four small plates, a knife each, and a handful of paper napkins. Opening the plastic containers she slid them into the centre of the table. The first contained thinly-sliced, cured ham and the second a large chunk of local cheese. She hacked away at the loaf, spraying tiny splinters of crust over the table.

'Tuck-in,' she ordered, as she sliced the chorizo into thin rounds.

Our acceptance to share in a glass of wine had turned into a hearty picnic. The cured ham melted on the tongue and the local cheese was strong and flavourful. A seductive aroma of wood-smoke filtered up from the spicy chorizo. We all tucked-in with gusto, especially Ramon. I felt a little guilty: after all, we had no intention of buying the house.

'Would you like another glass of wine?' asked our host, grabbing the wine bottle off the table.

Quickly, I placed a hand on top of my glass: it had taken me long enough to down the first one, I certainly didn't want another.

'No, thank you, that was delicious,' I said through a wry smile, before quickly adding, 'I'm afraid I have to drive.'

I had a feeling that Ramon would have stayed there all afternoon if we hadn't suggested moving on. Graciously we thanked our host for her warm hospitality.

'You must come and see me again,' she said, 'the next time you're passing, even if you don't buy the house,' she added.

This telling addition helped alleviate my niggling guilt. Like grannies the world over, I think she knew exactly what we were thinking.

Leaving the quiet village behind us we headed off, once again whizzing along narrow country lanes chasing Ramon. Mile after mile we drove, along traffic-free lanes, up hill and down dale. After about 20 minutes, Ramon pulled to the side of an unmade track. As it narrowed, it dropped steeply from view. Pulling up behind him we stepped from the car.

'We'll have to walk from here,' he called. 'There's nowhere to turn around at the end of the track.'

Not an ideal start to our final viewing of the day: who would want to live in a house where there was no parking! Having travelled all this way we were determined to see what he had in-store this time. After a short walk the panorama opened out, a truly breath taking view. We paused for a moment on the track, soaking up this idyllic landscape.

The air was warm and still, broken only by the lively chattering of busy songbirds. Below us were the steep valley sides of the river Miño. Rising from the valley floor, like a staircase to the clouds, were neatly walled terraces following the valley's contours. These dry stone walls were partially hidden by a bright-green canopy of vine leaves: this season's growth from the area's mature vineyards. The cool river mirrored the scene with ghostly images shimmering in the dark water. Overhead, a cloudless blue sky added to this artist's palette of vibrant colours and deep shades.

The tiny house was very disappointing, nothing more than a crumbling, stone shed, built from uncut pieces of local granite. Its current layout provided one large room upstairs and one down. Attached to one side was a kind of lean-to and the asking price included a small vineyard. The location was idyllic, peaceful and tranquil, but the house was way too small, far too isolated and totally impractical as a home or even to renovate as a holiday let.

By the time we drove away, the sun was setting in the western sky. We had spent the whole day with Ramon and seen only one property of note: the large manor house. We had hoped that Ramon would have a better idea of what we were looking for, especially considering our trip here earlier in the year. It looked as though Ramon wasn't the estate agent for us: perhaps we needed to broaden our horizons.

6

Flossing the Pig

House viewing with Ramon had given us a clear picture of exactly what we were looking for. We harboured dreams of living in an old, stone farmhouse, preferably restored and ready for occupation. Undertaking a modest amount of renovation work wasn't out of the question but ideally we were looking to move straight in. We also wanted several outbuildings that, long-term, we could convert into cottage-style accommodation similar to the romantic countryside retreat we stayed at on our first visit to Galicia. Was this too much to ask for!

Viewings with Ramon were limited to weekends; during the week he was away at his coastal home. We decided to branch out and see what the local agents in Monforte had to offer. On previous visits to the town, I'd noticed an estate agency tucked away down a narrow street; this would be our first port of call.

The morning was bright and sunny as we drove into

town. I parked in the central car park next to the college. A picturesque footpath follows the course of the river Cabe into the town centre. We crossed the main road, scene of my earlier dash-for-cash, and headed down a side street.

Standing outside on the pavement, the estate agents looked similar to those in the UK. Hanging in the window were printed information sheets: each one showed a photo of the property and gave a brief description.

'This looks more like it,' I said, glancing at the display. 'Come on; let's see what they've got.'

We entered the office expecting to find more of the same: neatly merchandised sheets, systematically displayed in order of escalating price. Imagine our surprise when all we found were three desks, a row of filing cabinets, and a few shelves of alphabetically labelled box-files. Pinned on the wall behind one desk, were architects drawings: intricate plans for yet another dreary apartment block.

All we wanted to do was pick up some information sheets, take them away, and draw up a shortlist at our convenience. Frustrated but undeterred, we approached a young lady sitting behind a desk. She greeted our nervous approach with a beaming smile and a loud and melodic, 'Hola!'

'Hola,' we replied.

'Do you have any information on houses for sale?' asked Melanie.

'Yes of course, take a seat,' replied the assistant, gesturing us to sit down. 'My name is Maria. What are you looking for?' she added.

Maria was a young woman in her early 20's. She had dark hair and a round, happy-looking face.

'Do you speak English?' asked Melanie.

'No,' replied Maria.

'Does anyone here speak English?' we asked hopefully.

Maria turned to her three colleagues and asked; the answer was a resounding, 'No'.

This is going to be interesting, I thought to myself.

For the next hour or so, we threw ourselves headlong into the task of communication. We used a combination of broken Spanish, stammered English, written English, hand signals, facial expressions, mime, and even scribbled sketches, in order to make ourselves understood. When most people would have given up, Maria remained positive, helpful and upbeat.

'Can we look at some houses now?' I asked, confident that she now knew what we were looking for.

'That's not possible,' she replied.

She explained that mornings were their busiest period; if we returned this afternoon she could accompany us on some viewings. My frustration was almost palpable: nothing was ever straightforward. Delays and waiting were the order of the day. Losing my composure wouldn't help: I had to remain calm. We were making progress, slow progress but progress nonetheless. We thanked Maria for her patience and left, agreeing to return that afternoon.

We strolled back to the car. By now the sun was high in the sky: another cloudless day, warm and still.

Things could be worse, I thought to myself.

That afternoon we returned: it felt strange, starting the afternoon at 4:30. It's almost early evening in the UK. Once again Maria greeted us warmly. I pulled up a chair with a sense of déjà vu.

'Do you have a car?' she asked.

'Yes,' I replied, eager to get started.

'That's good,' replied Maria. 'Take a seat,' she added.

What now? I thought to myself.

I presumed that after this morning's lengthy and

arduous extraction of information, Maria would have prepared a list of suitable properties for us to view. How wrong could I be?

Once seated, Maria sauntered across the office to three heavily laden shelves. Wedged between two black box-files on the top shelf was an old, brown ring-binder. Tiny dust particles floated through the air as she pulled it from the shelf. The scruffy, old binder contained tatty scraps of hand written paper, forced into two chrome retention rings. This lazy approach to filing had caused each punctured hole to tear. Through persistent use, these small tears had elongated to the point where most were completely ripped. Each slip of paper contained basic descriptive property details: style of property, type of building materials, the number of bedrooms, plot size, location, contact phone number, and price.

One-by-one she studiously checked the details on every leaf. Each turn of a page resulted in yet another small tear. The tatty leaves were a hotchpotch of different types of paper. Most were that old that they'd faded to a yellowy-brown. Finally, she flipped over the last scrappy page.

I found it puzzling that throughout her search she hadn't made any notes or asked one question. Then, to our frustration, she began the whole process in reverse: one-by-one flipping the pages from back to front. Suddenly, and without warning, the two chromed rings sprang open. The scrappy sheets scattered across the desk like the upturned contents of a wastepaper basket. Maria found the whole incident amusing. Melanie and I did not. Slowly and tediously she began reinserting the scraps of paper into the binder.

We simply weren't used to this laid-back approach to customer service and were struggling to adjust. We forced ourselves to grin and bear it. What choice did we have?

Oblivious to our rising frustration, Maria continued reinserting the ejected sheets. With the task complete, she began flicking through the pages once again. By now my blood was boiling. I could feel the pressure of frustration building up behind my eyes as if my head was about to explode.

As if aware of our mounting tension, Maria flipped over another page and stopped. After a period of measured contemplation, she walked across the office to a row of four grey filing cabinets on the opposite wall. She pulled open the top drawer on one of the cabinets, leant in, carefully lifted out a small wooden box and brought it back to the desk. It contained an assortment of keys, a rather large assortment. One-by-one she pulled the keys from the box and checked their aged labels. Instead of setting the rejected keys aside and continuing her search, she dropped them back into the box and pulled out another.

This could literally take forever, I thought to myself.

I toyed with the idea of leaping over the desk, upturning the box of keys and rifling through them in a frenzied fit. Just as I was about to pounce Maria squeaked, 'Ha ha.'

Thankfully, she had found the key that matched her property choice. My mounting frustration began to recede. This crazy routine continued at a snails-pace for over an hour. Eventually, Maria found four suitable properties and their corresponding keys.

'OK, let's go,' she chirped happily.

We spent the rest of the afternoon driving around the Galician countryside only to find that none of the properties were suitable. Out of the four, two of them were far too modern; and although the other two were old stone-built houses, both of them were in a poor location and neither had any outbuildings. With daylight fading, we returned to the agency. Maria was eager to point out that they had many more properties to show us. We had clearly provided a welcome distraction from her normal working routine. We thanked her for her time and promised to return another day.

We were disappointed by our first excursion into the local property market. Maria's choice of houses fell well short of our expectations. Either we had failed to communicate our requirements properly, or Maria had failed to understand us. Either way, today's viewings had been an unmitigated disaster. We had to learn from this experience and learn fast.

Many more trips to see Maria followed. Before long we were familiar with the local estate agency speak. Most properties fell into one of four categories:

New Construction – Newly built but unfinished, the exterior brickwork would be un-rendered and the interior walls un-plastered. The buyer would decide how they wanted the house finished and the builder would complete the work at an agreed price.

Habitable – But for the fact that this description was accurate, it would be quite amusing. Without exception, none of the properties described to us as habitable, were. I wouldn't have kept animals in most of them, never mind lived there. Sadly this description was true but the conditions of habitation were appalling.

To Restore – To demolish would be a more accurate description. Properties in this category were barely recognizable as houses. If it wasn't for the final category, ruinous would have been more appropriate.

Ruin – These were quite literally a pile of stones in the middle of a field. They were completely unrecognizable as buildings. Any plot of land that contained a mound of rubble was categorized as a ruin.

Fortunately, these four categories covered a comprehensive range of properties with some notable exceptions. One such exception came from an unusual source. On one of our regular visits to see Maria, we were introduced to Jamie.

'This is Jamie,' announced Maria as we entered the agents. 'His parents have a house for sale in the country. Would you like to see it?' she asked.

'Of course,' we replied, eager to see what he had to offer.

'His car is parked at the other end of town,' said Maria. 'Can you take him to his car and then follow him to the house?' she asked.

This unconventional request would have seemed very strange a few weeks ago but not anymore. When it comes to viewing houses in Galicia, nothing comes as a surprise anymore. Jamie guided us to his parked car and then we were off.

Leaving Monforte we headed into the countryside, climbing steadily for over a quarter of an hour. By the time we reached our destination, it felt as though we were on top of the world. Jamie pulled into the driveway of a modern-looking house and parked.

'This is my parents' house,' he said, as he stepped from the car. 'Just wait here a moment and I'll get the keys to their old house,' he added.

Quickly he returned.

'Their old house is at the end of the lane.'

Following Jamie, we strolled down the lane. To the right were two or three older properties hidden behind high boundary walls. Fleeting glimpses of their new roofs and cleaned stonework, gave me the impression that they had recently been renovated and to a high standard. Things were looking promising.

At the far end of the lane was the house we'd come to see. We entered through a pair of large wooden gates which opened into a small, irregular shaped courtyard. To the left was an open-sided barn, typical of this type of property. Directly in front was an external staircase which led to the first floor accommodation. Following our host, we climbed the steps. Using a rusty old key, the size of a small bread knife, Jamie unlocked the old wooden door and pushed it open.

'Come in,' he said, holding open the door.

We stepped over the threshold into a dark, cool hallway. A choking smell overpowered our senses. The stink was horrendous. Melanie and I looked at each other quizzically. What on earth could make such a stomach-churning stench?

It certainly wasn't the floors. The boards were immaculately clean and free from the tell-tale piles of dust associated with hungry woodworm.

I just wish I'd taken a deeper breath of clean air before entering.

Smell aside, walking through the house was a unique experience. Underfoot the planked flooring had a spongy feel, as if we were walking on a giant mattress. With these notable exceptions, the interior was in a reasonable condition; far better than most we'd seen.

'This way,' said Jamie, guiding us through the back door and down a flight of steps into the garden.

At last, some fresh air. How we managed to make our way through the house without fainting was anyone's guess.

The outlook from the back garden was lovely: rolling

green meadows sprinkled with patches of woodland and tiny hamlets. While admiring this picturesque landscape Jamie's parents appeared.

'This is good earth,' insisted his father, pointing to an allotment in the garden. 'Good trees, apples and pears and water, good water from the well.'

A passion for the land, and the bounty it provides, was a common theme running through most of our viewings. It's a passion we don't share. As far as I'm concerned, gardens are for mowing and fruit and vegetables come from the supermarket.

Built against the back wall of the house was a garden shed. Its walls were built from grey breeze-blocks which supported a corrugated tin roof. With the arrival of Jamie's dad, viewing responsibilities transferred from son to father. He pulled a small bunch of keys from his pocket and unlocked the shed's galvanized steel door.

'Come and take a look in here,' he said excitedly, gesturing us to enter the little shed.

The old man led the way, flicking a light switch on as he entered, Melanie followed and I brought up the rear. It took a few moments for my eyes to adjust from the bright sunlight, to the dimly lit shed. By the time they had, I was shocked to see three severed limbs hanging from the ceiling. Thankfully they were the legs of a pig. Having regained my composure I searched for evidence of a fourth.

They must have eaten it, I thought to myself. Either that or it was a three legged pig.

While scanning the shed for the fourth leg, I came across something even more macabre: the pig's head, hanging from the ceiling by a large steel hook, punctured through its forehead. Small salt crystals had formed on its long snout, sparkling like tiny diamonds in the dim light.

Its pointed ears projected rigidly upward, like the clipped ears of a Doberman, and its dry and wrinkled eyelids were closed as if asleep. Gruesomely, its bottom jaw had been hacked away exposing a row of stained upper teeth. Unbeknown to Melanie, this grisly find was hanging immediately behind her.

'Just watch out,' I said to Melanie as we turned to leave.

My warning had come too late. In her eagerness to depart this porcine mortuary, she had turned too quickly and caught flailing strands of hair in the pigs gaping jaw. This disgusting, and unintentional, tooth flossing had sealed this property's fate. Quickly she pulled her hair free and ran into the garden. I knew then that we wouldn't be making an offer on this house.

However, before leaving we did find the source of the horrendous stink. The open-sided barn that we had seen from the courtyard ran the full length of the house. Rather than bouncing our way back through the stinking upstairs rooms, we walked around the side and through the barn. The floor was littered with piles of rotting potatoes and turnips. The stink from these was bad enough but something was missing. After wading through this mire of rotting vegetables, we discovered the missing ingredients.

To the right of the stone steps, which led to the upstairs accommodation, was a pair of stable doors. Armed with the key, Jamie's father opened one of the doors and asked if we would like to take a look inside.

'Father, they don't want to look in there,' said Jamie, obviously embarrassed that his father had even suggested such a thing. 'And anyway, they don't have the right clothes on,' he added.

Gingerly we approached the open door. Housed inside was a small herd of cows, covered in their own effluent and living directly below the upstairs accommodation. The floor was literally swimming in cow shit. The stink from the rotting vegetables, combined with the rising, methane-fuelled odours of the effluent, was festering in the living accommodation above: Finally, we had found the source of this sickly ether. Politely we declined the old man's offer of a more thorough examination.

As we walked slowly back to the car Jamie assured us that should we decide to buy the house, the stables would be thoroughly cleaned. His comments reminded me of the old adage that, "a good smell sells". It usually refers to the rich aroma of freshly made coffee or newly baked bread. I doubt the Galician recipe of rotting vegetables and cow shit will ever catch on.

'Before you leave come and take a glass of wine with me,' insisted Jamie's father.

We were a bit hesitant, particularly after our experience with Ramon, but eventually we accepted: after all, it would be impolite not to.

Jamie's father's *bodega* was across the lane from their new house. From the outside it looked like many others in the area: a traditionally built, single storey, stone-built barn, but inside things were very different. The concrete floor was painted a cool-grey colour and looked clinically clean. Modern, fluorescent tube-lighting reflected off the spotlessly clean, white-washed walls. Along two sides stood six stainless steel wine vats and in one corner a neatly stacked pallet of empty bottles. Jamie's father clearly took his winemaking very seriously.

'Would you like red, or white?' he asked.

Melanie chose white and I opted for red. His wine was delicious; by far the best homemade wine we'd tasted. Our genuine praise for its quality didn't go unrewarded. On leaving, he gave us a bottle of red and white to take home with us.

'Would you like to see my father's vineyards?' asked Jamie as we strolled back to the car.

'Yes please,' we replied enthusiastically.

The vineyards are located in an area called Amandi. It's the most prestigious grape growing zone in the Ribeira Sacra. The vines grow in narrow terraces on the steep slopes of the Canyon of the river Sil.

'We'll take my car,' said Jamie. 'The road down the gorge is no more than a dirt track in some places,' he added.

We all jumped in his little 4x4 and before we knew it, were driving through another small village.

'Have you seen the Cañon de Sil?' asked Jamie.

'No not yet,' I replied.

'In that case I'll take you to the viewing point at Cadeiras before we visit the vineyards,' he said.

We followed a narrow lane out of the village and along a track to an open wooded area. Beyond this lay a charming Romanesque church. Granite picnic tables were scattered amongst the trees, each with a charcoal-blackened stone barbecue located nearby.

'This is where the annual fiesta is held,' explained Jamie.

He parked the car and led us along a well trodden footpath to the viewing platform. Built on a natural rocky outcrop, it gave us an unrestricted view both upstream and downstream. The panorama was breathtaking.

Overhead, a deep-blue sky displayed a patchwork of cotton-wool clouds. The vast horizon was limited only by the clarity of one's vision: hill upon hill, mountain upon mountain, fading shades of grey that merged with the sky at the outer limits of visibility. A thousand feet below us, was the cool, dark water of the river Sil, meandering its way through the canyon like a giant black Anaconda.

Upstream the steep valley sides were terraced with vines that rose from the water's edge to the top of the tallest peak. Downstream the near vertical, fractured rock-face of the canyon looked grey and forbidding and seemed devoid of life. We stood there speechless, soaking up the splendour and enormity of our natural surroundings. Tourist guides describe the canyon as Fjord like: a clear understatement of the immense and dramatic beauty of this gorge. After a few minutes we returned to the car and continued on our tour.

Moments later we were descending the valley. The lower we went, the narrower the lane became. Dry stone walls lined our descent. The occasional gateway gave passing glimpses of the terraced vineyards and the river below. After passing through a small hamlet half way down the valley, the narrow lane became an unmade and bumpy track. The roadside walls disappeared, affording a beautiful view of the vibrant vineyards, the calm river, and the steep valley sides. Occasionally, Jamie stopped to have a quick word with familiar faces, working in their vineyards. Before long we were literally at the water's edge. From here, we quickly began our steep and bumpy ascent. It wasn't long before we were back at his parents, thanking them all for their time.

Our departure was tinged with disappointment. After weeks of searching we had found nothing that met our requirements. If we were going to make a home in Galicia, we would have to make some compromises. Finding a property, fit for immediate occupation and within our budget, was proving impossible. Perhaps we would have to consider a restoration project.

7

Tasting Village Life

Life in Ferreira, at *Casa de Elo,* was usually peaceful and quiet. One exception to this was market day. Come rain or shine, on the first and fifteenth of every month, local traders gather on the village green to sell anything from freshly baked bread to livestock. At one o'clock, villagers from the surrounding area descend on the market for lunch. Their choice is quite limited but no one seems to mind. The most popular dish is a plate of *pulpo* (octopus).

First thing in the morning the *pulperias,* as they are known, erect a table on the pavement and load it with circular wooden platters. Next, they place a large copper pot, the size of a witch's caldron, on top of a gas burner. The pot is filled with water and left to boil. Once boiled, two or three octopuses are tossed in and left to simmer until lunchtime. To serve this regional delicacy, the tenderised octopus is hauled out of the bubbling pot. Its tentacles are snipped into centimetre thick rounds, using a pair of sharp scissors, piled high on a wooden plate and doused in olive oil. A sprinkling of *pimiento* (paprika) is optional.

Pulpo is as traditional to Galicians as fish and chips are to us. We were often asked if we'd tried it; our answer was always the same, no. The conversation would then drone on about the gastronomic delights of this slippery creature, followed by a hotly disputed list of preferred eateries.

'We must try *pulpo*,' I said to Melanie, after one such encounter with an enthusiastic neighbour. 'At least if we try it we can tell people whether we like it or not.'

With this in mind, the next time the market was in town we did just that. After patiently queuing on the pavement, I handed over the money and strolled back to the house with a platter of oiled *pulpo*. We decided that one plate would be enough as a taster. Melanie watched my progress from the terrace at the front of the house.

'That looks disgusting,' said Melanie as I placed the wooden platter on the table.

The outside skin is a pinkie-purple colour; inside the flesh is smooth and white. There were small cylindrical suckers clearly visible on the fleshy edges of the snipped rounds.

'What's that?' asked Melanie, pointing at the dish.

'It's a sucker,' I replied.

'I'm not eating that,' she said, clearly uneasy at the thought.

'Don't be silly, it won't kill you,' at least I didn't think it would.

Melanie was having none of it and promptly set about severing each individual sucker from the flesh. Hesitantly, I stabbed my fork into the smallest piece I could find, lifted it slowly to my mouth and popped it in. The texture felt like an oily piece of rubber. I chewed on it for a while, as if chewing on a piece of gum, and then swallowed it whole.

'What's it like?' asked Melanie.

'It's OK,' I said, trying hard to disguise my disgust.

Having removed any trace of suckers, Melanie cut what remained into four tiny pieces. Slowly, she lifted one of the morsels from the platter and tentatively put it into her mouth. She started retching immediately. Moments later she leapt to her feet, sprinted across the terrace and spat it into a flower bed.

'That's disgusting,' she cried. 'I'm not eating that.'

I had to agree, it really was disgusting: even the dog refused to eat it.

In addition to market days, the only other disruption to our peace and tranquillity was Elo's fortnightly visit to tend the garden and mow the lawn. Melanie loathed the intrusion. She hadn't realised that admitting to understanding a little Spanish meant that Elo would direct all her conversation to her. I on the other hand maintained the illusion of linguistic ignorance, an illusion not that far from the truth. With Elo around the house, Melanie had no escape. The slightest mispronunciation of a Spanish word would be pounced on like a hungry lion and corrected in the most brutal manner.

'*Repetes* M-e-l-a-n-i-e, *repetes*,' (repeat Melanie repeat) would echo around the house as Elo attempted to mentor Melanie in the art of perfect pronunciation. This annoying instruction became her catchphrase. Whenever we added a new word to our expanding vocabulary we would tease each other with, *repetes, repetes*.

Although Elo could be quite irritating at times, she was well intentioned and occasionally had something interesting to contribute.

'Next weekend is the annual Ferreira wine fiesta,' she announced, on one visit.

Now you're talking, I thought to myself.

'It takes place on the village green on the first weekend in June,' she added.

Thoughtfully, she had arranged for Antoniño to call at the house and accompany us to the event.

With less than a week to go, the only sign of activity on the green was a small trailer parked opposite. It was covered with a faded blue tarpaulin; a bright placard poking out of the top read, *'Camas Elasticas 1€'*. The literal translation is elastic beds or more accurately, trampolines. It looked as though the fair was coming to town. On Tuesday another two trailers arrived and by Wednesday a crudely converted camper-van had taken up residence in the middle of the park.

The week's activity came to a head on Friday morning when several council workers began erecting steel framed booths on the green. Later in the day, half a dozen local wine producers arrived and began personalising their individual booths. At one end of the green, a mobile bar the size of a wedding marquee was being hurriedly erected. Its blue and white striped tarpaulin roof made it look more like a Big Top than a bar. Opposite the bar was a mobile tourist information office and promotional centre, and next to that, a mobile candy shop. On the far side of the green, a huge bouncy castle was in the latter stages of inflation. By sundown on Friday, the area was ready and the stage set.

The following morning we were woken by an ear splitting explosion.

'What the hell was that,' I shouted.

Before Melanie had time to reply there was another -
Whoooosh BANG!

'What's going on?'

Melanie jumped out of bed and rushed across to the
window. She pulled the *persiana* up just in time to see a
middle aged man, in the park opposite, lighting a rocket.

'There's a bloke in the park lighting a firework,' she
said.

'Firework, it sounds more like military ordnance.'

No sooner had I uttered the words than another one
took to the air – *Whoooosh BANG!* And then it fell silent.

'He's wandered off,' said Melanie, returning to bed.

We found out later that fireworks are used to signal the
start of fiestas and the end of fiestas, and sometimes the in
between bits of fiestas. In fact, any chance they get to
frighten the living daylights out of man or beast, they do.

After this abrupt awakening the morning's events
started slowly. One after another, local wine producers
drove onto the green in small vans. Boxes of wine were
unloaded and neatly stacked in their respective booths. By
midday the temporary bar had opened. Several attractive
young ladies occupied the council's mobile information
centre and members of the public had begun filtering into
the green from all directions. The fairground rides were
ready for business and road-side stalls displayed handmade
arts and crafts. Latino music floated across the green from
tatty old speakers hanging in the bar.

Melanie and I sat on the front terrace, overlooking the
green, watching the afternoon's events unfold. Smartly
dressed visitors chatted over a glass of wine. Equally well
dressed children ran playfully in and out of the crowds,
occasionally tumbling to the ground. There were groups of
people huddled around the craft stalls browsing their
wares. Across the green, a few young children bounced

playfully on the bouncy castle and others sat contentedly, circling on a small merry-go-round. It all seemed rather low-key and sedate, more reminiscent of an English garden party than a Spanish fiesta. The attendance was low and I couldn't help thinking that all the effort hadn't really been worth it. By half past one, most of the crowd had sauntered off to a local restaurant or back to their family homes for lunch. The stalls closed and as quickly as the event had started, it finished.

We were left feeling a little deflated. Our initial enthusiasm for the village wine fiesta had waned slightly. I'm not sure what we expected but this had been a bit of a wash-out. Perhaps things would liven up later in the day.

Six o'clock prompted another series of fierce explosions. The fallout was so severe that the windows rattled and Jazz sprinted for cover in sheer terror.

'It sounds like the fiesta is starting up again,' I quipped to Melanie, as she tried in vain to coax Jazz from the house.

Unlike the morning, this evening's events started off far livelier. The music from the bar blasted out, creating a much bubblier atmosphere. By nine o'clock the place was buzzing. The consumption of copious amounts of wine had transformed this sedate gathering into a vivacious and good humoured party.

Not wanting to be out done by stylishly dressed Spaniards, Melanie and I chose suitably smart attire and waited patiently on the terrace for Antoniño to arrive. We were so busy watching events unfold, that we didn't see him standing at the gates.

'Hola!' he called. 'Are you ready?'

Eager to join in the festivities we marched up the drive to meet him.

The row of tasting booths started just outside the gates.

Cheekily, Antoniño manoeuvred himself through the crowd and up to the serving counter.

'Three reds,' he demanded, firmly yet polite.

His velvety bass-tones echoed through the throng. Melanie and I looked on as he made his way back, carrying three glasses high above his head.

'Here you go, try this,' said Antoniño, passing us a glass.

'How much do I owe you,' I asked, not wanting to seem ungrateful.

'It's free,' he announced.

Free, I thought to myself. Surely it can't be free. No wonder the place is rocking.

Before we finished the first glass Antoniño was off, heading for the next booth. He was clearly on a mission this evening and why not? Quickly we guzzled down the remaining mouthful. Sheepishly I returned our glasses to the first booth while Antoniño wrestled his way to the front of the crowd at the next one. By the time we reached the sixth and final booth in the row, I was feeling quite guilty: all this wine and we hadn't spent a penny; Antoniño was having none of it.

'Back we go,' he said, pushing his way to the front once again. 'We have to do them all at least four or even five times,' he added.

We weren't sure whether he was joking or not but had no intention of quitting. It seemed inconceivable that such an event could ever take place in England. Despite the limitless amount of free wine, the atmosphere here was one of jovial fun. From grandparents through to grandkids, people of all ages were enjoying this family fiesta. We saw no rowdiness or drunken behaviour, no one collapsed comatose on the pavement or peeing in the street. No one felt the need to start disrobing or worse still kick lumps out of each other and to top it off, not a policeman in sight.

Following Antoniño's lead we made our way back along the row, calling at every booth for another glass of wine.

'Back we go,' he shouted as we reached our initial starting point.

Perhaps he wasn't kidding after all.

'We'll just finish this one,' said Melanie hoping for a break.

Fortunately for us, Antoniño stumbled into an old friend. While they set about righting the world, Melanie and I sloped off and hid behind a large tree.

Midnight signalled another barrage of mortar-style fireworks. These unexpected, and incredibly loud detonations made us both jump. A giggled murmur echoed through the startled crowd. Our attempts to disappear from Antoniño's view had failed miserably.

'Come on,' he called, 'we're going for something to eat.'

By now he was looking a bit worse for wear. His eyes had that tell-tale glazed appearance and he swayed gently from side-to-side as he spoke. I thought he might be slurring his words but, as I could barely understand him at the best of times, I wasn't quite sure.

'My old friend Pablo is joining us,' he added.

The clock had gone past midnight by now but we were both starving, so quickly agreed. Our destination was the restaurant, O'Mosteiro, which sits opposite the town hall.

The town hall is a beautiful old building, restored with meticulous attention to detail. Together with the village library, post office, and tourist information office, it occupies two sides of the *Plaza Mayor* (Main Square). At night, the square and surrounding buildings are sympathetically lit creating a romantic backdrop.

Tonight; however, the square had been commandeered by a Spanish pop group. Bass-filled, Latino rhythms boomed out across the packed square from a temporary stage. Fans of all ages danced in the streets. Younger admirers lined up at the front, mimicking their idols dance movements and screaming out the vocals.

Outside the restaurant, partygoers sat at tables soaking up the festive atmosphere. Through small windows both sides of the entrance, the brightly lit restaurant looked warm and inviting. Following Antoniño and Pablo, we jostled our way through the throbbing bar area and into a small restaurant at the back. The place was packed with hungry diners.

'You'll have to wait,' said a waiter as we entered.

The waiter looked about sixty and was clearly struggling to cope with an influx of raucous partygoers. Antoniño was hungry and wanted to eat: a brief exchange followed. Antoniño was having a bit of fun with the old waiter but he was having none of it.

'You'll have to wait. Can't you see I'm busy!' demanded the waiter.

Antoniño was in no mood to hang around. As soon as the waiter had disappeared into the kitchen, he made his move.

'Wait here,' he said, with a cheeky smile and promptly marched back into the bar.

Moments later he returned, struggling with an empty table. Melanie and I looked on in disbelief.

'Don't worry,' he said, stumbling past us, 'I know the owner.'

Melanie and I stood at the side, glowing red with embarrassment as other diners looked on in amazement. Antoniño plonked the table down, blocking the only available floor space in the entire restaurant. The waiter was furious as he returned balancing several plates of food on each arm. By the time he finished serving, Antoniño had set the table and Pablo had requisitioned four chairs from the bar. Within the space of five minutes we were all sitting comfortably and munching on thick chunks of crusty bread. Even the waiter's frustration had waned as he thumped a bottle of house wine down on the table.

After sampling some of the best wines in the area, the house red tasted fairly disgusting. The colour was more reminiscent of a watery blackcurrant cordial than red wine. There were tiny, dark particles floating throughout and it tasted like a liquidised bag of damp, mouldy compost.

'This wine's terrible,' said Pablo, after taking a good mouthful. 'My homemade wine is much better than this,' he added

'Pablo makes excellent wine,' said Antoniño. 'It's completely natural, with no added chemicals.'

'That's right,' said Pablo, 'completely natural and no added chemicals.'

For reasons best known to them, the exclusion of chemicals from his wine was clearly of major significance.

Conversation around the table was difficult. Antoniño and Pablo babbled away to each other in Gallego, Galicia's regional language. It has as much in common with Portuguese as it does Spanish. They tried to include us and every so often asked us a question. They would begin their enquiry in Spanish at a very slow pace and end in Gallego at a gallop. At best, our responses were limited to one or two words. We tried to laugh at the right time and nod our heads when appropriate, but with a deafening backdrop conversation proved nigh on impossible.

To our relief, a motherly looking woman with a welcoming smile approached the table. Her name was Anna: landlady, cook, head waitress, and bottle washer.

She was here to take our order. The menu was despatched orally and at a head-spinning speed. Thankfully, Antoniño did the honours and ordered for us all. What we were about to get was anyone's guess.

Moments later Anna returned carrying a large platter.

'Here you go,' she said as she set the platter down in the middle of the table, *'entremeses.'*

The platter contained a selection of cured meats and various local cheeses. The meats included: *jamon iberico* (cured ham) *chorizo* (a spicy pork sausage) *lomo* (pork loin) *salchichon* (salami) and boiled ham.

'Tuck in,' said Antoniño, as he snatched a bit of *chorizo*.

We were all famished: no waiting on ceremony, just every man for himself.

Previous attempts at eating these uncooked delicacies had left me with an aching jaw and a mouthful of indigestible meat. Watching Antoniño and Pablo devour these tasty bites made me appreciate exactly how to enjoy this typical dish. A bite of meat followed by a nibble of crusty loaf made chewing easy. Each selection had its own distinctive flavour.

'This is delicious,' I said to Melanie, having grasped the basics of cured meat consumption.

'These aren't as nice as mine,' remarked Pablo.

'Pablo makes excellent *chorizo*,' added Antoniño. 'It's completely natural, with no added chemicals.'

'That's right,' repeated Pablo, 'completely natural and no added chemicals.'

A drunken theme was emerging from tonight's dinner conversation. We smiled at Pablo and nodded our head in acknowledgment of his environmentally friendly *chorizo*. We finished off the last of the *entremeses* to rousing echoes of, 'completely natural and no added chemicals.'

The main course turned out to be a real treat. Anna

emerged from the kitchen carrying two large plates and set them down on the table. Both plates contained the leg and shoulder of a young lamb. The portions were enormous, even to share. Each joint was big enough to feed Sunday lunch to a family of four and still have enough left over for a lamb curry the following day. They were beautifully roasted to a rich golden-brown. Natural juices filled the base of the plate and freshly fried chips completed the feast. While Antoniño and Pablo bickered over the age of the young animal, based on the size and thickness of its limbs, Melanie and I feasted on this seasonal sacrifice. The only ingredient lacking was a spoonful of mint sauce. By the time we had scraped the last pieces of tender meat off the bones, we were absolutely stuffed.

'What would you like for desert?' asked Anna as she cleared away the table.

Before we could speak, Antoniño had ordered *tarta de whisky* for us all.

After the delicious delights of the last two courses, desert was a bit disappointing: an inch-thick slab of ice cream sitting on a thin slice of sad-looking sponge, but even this dish had a splash of originality. Before I had lifted my spoon off the table, Anna returned clutching a bottle of Passport Scotch whisky. She twisted the cap off and poured a generous measure over everyone's softening dessert.

'Coffee,' she asked, after screwing the top back on the whisky.

'Of course,' replied Antoniño.

We finished our late night feast with a *café solo*: a tiny cup of strong black coffee. To accompany the coffee, Anna brought a bottle of clear spirit in a curious looking round bottle with a long thin neck and stainless steel shot-pouring spout.

'Try this,' insisted Antoniño, as he poured a generous measure into his coffee cup.

'What is it?' I asked.

'*Aguardiente,*' he replied, with more than a hint of menace in his voice.

Aguardiente is the local firewater, distilled from the remnants of the wine making process. It's a strong, harsh, throat-burning liqueur. I poured a drop into my cup then handed it to Melanie.

'No thanks,' she said. 'You can try it if you want, but I'll stick to plain coffee' she added.

Cautiously, I sipped the thick, black liquid but even after a night on the booze, it wasn't really to my taste. Thankfully, after two good sips, I'd downed the lot. Antoniño called for the bill but flatly refused to let us contribute. My pressing only served to annoy him so we thanked him graciously for his generosity.

Back in the bar, Antoniño joined a group of his friends and began playing cards. We thanked him again for his hospitality before returning to the square. It felt good to be outside in the fresh air. By now the time was approaching three in the morning but the party was still in full flow. We ambled across the street and sat on a low wall overlooking the square. The band was still playing to an appreciative audience. People of all ages, from young children to old grandparents, were dancing in the square, arm-in-arm to a salsa beat. Unlike the English, Spaniards have little inherited reserve; no stiff-upper-lip to spoil their enjoyment.

At 3:30 the band took its final bow and the square fell silent. We joined the departing crowds and made the short walk home. Tonight's events were an aspect of Spanish life that we hadn't participated in before, and were eager to sample more.

8

Out of our Depth

Finding a house fit for occupation that fell within our budget had so far proved elusive. If we were to remain in Galicia we would have to widen the parameters of our search and include renovation projects. Having made this decision we were keen to revisit one property, the *Pazo* we had viewed with Ramon.

'Let's go and take another look at the *Pazo*,' I said to Melanie over breakfast. 'It's not as if we need a key.'

'Are you sure?' replied Melanie, obviously worried about the consequences of getting caught.

'No one will ever know we've been there,' I replied, in an attempt to reassure her.

Later that morning, having eased her fears, we took the short drive to the house. Since our last visit the track leading to the *Pazo* had become even more overgrown. Fortunately, there were two parallel tracks of flattened undergrowth to walk along, a clear sign of agricultural activity in the fields beyond. The morning sunshine filtered through the leafy canopy of the adjacent wood. Patchy puddles of sunlight fell on the lush undergrowth covering the lane. We reached the gates and clambered through the narrow gap into the shaded courtyard beyond.

Imagining how it might one day look was easy. The possibilities were endless. Images of grandeur flashed through my mind, blinding me to the financial realities of restoring such an enormous building. We revisited the house time after time, each visit reinforcing our belief that we could transform this derelict mansion into a majestic Spanish home. We were living in a romantic fantasyland where money is no object and nothing is impossible. Having convinced ourselves that we had found the right place, we just had to speak with Ramon.

'We would like to make an offer on the *Pazo*,' I told him.

I tried to convey a mood of assured calmness when inside I was bursting with nervous excitement. Ramon seemed unmoved. After weeks of dragging us around the Galician countryside, with nothing but rejection I thought he might be a little more enthusiastic.

'I think the house is sold,' he replied.

My heart sank and a feeling of emptiness filled my stomach. Ramon greeted our offer with such disinterest because someone else was buying the *Pazo*.

'I'm waiting to hear from another party but I'm sure it is sold. I'll ring them tonight and let you know tomorrow' he added.

That evening we mulled over the events of the last few days. We had become so obsessed with the idea of renovating the *Pazo* that we had almost lost touch with reality. Hearing that the place was sold brought us back down to earth with an almighty bump. Practicality flooded through our thinking like an icy cold tidal wave. Taking on such an enormous restoration project could easily have led to financial ruin.

The following day Ramon confirmed that an offer had been accepted on the *Pazo*. In the nick of time we'd learnt a very valuable lesson. When it comes to property restoration, never let your heart rule your head.

Not long after this revelation, Maria took us to see a house in the tiny village of Gundivos: high in the hills overlooking Monforte. From the approach road its charm and beauty were undeniable. A traditional old farmhouse built from local stone with outstanding views.

'There it is,' said Maria, as we climbed the narrow road. 'Take the next right.'

The property was about one hundred metres from the road. As we approached we could see that it had been built using the finest quality masonry, some of which had been recycled from much earlier buildings. Finely chiselled Masonic symbols dated some of the blocks back to medieval times. The house was fronted by a high wall and a gated square archway. Maria unlocked the gates revealing a small enclosed courtyard.

The main house was on the left as we entered. A wooden balcony ran its length and opened out into a small raised terrace along the front. At both ends of this wooden walkway, a flight of worn and uneven stone steps led to the first floor accommodation. Directly in front of us, leading out of the courtyard, was a doorway through to an abandoned and overgrown kitchen-garden. To the right was a good sized barn that could be converted into separate accommodation. The place was charming, exactly what we were looking for, or was it?

Setting aside my rose-tinted glasses for a moment, I

took a fresh look through a more practical pair of eyes.

The entire building was in a dreadful condition. The roof had partially collapsed and all the floors and ceilings were either infested with woodworm or rotten through rain damage. There was no electricity supply and no sewerage system. The only water to the house came courtesy of a small, shallow well situated in the middle of the courtyard.

An emotional fight ensued: heart in the red corner and head in the blue. There was no denying that the house had charm and the site was idyllic, but equally the place needed a lot of work and the location was isolated. Not long into the bout, the bell rang; my mental boxing was rudely interrupted by a ferocious downpour.

'Maria, we love it,' I said as we ran back to the car. 'As soon as the weather improves we want to come back for a second viewing.'

A few days later we took another look at the place. The house was bigger than we thought. Other than that, everything was pretty much as we'd remembered: charming and very appealing. However, we had missed one thing on our first visit. Perched on a hill overlooking the house was another property. Although it looked in far worse condition than this house, the thought that one day we might have some noisy neighbours or worse still squatters, was a little off-putting.

'Maria, is the house behind for sale?' I asked hopefully.

'I don't think so but we can ask when we get back to the office.'

Back at the office the answer was a disappointing no.

Over the next few days we revisited the house several times. We gained access through an old wooden door leading into the barn. The security here consisted of a frayed piece of twine wound around a rusty nail. It gave us access to the barn and from there through into the house. This dilapidated old farmhouse was seducing us with its charm and character, even the possibility of being overlooked didn't deter us. But before we made an offer we needed to know that restoring this huge country mansion fell within our budget. We needed to find a builder and get a quote.

When it came to viewing houses our limited Spanish was fairly inconsequential. The thought of trying to explain detailed renovation work to a builder was frightening. That evening over dinner, we planned our course of action.

'Perhaps we can ask Pilar to recommend a builder,' suggested Melanie.

Pilar was co-owner of the estate agency where Maria worked. From our very first encounter, she had been a constant source of help and support.

I nodded in agreement. 'We're going to need an interpreter as well.'

'Perhaps Pilar can help us with that,' said Melanie.

The following morning we drove into Monforte. The patchy weather we had suffered over the last few weeks appeared to be changing for the better. Clear blue skies and comfortably warm temperatures were once again order of the day. As usual, we parked in the college car park and strolled along the river into the town centre.

'Good morning,' I announced, as we entered the estate agents.

A chorus of, 'good morning' echoed back from all present. We explained the situation to Pilar and hoped for a positive response.

'No problem, I'm sure I can find a builder to give you a quote,' she said confidently. 'But an interpreter,' she paused for a moment in concentrated thought. 'Come with me,' she said, leaping to her feet and heading for the door.

We jumped up quickly and followed. Pilar set-off up the street at a pace, acknowledging acquaintances with a broad smile and a quick: 'hola', as she raced along. She'd almost broken into a canter as she rounded the bend at the top of the street and collided headlong with a young man heading in the opposite direction. Thankfully no one was hurt and both parties saw the funny side of things. It seemed that they knew each other.

'You speak English, don't you Jose?' asked Pilar of the young man.

'Yes,' he replied hesitantly.

By sheer coincidence, Pilar had not only collided with someone she knew but also someone who spoke English: we were astonished. We'd lived here for over two months and, excluding Ramon, this young man was the first person we'd met who spoke any English: Pilar came straight to the point.

'My clients need someone to act as an interpreter for them,' she said.

Jose wasn't keen on the idea but Pilar had her prize and she wasn't letting go. After a little more persuasion Jose reluctantly agreed.

Later that week we returned to the agency as arranged. Jose was already there when we arrived. He greeted us nervously. We could tell from his shy and bashful demeanour that he wasn't relishing his press-ganged role as our interpreter. A short time later the builder arrived; Pilar introduced him as Manolo.

He was a confident and animated individual in his early fifties. When he spoke, his whole face seemed to smile. Deep-set wrinkles furrowed his tanned forehead and he had a coarse, gravelly voice. Accompanying Manolo was his son, a serious and studious young man in his mid-twenties. Pilar handed them the keys and we set off for the house.

The late evening sun was bright and warm. The light showers we dodged earlier in the month had sparked an explosion of colourful vegetation. Roadside verges were carpeted with wild flowers and tall grasses. Before long we were trundling along the lane on the approach to the house. Moments later the builder and his son arrived in a white pick-up truck.

For the next half an hour we exchanged renovation ideas; Jose was proving invaluable. He was clearly uncomfortable with his role as interpreter but failed to appreciate that his bashfulness and lack of confidence in using English, paled into insignificance compared to our grasp of Spanish. Throughout it all the builder remained confident. Wild arm movements signalled the position of new walls and the demolition of old ones. As time rolled on his antics became increasingly animated. We found it slightly disconcerting that, throughout our entire discussions, he failed to make any notes or take one single measurement. It ended with him agreeing to prepare a quote.

'How long will it take?' I asked, eagerly.

'I'll have it done by the end of next week,' he replied. 'Now let's go and have a drink.'

Doing business in Spain always seems to end over a glass of wine. A tradition we were happy to observe.

'Follow me back to Monforte, I know just the place,' announced Manolo.

By the time we arrived back, most of the town was in the shade. Only the tops of the tallest buildings reflected the brightness of the setting sun. We parked behind Manolo's pick-up truck outside a bar named JM. Manolo was clearly at home in these familiar surroundings. He joked with the barman as though they were old friends, before ordering the drinks.

'Would you like a tapa?' asked Manolo, pointing at a glass-fronted cabinet sat on the bar.

How could we refuse a tasty nibble to enjoy with our wine?

The cabinet was filled with a large selection of tapas: some we recognised and others that were less familiar.

'Would you like some pancetta?' asked Manolo.

We weren't quite sure what to expect but agreeing to his suggestion seemed preferable to second guessing the selection facing us.

'Five pancettas,' demanded Manolo.

The barman disappeared. A few minutes later he returned carrying five tiny saucers. Each one contained a small chunk of crusty bread topped with a rasher of sizzling pancetta; enthusiastically, we tucked in. There's something very English about the aroma of pan fried bacon. Even the fat-soaked crust tasted delicious. After wolfing down this tasty nibble, Manolo was eager to try another.

'Do you like *pulpo*?' he asked.

For once we could answer honestly.

'No we don't like it.'

'The *pulpo* here is very different, it's delicious,' said Manolo as he ordered five portions.

This dish was nothing like the rubbery rounds we'd trialled at the market in Ferreira. Here the delicacy was served cold, chopped into small pieces with onions and peppers and bathed in herby vinaigrette. I wouldn't say that I enjoyed it, but I could at least eat it. Melanie; however, was not for turning and flatly refused to try even a small piece, hardly surprising given her previous reaction.

A brief interlude in Manolo's showmanship gave Jose the opportunity to make his exit. We thanked him for his time. He didn't realise it but his contribution had been invaluable. Jose's departure gave Melanie and me an excuse to bid our farewell. I offered to settle the bar bill but Manolo adamantly refused; however, he was keen to play one last joke on the barman before we left.

'Watch this,' he said with a mischievous smile.

The bill amounted to 14 euros. From the back of his wallet Manolo pulled out a 500 euro note and nonchalantly placed it on the bar. When the barman returned he reached to take it and then paused in disbelief. I doubt he had ever seen such a high denomination banknote before. Suddenly the penny dropped: Manolo was playing a prank. The note was real enough but the thought that anyone would try and settle such a small bill with a 500 note had the pair of them in fits of laughter. Manolo thrived in front of an audience and although this simple, slap-stick humour didn't amuse us, watching two grown men acting like small children certainly brought a smile to our faces. With the note placed safely back in his wallet and the bill settled, we all left.

A week later Pilar rang. As promised, Manolo had completed the estimate and wanted to go through it with us.

'Can you call at the office tomorrow at seven?' asked Pilar.

This news was an exciting development.

'We'll have to get in touch with Jose and ask him to meet us at the office,' I said to Melanie as she came off the phone.

'I'll ring him straightaway.'

Try as she did, Jose was not responding. From our very first meeting he had been a reluctant recruit. We were beginning to realise just how reluctant. Having failed to contact him, we decided to arrive early for the meeting in the hope that Pilar might be able to find a replacement.

'Don't worry,' she said, after we explained our dilemma. 'I know an English teacher who might help.'

No sooner had she uttered the words than Manolo arrived. She explained our predicament to Maria and sent her in search of the English teacher. Meanwhile, Pilar led the three of us into a private office at the rear. We sat patiently, waiting for Maria to return. We tried to make small-talk but the language barrier proved difficult to breach. Conversations were limited to the weather, both here and in the UK, and family, an obligatory topic of all Spanish exchanges. After a while Manolo began to fidget in his seat like a restless schoolboy. To everyone's relief Maria returned.

'This is Sylvia,' she announced.

Sylvia was a young woman, large and bubbly. Her command of the English language was excellent and we hit it off immediately. Unlike Jose, she seemed thrilled at the prospect of putting her English to good use. She pulled up a chair next to us and the meeting was turned over to Manolo.

He arrived carrying a thin, cardboard file. Prompted by our glare, he opened it and pulled out the quote. Carefully, and thoroughly, he explained every detail. Sylvia's translation was excellent and never faltered. The whole process took about half an hour, concluding with the price.

'That will be seven million,' said Sylvia, 'seven million pesetas.'

This time we were prepared. One million pesetas is equal to 6000 euros or 4000 pounds. The calculation was simple.

This figure was well within budget: my heart fluttered

with excitement. We sat silently, digesting the news. Without warning Pilar began quizzing Manolo. We stared at Sylvia desperate to know what was being said.

'She's asking him about the windows and doors,' whispered Sylvia.

'Windows and doors', I thought to myself, and why is Sylvia whispering! We're the only people that can understand her.

'Now she's asking about the kitchen, and the ceilings, the plumbing, and the courtyard,' the list went on and on.

'Do you have any questions?' asked Pilar after a while.

'*Ermm...* No,' I stuttered.

Pilar had made it perfectly clear, through her interrogation of Manolo, that we should be asking questions, important questions; but we didn't have a clue what they were. Our lack of knowledge, experience and understanding of the building trade, could prove to be an expensive shortcoming.

We thanked Manolo for his time. We would consider his proposal and let him know our decision in due course. Once he had left, Pilar was keen to point out that Manolo's quote was missing some very important and potentially expensive details. We were clearly out of our depth in this alien environment. Pilar suggested we get another estimate. We thanked both her and Sylvia for their help and left to consider our options.

'Do you fancy a drink?' I asked as we strolled back to the car.

'I think I need one after that,' replied Melanie.

I knew just the place to lift our spirits.

Leaving Monforte we followed the signs for the town of Chantada. The main highway winds its way through picturesque countryside. A patchwork of lush meadows, ancient deciduous forests, and small conifer plantations, are stitched together with a network of dry-stone walls, wooden fencing, and unkempt thickets. Sprinkled over this landscape are the whitewashed walls of tiny hamlets and stone built farmhouses.

After driving for about 10 km, the road crosses the deep valley gorge of the river Miño. This magic carpet of tarmac is supported by concrete tablets rising hundreds of feet from the valley below. Before crossing the river we turned left. A narrow, tree-lined lane meanders down the valley side to the river bank: we continued on.

Spanning the river is a medieval stone bridge, its shadow reflected like a mirage in the still water. We bypassed this and continued along the river's edge to the village of Belesar. This tiny village is divided in two by the river, and linked by a steel-railed bridge. Immediately before entering the village a wooden sign marked *'Bodega'*, is nailed to a rocky outcrop at the roadside. Thirty-or-so granite steps lead to a quiet bar built on the riverbank.

As usual the bar was deserted. We took a seat at a window table, ordered a glass of local red wine and stared out at the spectacular scenery. The valley sides are contoured with terraced vineyards, rising hundreds of metres from the river's edge like a staircase to heaven. Ghostly reflections of the steel bridge and colourful village houses shimmered in the dark water.

'I needed that,' said Melanie, sipping her wine and soaking up the scenery.

'If we're going to buy a house to renovate, we're going to need professional help,' I said. 'There's no way we can do this on our own.'

'What sort of help?' asked Melanie.

'We need an architect.'

Today's meeting highlighted the fact that we were way

out of our depth. None of the houses we'd viewed in Galicia were DIY projects. All of them needed major restoration work that required professional expertise.

The following day we returned to the estate agents to ask Pilar if she could recommend an architect. As helpful and impartial as ever, she gave us the names of three.

'I haven't worked with any of them, so you'll have to decide for yourself who is most suitable,' she said, as she scribbled their names and telephone numbers down on a piece of paper.

Later that day we phoned Sylvia and asked if she could help us find and interview an architect.

'Of course,' she said. 'I'll meet you tomorrow and we'll take it from there.'

We didn't know it at the time, but that meeting would form the foundation of our future in Galicia.

'I've been thinking,' said Sylvia, when we met up the following day. 'I have a friend who's an architect. His name is Felipe, Felipe Maria Feijoo de Fontecha.'

I looked at the list that Pilar had given us; second name down was Felipe Fontecha. Perhaps fate had intervened, with nothing else to base our decision on we decided to start with him.

'Can you ring him to arrange a meeting?' I asked Sylvia.

'His office is just along the road. Let's walk on and see if he's in,' she replied. 'Come on, let's go.'

Before we had time to think about it we were climbing the stairs to his office and knocking on the door. After spending all my working life in England, I was struggling to adjust to the hit-and-hope approach to Spanish business. On this occasion we were lucky, Felipe was in, and available.

Through Sylvia, we outlined the situation and asked if

he could help. He explained his role within the practice and introduced us to his colleague Javier. Between them they agreed to help and arranged a meeting to view the property. We thanked them for their time and left, pleased with the day's progress.

The viewing with Felipe and Javier was in stark contrast to that of Manolo's. They were here to conduct a detailed and thorough site survey. They gave us precise recommendations on how best to use the available space and took a series of detailed measurements. The whole process lasted over two hours.

Felipe agreed to draw-up plans of the existing building, incorporating the changes we'd discussed. When complete we would meet again to consider any amendments. This was exactly the approach we were looking for: precise, professional, and structured. We thanked them for their time and headed back to Monforte with Sylvia.

'Thanks for your help Sylvia,' said Melanie on the drive back. 'We couldn't have done it without you.'

'It's no trouble,' she said. 'I'm glad I could help.'

Earlier in the day, Melanie and I had discussed asking Sylvia to act as our paid interpreter. This seemed as good a time as any to table our proposal.

'We would like to pay you for your time Sylvia,' I said, as we hit the outskirts of Monforte.

'Don't be silly,' she replied, 'I don't want paying.'

'Sylvia, we must insist. Let's call it a Spanish lesson,' I suggested. 'We'll pay you to give us a two hour lesson every Monday but if we need any translating or interpreting done, then we'll do that instead.'

Sylvia thought this was a great idea and happily agreed.

'See you on Monday,' said Melanie, as we dropped her off outside her apartment.

9

Too Clever by Half

Employing the services of an architect eased our concerns. We were still sailing through uncharted waters but now we had a pilot to guide us. While Felipe prepared the plans, we used the time to relax and enjoy the fine weather. Melanie was sunbathing in the garden, and I had just started to doze off when the doorbell rang.

'I'll go,' I said, leaping to my feet and heading towards the front gates.

Clutching the wrought iron bars of the gates and peering through like a jailed prisoner, was the familiar figure of Ramon.

'I have some new properties to show you,' he called, as I came into view.

'Thanks but we've found somewhere and we're going to make an offer on it,' I said, as I walked up the drive to meet him.

He was visibly shocked by the news. We had not seen or heard from him for over two weeks. Surely he didn't expect us to wait around and be at his beck and call, if so he was sadly mistaken.

Anxiously he quizzed me about the find. The prospect of losing a potential customer had focused his mind. For the first time since we'd met him, he seemed more interested in what we were looking for rather than what he had to show us. Without giving too much away, I explained what we'd found and a rough idea of its location. He wished us luck and left.

The very next morning he was back.

'I've found a stone house in the area you mentioned yesterday,' he said excitedly. 'Come and take a look, it's only eight million,' he added.

It couldn't harm to take a look and we had nothing else planned for the morning. Even the price was attractive: a million pesetas less than the farmhouse in Gundivos.

'Give us a few minutes to get ready and we'll be with you.'

A quick wash and change and we were ready for off.

'We need to pick someone up in Monforte before we visit the house,' said Ramon, as we locked the gates.

Collecting a key-holder, from a distant location, was a common feature of Ramon's viewings. By the time we reached the town Ramon's mystery guest was waiting on a street corner. Without delay we headed out of town and into the countryside.

'We usually have Maria with us on this road,' I joked, as we chased after Ramon.

'Perhaps he's taking us to see the same house,' quipped Melanie.

However unintentional our remarks, the facts were undeniable: Turn after turn, junction after junction. We'd taken this same route so many times before; I could almost negotiate it blindfolded. Ten minutes later our suspicions were realised as we turned off the lane in Gundivos and pulled up outside the farmhouse.

'Pretend we haven't seen it,' I said to Melanie. 'Let's see what they've got to say.'

The shadowy figure Ramon had picked up in town remained a mystery. He wasn't the key holder, although he'd clearly been to the house before. He knew exactly how to gain access through the unsecured doorway into the barn.

Who is he, and what is he doing here?

We kept up the pretence of ignorance by taking a good look around and asking all the usual questions, the answers to which we already knew. I felt a bit uncomfortable with the whole situation. Ramon was shifty enough but there was something more sinister about his new recruit.

Perhaps we can use their lower asking price to negotiate a better price with Pilar, I thought to myself.

All of a sudden I remembered about the house on the hill. The one that overlooks this property and the one that Pilar was unable to offer us. If Ramon's mate was some kind of unofficial agent, perhaps he could sort a deal out on that property as well.

'Is that house for sale?' I asked Ramon, pointing at the one on the hill.

A short discussion followed between Ramon and his side-kick.

'If you're interested in buying both of them, we can find out,' he replied.

'That would depend on the price,' I said, 'but yes, we are interested.'

Buying both would open up a host of new possibilities; it had to be worth a try. Ramon agreed to find out and let us know tomorrow. This new development was very exciting. Perhaps we could buy both properties after all.

The next day Ramon called around again. His colleague had found the owner of the house on the hill and he was willing to sell.

'How much does he want for it?' I asked eagerly.

'I don't know,' said Ramon. 'We need to go back to Monforte, pick up my associate and take a look at the other house.'

It all seemed very cloak and dagger to me. I could only presume that Ramon's colleague trusted him less than we did. Melanie and I were tiring of all this running around. Tying Ramon down was like chasing a bar of soap in a warm bath. The prospect of securing both properties was too good an opportunity to pass up. We just had to find out how much they would both cost.

Half an hour later, the four of us were wading through a field of tall grasses; climbing the hill towards the other house. From a distance it looked in reasonable condition but up close the place was a wreck. Most of the roof had collapsed inwards: under this weight, the rotten floors had given way, creating a mound of building rubble in the middle of the basement. The outside walls were still intact but that was about it. Its ruinous condition didn't really matter to us. All we wanted to do at this stage was stop anyone else getting their hands on it.

'So how much is it?' I asked Ramon.

He turned to his colleague for inspiration.

'Fourteen,' he said, after a while.

'Fourteen Million! You must be joking,' I replied sarcastically.

Melanie stormed off in a huff and I followed. Ramon came charging after us, stumbling through the long grasses in an effort to catch up.

'That includes another four acres of land,' he called.

We stopped and waited for him.

'Ramon, I've told you before, we don't want any more land,' I snapped in annoyance. 'That ruin is not worth *four* million,' I added cheekily.

The negotiations had begun.

Ramon let out a forced laugh, 'It might be possible to buy the house without the land,' he said, 'for maybe six'.

'Six million!' I repeated in astonishment. 'If we're going to buy both houses the most we can offer is thirteen for the pair.'

Ramon paused for a while considering my new offer. 'I'll have to ask my colleague,' he said, shuffling off in disappointment.

By now the sun was at its height. A warm, gentle breeze floated across the hay field creating a swaying sea of thigh-length grasses. Ramon's mystery man had wandered off, shading himself from the midday sun by sitting under the cool canopy of a large fig tree. We ambled across to meet him and gave him the offer. He shrugged his shoulders in a gesture of agreement. Ramon would call to see us in a few days to confirm that all parties were in agreement.

Is this it? I thought to myself.

We'd spent months searching, days viewing and hours waiting around. We'd risked life and limb, tip-toeing through dirty, derelict and dangerous buildings. We'd hung around in estate agents and on street corners waiting for home owners and key holders. Had we finally found the dream home we were looking for?

Something didn't feel quite right: negotiations had proved far too easy.

Who was this mystery middleman and what was he getting out of the deal?

They had started the negotiations at 22 million and I ended them at 13. I felt uneasy about the whole affair, and generally speaking: if something sounds too good to be true, it inevitably is.

We returned home to wait for a response. At the very least, Felipe was busy working on plans for the right house.

Later that afternoon Ramon turned up again. He was verging on becoming a nuisance. Accompanying him was his wife and another couple. He introduced them as clients of his from England. They had just returned from the notary office having completed the purchase of a house. I got the impression that he was trying to reassure us about his credentials as an estate agent. We weren't really that impressed. Melanie and I were simply thrilled to be speaking our native tongue. Chatting to others without the need of a dictionary or the preparation of a rehearsed statement was a rare luxury. When Ramon asked us to join them for dinner we jumped at the chance, giddy at the thought of an evening of spoken English.

Ramon's country home is a modest affair: a traditional, stone-built cottage just a short drive from the centre of Ferreira. It occupies an elevated position with magnificent panoramic views over the surrounding countryside and distant mountains. In front of the cottage is a small vineyard resting on a gentle slope.

'Do you make your own wine?' I asked politely.

'Of course,' he replied, 'Come and see.'

We followed him around the side of the house. An old wooden door guarded the entrance to his small *bodega*. He pushed it open and stepped inside.

'Here you go,' he said, as he handed four dusty bottles of red wine to Melanie and me.

'You take them and I'll carry the rest,' he said.

Clutching three more bottles, he closed the door. Tucked under one arm were a couple of one litre bottles of *aguardiente* and in his other hand a bottle of *licor café*.

Laden with alcohol, the three of us climbed the exterior stone steps to the first floor accommodation. A crudely constructed, chestnut panelled door led directly into the main living room. The place was simply furnished with a mismatch of secondhand furniture. The floor was planked with rough-planed and irregular sized hardwood boards. A tarnished brass chandelier hung from the ceiling, secured by a rusty nail. The ceiling was so low that everyone except Ramon had to tilt their head as they walked under the light fitting. If Ramon was making any money from his estate agency exploits, he certainly wasn't investing it in this little house.

There were three doors leading off the living area. Two of them led to bedrooms, both of which were equally as poorly furnished as the living room, and the third led into a small kitchen.

I couldn't help thinking that if Ramon had brought us here before taking us to view his sale properties, we would have had a much better understanding of his interpretation of habitable. As we followed him from room to room I half expected him to stamp on the floor and shout, 'Gud wud, gud wud'!

By the time Ramon had finished showing us around, his wife was in a real panic.

'What's the matter?' I asked Ramon.

'My wife had planned to make a tortilla for dinner but our neighbour is not at home.'

Melanie and I looked at each, confused by Ramon's statement.

'The neighbour's not home!' whispered Melanie quizzically.

Fearing a long, drawn-out explanation we remained silent. Perhaps something had been lost in translation.

'Here you go,' said Ramon, handing us both a tumbler of his home made wine.

The first sip of home brew is always the worst. After months of practice we'd learnt to disguise our repulsion with a contorted smile.

To the delight of our hostess the next door neighbour returned. Our earlier confusion was quickly explained as two dozen freshly laid eggs were passed over the garden fence. The two main ingredients of a tortilla are potatoes and eggs. Within half an hour, dinner was served. Traditional Spanish tortilla accompanied by a fresh mixed salad, smothered in olive oil and red wine vinegar and sprinkled with freshly chopped herbs and rock salt – delicious.

'For dessert we're going to have a Galician *quemada,'* announced Ramon, with a twinkle of devilment in his eye.

As soon as we'd devoured the main course, preparations began in earnest for our mystery pudding. At the back of the dining table was an old sideboard. Its bright lacquered veneer was rippled with damp and peeling away from its cheap chipboard carcass. Ramon opened one of the doors and pulled out a heavy earthenware dish. He placed it carefully in the centre of the table as if displaying a priceless family heirloom. It measured about a foot in diameter and five inches deep. The brown glaze was chipped around the rim and the inside scarred with scratches.

Into the dish he poured the two, litre bottles of *aguardiente* that he'd taken from the *bodega*. While Ramon finished this, his wife fetched a bag of sugar and two large lemons from the kitchen.

'It takes fourteen tablespoons of sugar,' said Ramon.

He reminded me of a naughty schoolboy messing around with dangerous chemicals in the science lab. We watched in bemused silence, undecided whether he was preparing a dessert or making a Molotov cocktail. Having spooned in the sugar he pulled a penknife from his pocket and picked up a lemon. Clutching it tightly, he began hacking away chunks of peel. The large lumps splashed into the bowl and floated to the surface. He finished by cutting the lemons in half and squeezing out the juice. Pips burst out in all directions as he pressed the last droplets of juice from the pulp. Like a witch in *Macbeth,* he stirred his alcoholic brew.

'Don't be alarmed,' he said, as he leant over and switched off the light.

The room was plunged into darkness, save for a narrow beam of light filtering under the kitchen door. After our initial surprise the room fell quiet. The silence was broken by the unmistakable rattle of a box of matches. The spark of a strike and the bright phosphorous glow of ignition illuminated the room. Ramon's ghostly shadow flickered in the yellow flame. He was leaning over the table, match in one hand and a ladle brimming with his alcoholic potion in the other. Surely he wasn't intending to light this flammable cocktail, not in a house made mainly of wood.

That was exactly his intention. With near perfect synchronicity, he raised the ladle high above the bowl and ignited its alcohol laden cup. The blue-green flame danced and skipped, casting ethereal shadows around the small room. Gently, Ramon tipped the ladle; a cascading waterfall of flaming alcohol tumbled into the bowl setting the whole thing alight. Time after time he scooped a ladleful of flaming liquid from the bowl, raising it within inches of the dry wooden ceiling before tipping it back in a fiery torrent. This tabletop pyrotechnic show lasted over five minutes. The flames were finally extinguished using a damp tea towel.

'Drink it while it's hot,' insisted Ramon, as he handed each of us a warm glass of liqueur.

Cautiously, I took a sip from the warm glass. This unique cocktail tasted like a warm mouthful of siphoned petrol mixed with a lemon-flavoured cold remedy. It was absolutely hideous. Its only redeeming feature was that after a second glass, I really didn't care what it tasted like.

Ramon had proved a good host. He'd showed us a different side to his character, something we hadn't seen before. I still wasn't convinced by his sincerity but it couldn't harm to give him the benefit of the doubt.

Two days later we still hadn't heard from him regarding the offer. Just as we were starting to wonder what had happened to him the doorbell rang.

'I bet that's him now,' I said to Melanie as I set off for the gates.

To my surprise, Pilar was standing there.

'Hello!' I called, as I marched up the drive. 'How are you?'

I invited her in and the three of us sat around the table on the front terrace.

'I'm afraid I have some bad news,' she said, after greeting Melanie. 'Someone has made an offer on the farmhouse.'

Melanie and I glanced across at each other: we were both feeling a little guilty. Pilar was not only the first agent to show us the house, but she had been a constant source of help and information since we first met. It seemed only fair that we come clean.

We did our best to explain about Ramon's unexpected appearance; the mystery man from Monforte, and most importantly, the fact that they were able to offer us both properties.

'How much are they asking for the two?' asked Pilar.

Her directness came as no surprise. In this respect, Galicians are very similar to Yorkshire folk. They call a spade a spade and if they want to know the answer to something, they ask. My surprise was in the tone of her question. She gave me the impression that she knew what my answer was going be before she'd asked the question. Perhaps our negotiations to buy these two houses weren't yet concluded. I decided to find out.

'We don't know,' I said gingerly. 'Ramon said he would get back to us in a few days and we haven't seen him since.'

Pilar seemed unconvinced by my answer but continued regardless. She explained that they had managed to find the owner of the house on the hill, and as a consequence she was now in a position to offer both properties to us.

'How much are they?' I asked.

'The farmhouse is seven million and the house on the hill a little over two.'

We were stunned. Pilar's combined asking price was almost four million pesetas less than Ramon's. From our very first encounter, I'd never fully trusted him. My instincts had proved correct; the way ahead was clear.

'We would like to buy them both,' I said to Pilar after a lengthy pause.

As far as we were concerned, Ramon and his sidekick could go to hell. It had taken us far too long to earn our little nest egg, to let some little squirt like him steal it from under our noses.

Pilar agreed to start the ball rolling as soon as she got back to the office. Her departure gave Melanie and me the opportunity to let off a little steam. I rang Ramon and summoned him to the house. I was in no mood to listen to feeble excuses. He pleaded his innocence but we were unconvinced and in no uncertain terms, dispensed with his services.

The following morning we were up early, excited by the prospect of finalising the deal. Things could not have turned out better: we had the houses we wanted, from the agent we preferred, and at the best possible price. Straight after breakfast we headed into town and on to the estate agents.

'There are a few problems with the two houses,' announced Pilar, after greeting us.

'A few problems,' I asked nervously.

After leaving us yesterday Pilar had contacted both house owners. The farmhouse was owned by two brothers. She was told that they'd already accepted an offer. To secure the house we would have to make an improved bid. By an ironic twist of fate, Pilar was asking us to gazump our own offer. How had we managed to get ourselves into such a predicament! If we wanted the house we had no alternative but to bite the bullet and up the offer. We nudged the offer up slightly and thankfully it was accepted.

'The other problem is a bit more complicated,' she said cautiously. 'The other house is under offer as well.'

We tried to look surprised but knew full well that once again we were the culprits. Having agreed to buy the house through Ramon, his creepy colleague had spoken with the owner and secured sole rights to sell it for a period of seven days. All we could do was wait, cross our fingers, and hope that he wouldn't find another buyer within the week.

This delay was a frustrating set-back; having come this far, we weren't going to buy the farmhouse without being sure of getting the other. It seemed that every time we got within touching distance of our goal, someone moved the posts.

The next few days dragged by, all our thoughts centred on the two houses. It came as a pleasant relief when, in the middle of the week, Sylvia rang with news.

'Felipe's finished the plans,' she said excitedly.

If only we could have shared her enthusiasm. With nothing but time on our hands, we agreed to meet up the very next day.

Felipe's offices are on the first floor of a residential apartment block in the centre of Monforte. It's quite indistinguishable from any other high-rise development, save for a tarnished brass plaque mounted on the wall outside. A smoked-glass panelled door leads into a cool and poorly lit lobby. On the right is a small elevator and to the left a flight of tiled steps. Sylvia flicked the light switch on at the bottom of the steps but nothing happened.

'Typical!' she snapped. 'They can't even be bothered to change the light bulbs.'

Unfazed by the darkness, she set off up the stairs followed by Melanie and me. Once on the first floor she rang the office doorbell and we waited patiently for a response. A few seconds later it opened and Felipe's secretary showed us inside. In contrast to the gloomy stairwell, the reception area was bright and airy. We hadn't been waiting long when Felipe popped his head around the corner. He welcomed us with a warm handshake and led us into his office.

He began by presenting the plans. Felipe had incorporated everything that we discussed on site and added a few ideas of his own. These detailed drawings breathed fresh life into the project. After the disappointment earlier in the week, seeing our ideas brought to life rekindled our enthusiasm.

'Sylvia, can you ask Felipe how much he thinks the work will cost?'

Her enquiry was met with a long and thoughtful pause. A conversation followed; Sylvia became frustrated. Felipe was reluctant to commit himself, hardly surprising given the stage we were at. She pushed him further.

'Felipe says that it's very difficult to quote a price at such an early stage but, based on similar projects, it will probably cost about 29 million,' she said. 'And that's just for the large house, nothing else,' she added.

We were stunned, we knew it wouldn't be cheap; but Felipe's estimate was more than three times the asking price of both properties. Before deciding what to do next we needed to know more.

'If we go ahead, how long will the work take?' I asked.

If we were going to invest so much of our nest egg in this project, we needed to know how long it would be before we could start recouping some of the money. Renting the proposed holiday let was key to our financial survival, to have any chance of securing bookings for next summer we would have to start advertising the rental property by Christmas at the latest. We were approaching the end of June: could all this work be finished by then.

'Felipe says, 'at least 12 months'', replied Silvia.

This was the biggest setback to date. Not only would we miss next summer's bookings but if there were any serious delays in the renovation work, we might miss the following year as well. Would our limited resources stretch so far! We thanked everyone for their time and left, with plenty to think about.

Once again we found ourselves swimming against the tide. We had set our hearts on restoring this charming old farmhouse but our heads were dragging us back to financial reality.

The seven day deadline had expired and we found ourselves driving back to the estate agents still unsure how we wanted to proceed. On arrival, Pilar ushered us into her private office at the back.

'The house is back on the market,' she said, in a muted tone.

Perhaps this is fate telling us to follow our hearts, I thought to myself.

'But there's some bad news,' she added.

Pilar explained that a third party wanted to buy the house. A mystery German bidder had entered the fray. If we wanted the house, the asking price had doubled to four million pesetas. It all sounded too staged to be true. We'd spent the last few days deliberating over our dilemma, tortuously considering every conceivable scenario.

Melanie glanced at me; she knew from my expression what the response would be. The answer was no. Our fragile reality had finally shattered and Melanie was struggling to cope. Unable to contain her emotions, she broke down in tears, sobbing uncontrollably at the loss of our dream and the prospect of starting the process all over again. We thanked Pilar for her efforts, withdrew our offer on the farmhouse and returned home to lick our wounds.

Will we ever find our dream home in Spain?

10

A Strategic Change

After the disappointments of the last few weeks, we decided that a break from house hunting would do us both good. We needed to reassess our position, recharge the batteries and weigh up all the options.

What better way to take my mind off things than to learn some new skills.

The title read, *'Cocina Tradicional de Español'*, (Traditional Spanish Cooking) exactly what I was looking for.

'What do you think of this?' I asked Melanie, as I picked the glossy covered book off the supermarket shelf and began flicking through it.

'What do I think to what?' replied Melanie.

'I'm going to teach myself to cook.'

'What do you know about cooking?'

'Nothing, that's why I need the book.'

She snatched it off me and started thumbing through.

'It's all in Spanish,' she said, having given it a derisory glance.

'I know it is. I can practice my Spanish while I'm learning to cook,' I added cheekily.

That afternoon I set about translating my first recipe, *Carne de vaca al estilo de Teruel*, a beef dish from the Aragon region of eastern Spain. The colourful photo showed an oval shaped platter circled with medallions of beef in a rich, brown gravy and centred with diced carrots. It looked delicious. Translating the ingredients was fairly straightforward. The preparation instructions proved slightly more taxing. The following day, armed with the list of ingredients, I drove into town and bought my supplies. My next task was to familiarise myself with the kitchen.

In England we had lived in a four storey terraced house built into the side of a hill. The basement kitchen was Melanie's domain: a place from which evening meals would miraculously appear. For me, the kitchen was an area I walked through on my way to the back garden. As for cooking, my skills in this department were limited to burning a few bangers on the barbecue: on that rare occasion an English summer would allow.

What I failed to appreciate, when choosing my new hobby, was the extent to which Melanie cherished her sovereignty over this domestic space. Foolishly, I thought that she would actively encourage my involvement in this area of daily domesticity. How wrong could I have been? My presence in the kitchen was viewed as a personal violation, an invasion of her space and worse, a pre-apocalyptic strike of unparalleled magnitude. How could I have missed the signs?

Undeterred by these negative vibes I began my preparations while Melanie retired to the garden. Slowly, I began to realise the seriousness of my actions. It took just 20 minutes for curiosity to get the better of her. Casually, she strolled back into the kitchen from the garden.

'Don't worry, I've only come to get a drink,' she snapped, as I glared across at her questioningly.

She poured herself a glass of juice and leant against the worktop sipping it slowly.

'Is there something else?' I asked teasingly.

Melanie was in no mood for baiting. She uttered a disgruntled tsk and marched back into the garden.

That evening we tucked in to the succulent beef. It tasted as good as it looked. A fact that even Melanie was forced to concede.

Buoyed by my success I decided to try my hand at creating a dessert. The very next day I set about translating the recipe for *Frangollo Canario,* chosen for no other reason other than its limited number of ingredients.

All the recipes in the book served six people. It hadn't posed a problem with the beef dish: I simply reduced the quantity of meat and kept all the other ingredients the same. This wasn't going to be possible with the dessert.

The ingredients were *Maíz* (maize flour), 1 kilo; *Leche* (milk), ½ litre; *Azúcar* (sugar), 100 grams; *Matalahuva* (aniseed), 2 teaspoons; and *Limon* (lemon), 1 lemon.

And the instructions couldn't have been simpler: *Add 1 ½ litres of water to a pan and bring to the boil. Add the maize flour and the rind of a lemon. Stir constantly for 1 hour. Place in a dish and allow to cool. Before serving add the sugar and serve with hot milk*

After a quick trip to the supermarket, I was ready to start. I began by boiling the water in a large saucepan. I opened the packet of maize flour and placed it next to the hob on the worktop. At this point things became a bit tricky: another pair of hands wouldn't have gone amiss. With a tablespoon in one hand and a wooden spoon in the other, I started to add the flour to the water. The instructions were clear, 'stir constantly': frantically I stirred the pan. Trying to co-ordinate the actions of stirring with one hand while spooning flour with the other, proved nigh on impossible. Little by little I added the flour, but the more I added the thicker the mixture became. Within seconds it became so coagulated that stirring the pan sent it whizzing around on the hob like a fairground waltzer. I dropped the tablespoon and grabbed the pan handle, stirring furiously. As soon as I released the pan to add more flour, it whizzed around on the burner. I simply didn't have enough hands.

'Melanie!' I called in desperation.

A few moments later Melanie appeared at the door.

'What?' she asked.

'Can you hold the pan while I stir?'

A faint grin of satisfaction filtered across her face as she strolled over to the hob. She knew all along that at some point I would need her help.

'Is it meant to be this thick?' she asked.

'All I've done is follow the instructions,' I said, trying desperately to seem blameless.

Melanie grabbed the pan handle while I continued to add the flour. After the addition of two more tablespoons, the mixture was so thick that my action to stir caused Melanie to call out in agony.

'Stop!' she screamed in pain. 'I can't hold it any longer, you're hurting my wrist. You must have done something wrong.'

She removed the pan from the heat and turned off the gas. By now, the gooey mass had set like reinforced concrete. The wooden spoon was stuck solid, jutting out of the pan like a miniature flagpole. Melanie checked the instructions.

'You seem to have done everything right,' she said, after carefully reading the recipe. 'What's this?' she asked, pointing at the packet of *maizena* perched on the worktop.

'That's the flour,' I replied.

'What flour?'

'The maize flour.'

'That's not maize flour,' she said. 'It's cornflour!'

'Cornflour'.

'Yes: Cornflour. It's used as a thickening agent.'

I had wrongly assumed that *maizena* was the same as *maiz*. Unsurprisingly, every spoonful of starchy cornflour I added thickened the mixture. Before long the pair of us were roaring with laughter at my naive mistake. Although the dessert was an unmitigated disaster, my culinary ignorance had succeeded in forging an uneasy kitchen alliance.

Although Melanie wasn't quite ready to accept me as a permanent member of the catering team, she actively encouraged my alfresco cooking. Earlier in the month we had invested in a paella burner and paella pan: The excellent summer weather gave me plenty of opportunity to hone my skills. Thankfully, it's a very simple dish to prepare; a typical Spanish meal, synonymous with outdoor dining.

Lazy days spent idling around the house gave us the opportunity to re-evaluate our house hunting strategy. There were plenty of old properties on the market but all of them were either too expensive or would be too time consuming to renovate. If Galicia was to become our home we needed a complete rethink.

After days of deliberation, our course became clear. We loved Galicia, it felt like home. The locals are welcoming and the countryside is stunning. We needed two properties, one to live in and the other for letting; and we needed to forget romantic notions of restoring ruins and look at more practical places to live. Having forged our plans we picked ourselves up, dusted ourselves down, and were now ready to start looking again.

From memory, the first two houses Maria had ever shown us might well fit our new search criteria. Recharged and re-energised, we headed off to Monforte to request a second viewing. Having spent the previous nine weeks stumbling through dilapidated shacks, our new requirements came as a bit of a shock.

'Hola Pilar!' I announced, as we entered the agents. 'We would like to go back and see the first two houses we were ever shown,' I added.

'The first two,' repeated Pilar, surprised at our change of heart.

'That is, if they're still for sale,' I was sure they would be but it seemed impolite to assume.

Within minutes we were off, heading out of town and into the countryside. The day was hot, very hot. The thermometer in the car indicated an outside temperature approaching 40°C. The two houses were fairly close together; both fell under the administrative council of Sober. Given our fondness for the fruits of the vine, I could just imagine the merriment such a postal address would cause among family and friends back in England.

The first house was just outside the village of Sober. It was quite a modern property, built from concrete and brick. It certainly wasn't as appealing as an old, stone farmhouse but it was far more practical. The place needed some work but nothing we couldn't handle ourselves. By far its most outstanding feature was the view: 180 degrees of unbroken panorama, looking out towards Monforte and the mountains beyond. If the vendor was open to offers, this could soon become our new home.

The second property was a small bungalow less than

two minutes drive away. It was quite a charming little place, resting inside its own walled gardens. In the garden, tall, dry grasses swayed gently in the breeze. There were fruit trees in the front and a thirsty-looking willow, weeping in the back. Planted at regular intervals around the boundary walls were mature grapevines. Their leaves were a rich green colour and young bunches of grapes hung from rusty training wires. The house was square in shape with a pyramidal, terracotta tiled roof. Attached to one side was a single-storey garage. Three steps led to the front door, sheltered by a tiny porch. Either side of the door was a window, covered from the outside by a sun-bleached wooden shutter. Inside there were five rooms leading off a short, central hallway: kitchen, lounge, two bedrooms and a small shower room. Every room was fully furnished and in the bedrooms, clothes were hanging in the wardrobes. It looked as if the owners had just upped and left. The house had potential and if we could do something with the garage, it could be an ideal holiday let.

'Maria, can we have a look inside the garage?'

'Sure,' she said, clearly baffled at the prospect of us actually wanting to buy the place.

The garage was an *Aladdin's* cave: a lifetime of junk kept just in case it was ever needed. It ran the width of the house. By converting this space into a kitchen/diner and adding a similar structure to the opposite side of the house, we could create a three bedroom, three bathroom holiday let. The back garden was certainly big enough for a swimming pool. This property had real potential. We dropped Maria back at the office and headed home to mull things over.

The more we thought about it, the more convinced we became that these were the right choices for us.

'Before we make an offer, let's ask Felipe to take a look

at the small house and make sure that our plans are realistic,' I said to Melanie.

'We'll go to Sylvia's tomorrow morning and ask her to help,' she suggested.

By 9:30 the next morning we were standing outside Sylvia's apartment buzzing her on the intercom.

'Hola,' Sylvia's voice crackled through the speaker.

'Hello Sylvia it's Melanie.'

'Come up,' she called.

The locking mechanism buzzed on the door, signalling us to push it open. We climbed the steps to the first floor. Sylvia's door was slightly ajar.

'Hello!' called Melanie as she pushed open the door and cautiously entered.

'Come in,' called Sylvia. 'What can I do for you?' she asked.

We explained about the small house and asked if she could ring Felipe to arrange an appointment for us.

'We don't need an appointment,' she remarked. 'Let's go and see if he's in.'

Minutes later we were outside Felipe's office, knocking on the door. His secretary answered.

'Is Felipe in?' asked Sylvia.

'He has someone with him at the moment but you're welcome to wait.'

The waiting area was light and airy. On the left were two black leatherette chairs, separated by a low table cluttered with glossy trade magazines. Acting the gentleman, I ushered Melanie and Sylvia to take a seat. My selfless act was quickly overshadowed by the reappearance of the secretary carrying a redundant office chair. Before too long, Felipe had concluded his other business and was leading us into his office. Sylvia explained our find and asked if he could come and take a look.

'He can come later today,' said Sylvia. 'Would you like me to come as well?' she asked eagerly.

'If you wouldn't mind,' I replied, trying not to sound presumptuous.

Later that afternoon we all met at the estate agents. Such was the importance Pilar placed on this viewing that she decided to join our little party. Before long we were trundling through the village and pulling up outside the house. Felipe had a curious expression across his face as he walked through the gates and stopped to survey this little property. He glanced back at us, clearly confused by our change of heart. We'd gone from restoring an enormous farmhouse to tidying up a tiny bungalow.

Through Sylvia we explained our ideas for developing the house and adding a swimming pool. His expression changed from that of confusion to one of sheer disbelief. While Pilar unlocked the front door we toured the gardens, looking at the place from every possible angle. Over the next hour, Felipe listened carefully to our proposals and gave them due consideration.

'He can't see any problems with the modifications,' said Sylvia.

This great news meant that we could make an offer on both houses today but we waited until we were back at the estate agents to table them.

'We would like to make an offer for both houses,' I said calmly.

Pilar seemed unmoved: not quite the response we were expecting, particularly considering our pitifully low offers. She looked across at Maria and called her to the desk.

'Maria, will you ring the owners with these offers,' she said coolly, perhaps too embarrassed to deliver them herself.

First on Maria's list was the house outside the village.

The one we hoped would become our home. The response from the vendor was unbelievable.

'He wants two million more than his original asking price,' whispered Maria, holding her hand firmly over the mouthpiece.

'Another two million,' I said, exasperated by the response. 'He must be joking,' I added.

Maria pleaded our case. Ten weeks earlier she had rung the vendor to confirm the price. We were sitting right opposite her at the time. Now the vendor had someone interested in buying it, he wanted more money. We did not realise that it would prove so difficult to buy a house.

'I'll try this other one,' said Maria, clearly as frustrated as we were.

Purposefully she tapped out the contact number on the telephone key pad and waited for a response. The vendor answered the call and Maria slipped into her sales patter.

'He says that they couldn't possibly accept so little,' she said, after relaying our offer. 'It cost them more than that to build,' she added.

It took a while for the implications of her last comment to sink in, but eventually it did. Surely, the fact that they were unable to accept such a low offer actually meant that they were prepared to accept a reduced offer.

'How much will they accept?' I asked, having recovered my composure.

A short conversation followed.

'They're prepared to accept one million pesetas less, on the proviso that you pay their selling costs.'

That sounded ominous: most guides to buying a home in Spain suggest allowing 10 percent for buying costs.

Will that be the same for the seller, I thought?

'We'll have to think about it and get back to them,' I said.

Maria explained our position to the vendor and ended the call.

'How much are their costs?' I asked Maria eagerly.

She called to Pilar who came across to explain.

'They're very small,' she said, 'about one or two hundred euros. The only costs for the vendor are the Notary fees. It's nothing to worry about,' she added.

Pilar had a genuine sincerity not normally associated with estate agents. She was softly spoken with a very calm and trusting tone.

'Think it over and let me know in the morning,' said Pilar, 'there's no rush.'

We left and headed home. Finding a vendor who seemed keen to sell was a new experience. All we had to do was agree a price and the house was ours. A shadow of uncertainty cloaked my thoughts. Once we agreed there was no turning back. Were we changing our ideas to fit the available properties, or were our new ideas dictating our choice of house: how could we be certain?

'Do you think we're doing the right thing?' I asked over dinner.

'Don't you?' asked Melanie.

'I think we are, but how can we be sure?'

'Do you have any doubts?' she asked, clearly surprised at the prospect that I might have.

'I wouldn't be human if I didn't have doubts,' I said. 'I love the area, I think it's great.'

'But?' asked Melanie.

'But I'm not sure; I'm not sure it's possible to be completely sure,' I added.

'But this is what we want, isn't it?'

'This is exactly what we want,' I replied.

'Then let's go for it.'

The following morning we returned to see Pilar, excited at the prospect of buying our first house. We were happy to pay the revised asking price but the little dealer inside me just had to try and get a bit more knocked off. I chanced my arm at another half a million. Pilar smiled at my cheek but nevertheless, forwarded our new offer.

'OK,' she said after a short telephone call. 'They'll accept your new offer.'

We were over the moon: we had finally done it, even Pilar seemed excited.

'I'll start preparing the paperwork straight away,' she said. 'It should be ready in about two weeks.'

'Do you know a good solicitor that we can use?' I asked.

Without exception, every guide book I'd ever read about buying a home abroad strongly recommended using a local solicitor to complete the transaction.

'You don't need a solicitor,' insisted Pilar. 'The *notario* (notary) does all the work for you,' she added.

Melanie and I glanced at each other. Pilar had been so helpful and trustworthy, perhaps the guide books were wrong; maybe Galicia was an exception. We were about to find out.

11

A Brush with the Law

Solicitors: To some people they're a necessary evil, to others, legalised bandits. Years in business, dealing with these hungry vultures, aligned me firmly with the latter view. We had no reason to doubt Pilar's opinion but everything I'd ever read about foreign property purchase, strongly advised the use of a local solicitor. Couple this fact to vivid memories of tabloid headlines warning of Spanish property scams and a nervous unease drifted into our thinking. The paperwork wouldn't be ready for a couple of weeks so we decided to make some discreet enquiries. Unusually, Sylvia was unable to help.

'Didn't you use a solicitor when you bought your apartment?' I asked, at our next Spanish lesson.

'A solicitor,' said Sylvia, curiously. 'You don't need a solicitor. The *notario* does all that.'

After the lesson we visited Felipe, surely he would know one.

'A solicitor,' said Felipe. 'You don't need a solicitor. The *notario* does all that.'

Tabloid editors have their own mischievous reasons for publishing sensational headlines but surely more mainstream authors would be less biased. We were beginning to doubt even their advice. Having thanked Felipe we decided to try and locate a solicitor ourselves.

'Let's just walk around town,' I said, 'there's bound to be a solicitor's office somewhere.'

We walked up the pedestrian precinct looking at all the polished nameplates.

'There's one,' said Melanie. 'M Alvarez - *Abogado.*'

We pushed open the door. The entrance hall was dark and uninviting. I flicked the light switch on at the bottom of the stairs and we climbed them to the first floor.

'There it is,' said Melanie, pointing at a door on the left.

We knocked and entered. After a short and difficult conversation it was clear that señor Alvarez couldn't speak a word of English: not much use to us. We left and continued our search. A little way up the precinct we found another; the response was the same. Perhaps we didn't need a solicitor after all. Pilar had agreed to provide us with a copy of the sale contract prior to signing. We decided to try again once we had it.

By the time Pilar rang, late on Friday afternoon, we'd almost given up hope of the paperwork being ready. I could tell from the sound of children playing noisily in the background that she was phoning from home. At least she hadn't forgotten us completely, and we agreed to call into the office on Monday morning.

That Monday we were up early. The prospect of coming face to face with the actual contract was both exciting and quite frightening.

'Good morning,' said Pilar, as we entered the estate agents. 'How are you?'

We anticipated a quick in and out; we should have known better.

'There's a small problem,' she said, after we'd taken a seat. 'Well, not really a problem, more a peculiarity,' she added.

Here we go again, I thought to myself.

It was always the same; one minute we believed everything was fine and the next, disaster.

'A problem,' I asked.

Pilar opened a brown file and handed us a copy of the contract. She did her best to explain but we were struggling to understand. From our blank expressions and gaping mouths, she could see our dilemma.

'Come with me,' she said, jumping to her feet and heading for the door. 'We'll go and talk with the *notario*. He speaks English.'

Pilar headed off up the street like a startled jack rabbit, dodging in and out of pedestrians like an Alpine skier. Melanie and I raced after her, trying desperately to keep up.

Other than a weathered, brass nameplate embossed with the word *Notario,* there was nothing to distinguish this building from any other town centre apartment block. Pilar pushed open the door and we entered a dark and dreary lobby. It felt refreshingly cool after racing through the hot and humid streets of Monforte. We climbed the stairs to the first floor.

Mounted on the wall, next to a scarred and scraped wooden door, was a clear resin plaque bearing the word *Notario.* Pilar's familiarity with this place was obvious; without hesitation she shouldered open the heavy door and marched into the room.

'*Buenos Dias,*' she announced on entering the busy waiting room.

A reciprocal chorus of acknowledgment echoed around the office. She squeezed through the crowded room to the reception counter. Melanie and I waited near the door, feeling slightly awkward. A few moments later she returned.

'We can speak with the *notario* in a few minutes,' she said.

We waited patiently and quietly. After a short while a door opened in the far corner and two men stepped out. They shook hands and the older of the two manoeuvred his way through the crowded room and left. The other, a younger looking man, glanced across at the receptionist to identify his next appointment. To my surprise, and slight embarrassment, he called over to us. We edged forward conscious of glaring eyes.

The young man shook our hands and invited us into his office. He was impeccably dressed with a dark suit, gleaming white shirt, silk tie and matching handkerchief in his top pocket. In stark contrast to the dated and shabby waiting room, his office was spotlessly clean with contemporary furniture arranged in a minimalist style. He rounded his desk and cushioned himself into an executive, leather-clad chair. In a softly spoken voice he asked Pilar how he might help us. While she explained, he listened intently and then turned to us.

'Please excuse my English,' he said, in a near perfect, unaccented tone. 'I don't often get the opportunity to speak it.'

If only my Spanish was as bad as his English, I thought enviously.

For the next few minutes we listened carefully to his advice. He began by explaining the minor problem. The house had never been officially registered. In this respect, we would be the first legal owners. A full and detailed explanation of the whole sales process followed. His manner was clear, precise and thorough: exactly what one would expect from a legal professional.

'When would you like to conclude the purchase?' he asked.

The question came as quite a surprise. It hadn't crossed my mind that the decision would be ours.

'As soon as possible,' I replied.

A painful frown filtered across his face. 'That could be a problem.'

Not another bloody problem. No sooner had we resolved one than another raised its ugly head. What now!

'I'm on holiday in August,' he said, opening a leather-bound Filofax on the desk in front of him. 'Let me see.'

He paused for a moment flicking the August sheets back and forth, 'It might be possible. How does the 14th of August sound?'

'That's fine by us,' I replied hastily, before he had chance to change his mind.

'I'm on holiday that week but I don't mind coming into the office for a short time.'

After scribbling a note in his Filofax, he handed us a business card – Manuel Arturo - *Notario*. It was a noble name, an honourable name. Images of a Roman centurion leading his men into battle flashed through my mind. We thanked Pilar for her time, and more importantly, introducing us to Don Arturo.

Meeting the *notario* had eased our fears and convinced us that we really didn't need a solicitor. We were happy to put our faith in the locals and trust their honesty.

It was time to get some architectural plans drawn up.

After the disastrous outcome of the farmhouse in Gundivos, we decided not to tempt fate by asking Felipe to start work before we were sure of progressing with the sale. With the completion date set, we thought it safe to proceed. Our Spanish lesson later that day gave us the ideal opportunity to set the ball rolling.

'Sylvia, can we go and see Felipe to ask him to draw some plans for the new house?' I asked.

'Of course; come on, let's go,' she replied eagerly.

To date, we'd managed just one full Spanish lesson; the rest of the time we'd used Sylvia as our personal interpreter. Not that it bothered her, she was more than happy to help us along the road to home ownership. If truth be known, so was I. When it comes to learning languages, some people seem to possess an almost genetic talent. Unfortunately, I'm not one of them.

We left the apartment and headed for Felipe's. The clock hadn't quite reached 4:30, so the streets were almost deserted. Fortunately, he'd returned early from lunch. Sylvia set about explaining our requirements and we agreed to meet at the house the following afternoon.

The next day we arrived early. The sun was high in the sky and the area around the house was breathless and still. A chorus of chirping cicadas drifted on the heavy air. Opposite the house, a choir of croaking frogs echoed across a small lake. We peered through the locked gates at the unloved bungalow, dreaming of how it might one day look. Before long Felipe, Javier, Sylvia and an office junior from the estate agents arrived. She introduced herself as Olga and opened the gates. Javier hadn't seen the place before and he seemed very surprised by our change of heart. Without delay they set about measuring up. An hour and a half later, they'd finished.

'Felipe wants to know what changes you want to make,' said Sylvia.

Over a decade of holidaying in other peoples homes had given us a clear vision of exactly what we wanted to achieve. We marched around the house opening theoretical doorways and building imaginary walls. We wanted three bedrooms, each with its own en-suite bathroom. A long covered terrace overlooking a large swimming pool and direct access from there into the kitchen. Sylvia translated and Felipe made notes.

'How soon can we have the initial plans?' I asked.

Sylvia relayed our impatient request, 'He says next Tuesday.'

We were surprised but delighted by this unexpected news. That concluded the afternoon's business.

We drifted through the following week, filling our days with long lunchtime barbecues and afternoons basking in the summer sun. We skipped our Monday Spanish lesson as Sylvia had agreed to join us at Felipe's the following day. That morning we woke with a sense of nervous anticipation. We'd been here before and look how that turned out. We sped off to Monforte, excited yet anxious.

Sylvia was already there when we arrived. Felipe seemed quite organised for a change: his desk was neat and tidy, save for a solitary grey file. He opened it and pulled out a folded piece of paper. Carefully he flattened it out, spun it around and slid it towards us. Melanie and I bent over and peered at the drawing, it was amazing. Not a trace of the old house remained. The adjoined garage had been replaced with a new wing, balancing this was an extension of equal size on the opposite side of the house: the place looked huge. The tiny entrance porch had been replaced with a large, triple-arched, terracotta-tiled, covered terrace extending the length of the old house. At the rear, a new covered terrace looked out onto a large swimming pool surrounded by a paved patio.

Felipe pulled another sheet out of the file. This showed the planned layout of the new interior. There were three, en-suite bedrooms, two dressing rooms, an entrance hall, sitting room, and a kitchen/diner divided by an American-style breakfast bar. We chatted over the plans, throwing ideas around and making a few minor changes. Overall we were absolutely delighted, he'd listened carefully to our ideas and created our dream home.

'Felipe says that after he's amended the plans he'll place the work out to tender.'

Sylvia's statement brought the meeting to a close. We thanked Felipe for his work and Sylvia for her patience. All we had to do now was order the money from the bank and wait. We were almost there, just two more days to go. Surely nothing could go wrong at this late stage.

The following morning we decided to take our minds off things by doing a bit of sightseeing.

'What about Vigo?' I suggested. 'It's on the coast, so there's bound to be a marina or something.'

'OK,' replied Melanie, 'let's go to Vigo.'

By law, drivers in Spain are required to carry certain documents in the car at all times. We weren't exactly sure which documents. To avoid falling foul of the law, we carried anything and everything of relevance. The glovebox was literally bursting with bits of paper. In addition to the paperwork, every vehicle has to carry a spare set of light bulbs, two hazard-warning triangles, and a fluorescent jacket for every occupant.

The road from Ferreira climbs steadily to the summit of the river Miño valley before falling spectacularly to the river's edge. A snaking carpet of tarmac hugs the contours of the valley, twisting and turning as it plummets steeply towards the river. The widest gorges are breached by raised concrete platforms. It's a magnificent piece of roadway engineering. At the bottom of the valley the road meanders along the course of the river where it's flat and smooth. Breaks in the roadside foliage allow fleeting glimpses of the river. Shimmering images of the opposite bank were mirrored in the dark water as we sped along. Once through the city of Ourense we continued along the river's edge rather than travel on the highway. As we headed west the valley widened and its steep sides were replaced with a broad floodplain and rolling hills. The narrow road wound its way through small villages and tiny hamlets. The countryside is covered with ordered vineyards, thick with their summer foliage and ripening fruit.

After an hour or so we rejoined the main highway speeding toward our destination. From the southeast, the city of Vigo is surrounded by hills. A tightly winding dual carriageway rises steeply to the summit. From here visitors are treated to a stunning, uninterrupted view of the entire city and the rugged Atlantic coastline. All too soon this spectacular panorama vanished from view as we descended the hill and headed towards the city centre. As we jostled our way through the busy city streets, the fuel-fill light lit up on the dashboard.

'We could do with some petrol if you see a filling station,' I said, as we continued along.

We'd almost given up hope of seeing the Atlantic when, to our surprise, we crested a hill and found the cool-blue sea stretching out in front of us as far as the eye could see. At the next junction we had a clear choice, beach to the left or port to the right. It seemed reasonable to assume that the marina would be nearer to the port than the beach, so we turned right. Before long, my toss-of-a-coin decision began to look like a mistake.

A more accurate description of port would have been docks. A steel security fence lined one side of the road: behind this, rusting cargo vessels were moored along the quayside. Huge iron cranes set in steel tracks stood idly watching over these weathering hulks. Opposite the quay, an endless row of seedy looking warehouses with filthy windows and peeling paintwork lined the road.

'There's a petrol station!' shouted Melanie, pointing to the right.

Her sudden outburst caught me by surprise. We'd almost passed it. Quickly, I glanced in the mirror, signalled and under heavy braking began my manoeuvre.

No sooner had I turned the steering wheel than that unmistakable sound of twisting metal and breaking glass echoed through the car. Following this depressing noise came the aftermath.

In moments like this, time enters a new dimension, a surreal world of slowed images and vivid thoughts. A motorcycle skidded past us, sparking as it grated down the road. Its rider followed, rolling and tumbling along the tarmac like a rag doll. Melanie gasped with shock and burst into tears. Instinctively, I rolled the car onto the station forecourt and stopped. Like the frantic pounding of a hydraulic hammer, my heartbeat raced: I was in shock. To try and stop my body from shaking, I tightened my grip on the steering wheel and peered down the road with dread.

To my surprise, and great relief, the motorcyclist had picked himself up and was hobbling down the road to survey his wrecked machine. Even from this distance, I could tell that the bike was dead. Fortunately, the rider would live to recount his tale. By now my galloping heart beat had slowed to a canter and my attention turned to Melanie.

'Don't worry love,' I said in an effort to calm her. 'He's up and about.'

Having checked on the welfare of his bike, his attention turned to me. His pitiful hobble turned into a purposeful limp, as he headed for the car. I thought it wise to remain seated and lowered the window slightly as he neared. For a young man who'd just lost his beloved motorbike and sustained a few cuts, bruises and friction burns, he seemed reasonably calm. He rambled on for a while, repeating the words *seguro* (insurance) and *policia* (police) before telling me to wait and heading for the public phone.

By now my heart rate had returned to normal and the reality of our situation was starting to sink in. We knew that all traffic accidents in Spain have to be reported to the police and wherever possible those involved, including witnesses, have to remain at the scene. We would just have to wait and place our trust in the law. The thermometer reached a blistering 35°C.

'I'm going to get some water,' said Melanie, who by now had regained her composure.

While Melanie went into the petrol station to buy a bottle of water, I rolled the car into the shade and stepped out to survey the damage. With the exception of a layer of black rubber, stuck to the centre of my gleaming red rear bumper, there was nothing. Not a dent or a scratch, a discovery that extinguished any lingering sympathy I felt for this unfortunate rider. He had clearly been travelling too close and too fast. As I braked to enter the petrol station, he had been unable to slow down in time and driven straight into the back of us. Thankfully, we wouldn't have to rely on our inadequate Spanish to explain what had happened: the evidence was irrefutable.

Melanie returned with a refreshing bottle of ice-cold water. The rider maintained his roadside vigil, hobbling up and down the pavement in the baking heat. Our wait passed the hour mark and still the rider limped up and down, staring at the remains of his prized possession every time he passed it. Just as I started to think that the police would never turn up, a white van stopped at the kerbside on the opposite carriageway. I could see a small crest on the side with the words *Policia Locales* written underneath. I was quite surprised: I'd expected to see a high performance traffic car with flashing lights and sirens. This looked more like a delivery van than a police vehicle. Two smartly dressed officers stepped from the van. They straightened their hats and brushed the creases from their trousers.

Unsure of the protocol, we stepped from the car and waited at the kerbside for one of the officers to cross the road. Taking great care, he negotiated the busy, four-lane road and ordered us to accompany him back to the van. This looked ominous, a foreign bobby carrying a loaded pistol. Any thoughts of escape were quickly extinguished. Surely we weren't going to spend a night in the cells over a minor traffic accident. We followed him back, dodging in and out of the speeding traffic.

As we rounded the back of the van the second officer appeared. He tugged hard on the van's central door handle and it slid open. Melanie and I glanced at each other in alarm, as he invited us to enter.

To our relief, and amazement, the interior was fitted out as a mobile interview room. Positioned centrally was a Formica-topped table with bench seating on both sides. It looked more like a camper van than a prison van. All we needed now was a round of sandwiches and an ice-cold beer.

'Do either of you speak Spanish?' asked the first officer.

His command of English came as quite a surprise.

'No,' I replied, thinking it would be better for us to conduct the interview in our native tongue.

A short exchange followed between the two cops to decide who would draw the short straw and have to interview us in English. The die was cast and the loser began his questioning. All our answers were neatly recorded on the appropriate form. Meanwhile, the second officer stood menacingly in the open doorway, casually resting the palm of his hand on the butt of his automatic pistol, like a sheriff from the Wild West.

An endless stream of questions followed, none of which related to the accident. All my vehicle documentation was checked and everything was in order. After 10 minutes of note taking, he finally asked about the accident. We did our best to explain but he seemed far more interested in the bureaucracy than the actual event. After the briefest of explanations we were asked to wait outside.

The motorcyclist was next into the interrogation room. Within minutes of taking his seat, one of the officers marched back across the road and carefully examined the car. Slowly and purposefully he circled it, scanning every inch. It seemed that the biker's story didn't match ours. Once checked he headed back across the road, dodging oncoming traffic. I couldn't help thinking that if this carried on much longer, someone really was going to get hurt.

'Where is the damage?' he asked, abruptly

'It's on the back bumper,' I replied.

'Come and show me.'

We set off across the road, running the gauntlet of four

lanes of speeding traffic. I pointed out the imprint of a motorcycle tyre on the rear bumper.

'What other damage is there?' he demanded.

'None,' I replied. 'That's all there is.'

Dissatisfied with my answer, he rechecked the car. Thankfully, she was in great shape: A few days earlier, I'd washed and waxed her. The gleaming, red paintwork looked like new. Once he'd completed his inspection we dodged back across the road. He wasted no time in informing the biker of his findings. Seconds later, our luckless friend had confessed to his crime and we were free to go.

The time was approaching 9:30 in the evening, and the stifling heat of earlier was on the wane. An hour and a half later we were back home, exhausted by the day's events. We had a quick bite to eat and a glass of wine before hitting the sack.

Not quite what I had in mind when I suggested visiting Vigo to take our minds off things, but it had certainly done the trick. Tomorrow was our big day, a life changing day, hopefully it will go a bit smoother than this one.

The piercing tone of Melanie's alarm clock shattered my dozing fantasy. Angled beams of sunlight filtered through the partially raised *persiana*. Today was one day we didn't want to be late. Our appointment with Don Arturo, the *notario*, wasn't until 11:30; but we had plenty to do before then. I thought I might feel excited by the prospect of buying a house but I couldn't shake off the fear that something was bound to go wrong.

We decided on smart/casual attire. I'm not sure why, it just seemed appropriate. I enhanced my business-like appearance with my leather laptop bag, which now doubled as a briefcase. If nothing else, I could carry the money in it. Our first stop of the morning was the Banesto bank.

The morning sunshine was warm and bright as we headed for Monforte. We parked the car, strolled along the river bank and into the town centre. On entering the bank the manager caught my eye.

'Good morning,' he called, rising from his chair and striding across to greet us. 'Come with me.'

He ushered us into his private office and gestured us to take a seat.

'Are you here for the money?' he asked, in a rhetorical manner.

I nodded politely. There was a flurry of activity as we took a seat. The cash office was situated adjacent. An automated counting machine rifled through the notes like a distant machine gun. The manager left, returning a few minutes later with a bulging white envelope stuffed with cash.

'Here you are,' he said, handing me the notes. 'Now *you* must count it.'

I'd just watched the machine rattle off the count; I doubted a repeat was necessary, but the manager insisted. I tipped the neatly banded bundles of cash onto the table and began counting: unsurprisingly, it was all present and correct. With the count complete, I started stuffing the bundles into my briefcase.

'Would you like to leave the money with us and ask the vendor to come back here to count it?' interrupted the manager.

Trying to part a Yorkshireman from his money is like separating fingers after they've been superglued. I was as likely to leave the cash with him as I was to walk into the street and toss it in the air. Of course he wasn't to know this, so I politely declined his gracious offer and continued to stuff the briefcase. I hadn't seen this much cash since managing a supermarket over fifteen years ago.

There's a strange paranoia that goes with carrying a lot of cash, I felt it then and I could feel it now. All eyes seemed to stare at my bulging briefcase. I felt as if everyone knew what I was carrying. We fled the bank and rushed across to the estate agents.

The tightness of my grip left my hand sweating as we entered the agents. Pilar was conspicuous by her absence. I looked across at Maria in despair.

'She'll be back in five minutes,' chirped Maria. 'Take a seat.'

I couldn't believe that Pilar would be late for the most important day since our arrival in Spain. Clutching the briefcase as if my life depended on it, we plonked our frames down. As usual the office was quiet, just one old woman wearing spectacles the thickness of milk bottle bottoms and a couple in their fifties. Paranoid that armed robbers might attempt a smash and grab, I kept one eye on the door. Thankfully, Pilar was the first to enter. After greeting us she invited the other three to join us.

'This is the owner of the house,' she said, gently taking the arm of the old lady, 'and this is her son and daughter-in-law.'

We exchanged pleasantries before heading off to the Notary.

'The *notario* hasn't arrived yet,' said Pilar, after checking at reception.

Even he was late. I suppose he was doing us a favour by coming into work on his holiday, so we shouldn't complain. Our wait was short and within minutes of his arrival the six of us had squeezed into his office. He started by confirming the identity of the old woman, followed by a short summation of the contract. The old lady nodded in agreement. Then he turned his attention to us. This time he confirmed our identity followed by an equally short contract summary, albeit this time in English. With both parties satisfied and due diligence served, he asked the three of us to sign.

'That's it,' he said. 'All you have to do now is learn Spanish,' he added jokingly.

That's it: we'd finally done it. After all the waiting around, all the disappointment and heartache, we had finally bought a Spanish home. The whole process had taken less than five minutes. We thanked Don Arturo for sacrificing his time and filed out of his office behind the dithering old dear.

As we ambled back to the estate agents, Pilar explained that we would have to return to the Notary in a couple of weeks. To finalise the process, we needed to take the completed contract to the registry office. There would be a small fee to pay for the *notario's* services and 7% tax to the government. That was all very well, but I'd spent the best part of an hour wandering around the streets of Monforte with a briefcase full of used notes: didn't anybody want it!

Back at the estate agents, Pilar ushered us into her private office. She closed the blinds and shut the door.

'Now for the money,' she said, with a Fagin-like rub of her hands and a crafty smile.

I sensed that Pilar had been waiting for this moment for months. Everyone stared at the case as I rested it on my lap and opened the buckle. I felt like tipping its contents out on the desk like a successful bank robber but resisted the temptation. Slowly and methodically the daughter-in-law counted out the notes as Melanie and I watched in silence, it seemed to take forever. As we rose to leave, the old lady burst into tears. Blubbering through her emotions, she wished us good luck and much happiness. We thanked her for her kind wishes and turned to leave.

'Wait,' said Pilar suddenly.

What now? I thought to myself.

'You haven't got the keys,' she added.

In our rush to leave, we had almost forgotten why we were there. The old lady handed them over and off we went.

We walked briskly back to the car and drove swiftly home. There had been a bottle of champagne chilling in the fridge for weeks. Armed with this, and a couple of flutes, we headed off to the house. Before long we were sitting on the steps of our small porch, cork popped, and bubbles tickling the end of our noses.

12

Wall to Wall Sound

For the last few weeks our neighbours in Ferreira had used every available opportunity to tease us about the forthcoming village fiesta. We hadn't taken much notice at the time; we had far more pressing matters to consider, but having completed the house purchase our focus changed. Curiosity got the better of us and we were eager to find out exactly what to expect from a Spanish fiesta.

'Let's go into Monforte tonight and find out what all the fuss is about over the fiesta,' I suggested to Melanie over lunch.

Monforte was almost half way through their five day annual fiesta. The final day of their festivities, coincided with the first day of Ferreira's.

That night we left home at 11 o'clock and drove the 15 km into town. We'd never seen the place so busy. We joined a queue of traffic, creeping towards the town centre. Every available parking space was taken.

The focal point for the evening's festivities was the

impressive college, *Nosa Señora da Antiga*. All approach roads were temporarily closed and roadside bars had commandeered the streets. Each establishment had their own distinctive colour-coded tables and chairs. To ease traffic flow around the college, the one-way system had become two-way. Wider town centre roads doubled as temporary car parks with abandoned vehicles littering the centre of the road. Excited revellers wandered in and out of the traffic. The scene was one of disorganised chaos but nobody seemed to mind.

Carefully, we negotiated our way through the abandoned vehicles and headed for a quieter part of town. Fortunately for us, 11:30 at night is still quite early for Spanish partygoers. Before long we found a relatively quiet street not too far away from the action and parked.

The streets leading to the college were heaving with people. We joined the crowds and drifted along on a wave of excited fervour. Latino rhythms bounced off apartment blocks and echoed through the streets. As we neared the college the volume increased. Roadside traders filled the pavements. The sweet aroma of *churro's* floated on the warm night air. These deep-fried, doughy fingers, dipped in chocolate, are a Spanish favourite.

To the right of the college, a travelling funfair was in full swing. Bright flashing lights and loud popular music heightened the senses. All manner of mechanical inventions thrust their occupants this way and that, jerking their flexible frames up and down, left and right. Young children bounced around in a large inflatable castle, while watching parents guarded sweet, sticky candy-floss and hydrogen-filled balloons.

We wandered around the bustling fairground pausing occasionally to watch excited children being tossed from side-to-side on magical mechanical rides. Periodically, nervous screams of enjoyment pierced the pounding rhythms of modern Latino music blasting out from every direction. After a while we strolled back towards the college. Market stalls lined both sides of the street on the approaches to the square.

These orderly lines of poorly-lit trinket stalls were punctuated with Peruvian-looking families selling the most alluring knitwear. A kaleidoscopic display of luxury garments, knitted from precious Alpaca wool, was strewn across the pavement on a patchwork of old blankets. The haunting tones of distant panpipes crackled out from a baseless ghetto blaster. These beautiful woollens attracted a premium price. Unfortunately for the sellers, that was all they were attracting. The last thing on anyone's mind, on a warm summer evening, was a cold and depressing winter. I couldn't help but feel a bit sorry for them, especially the young girls. They were traditionally dressed with trousers, fur-lined boots and a thick Alpaca knitted jumper, not the ideal attire for a summer fiesta in Spain.

Over the melee of pumping Latino rhythms, haunting Peruvian panpipes, timeless Bob Marley classics and excited children, came the unmistakable amplified blasts of musicians warming up for a performance. Like Ancient Greek sailors enchanted by alluring Sirens, we bumped our way through the swollen masses and headed towards the square in front of the college. Erected at one end was an enormous stage. By the time we had strolled across the square to a suitable vantage point, the band was in full swing.

A male and female vocalist fronted the group. He was a striking Adonis, young and athletic with jet-black hair and perfectly air-brushed olive-toned skin. He sported a white, loose-fitting silk shirt which projected a radial glow as he twisted and turned in the bright spotlights. His matt-black trousers hugged his muscular thighs before flaring out below the knee. The finishing touch to this perfect media image of manliness was a pair of black, patent-leather shoes that mirrored the greasy shine of his slicked back hair. His partner provided the perfect nemesis.

She was a beautiful young woman with a perfect form. Her hair was skilfully managed, giving the impression of passionate abandonment: wild and free yet ordered and controlled. She wore a figure-hugging, strapless cocktail-dress. The dark, sequin-covered costume portrayed a shimmering lucidity as her choreographed routine swept her across the stage. Delicate stiletto sandals provided the platform for slender, bronzed legs that angled into the forbidden darkness of her pulsating waistline.

The remaining band members consisted of a lead guitarist, two rhythm guitarists, a bass guitarist, an organist, a synthesizer player, a percussionist and drummer, two saxophonists and a trombonist. Between them, they were able to recreate that recording studio sound. The quality of the performance was exceptional and all of it paid for by local residents and business owners. Could our village fiesta live up to these high standards? Only time would tell. We headed home in the early hours, excited at the prospect.

The only indication that Ferreira would soon have its annual fiesta was the overnight appearance of clandestine vehicles. As if by magic, tarpaulin-covered trailers and mobile trader vans had begun assembling on the outskirts of the village and around the fringes of the village green. Most were conspicuous by the absence of advertising logos but one dreary, sun-bleached cover carried the words, *Camas Elasticas*: the old favourite had returned. Not quite the throbbing excitement of a travelling funfair, but perhaps things might change within the next few days.

We returned home one afternoon to find an enormous electrical transformer sitting less than 10 metres from the front gates. The machine was the size of a small caravan and painted a hideous bright orange. Within a few days of its mysterious arrival an engineer from Fenosa, the national electricity company, connected it to the national grid. I couldn't help thinking that whatever needed this much power was going to be big, very big.

Sunday morning we were brutally awoken by the ear-shattering sound of ordnance-like fireworks, signalling the start of the fiesta. Having wiped the sleep from our eyes, we expected to see signs of activity: after all, events were due to start that evening.

To our surprise the only noticeable change was the unveiling of the *Camas Elasticas* and next to that, a half inflated bouncy castle. Its four corner turrets hung limply as an underpowered electric generator attempted to breathe life into its form. Before long the first plastic turret popped to attention: then the second, followed lazily by the third and fourth. Four erect pillars pointing skyward like ballistic missiles. Next to this, a traditional children's merry-go-round arrived. Secured to its 12-foot diameter base was an assortment of colourfully painted model vehicles, each one, just large enough to accommodate a small child. I could hardly have imagined a greater contrast from the bustling mechanised funfair that we'd enjoyed a few days earlier.

By the time we'd washed and dressed the village green was even quieter. The electric generator was silent and all signs of life had disappeared. Although we were looking forward to the coming events, we were also pleased that we wouldn't have to alter our Sunday morning ritual. An alfresco breakfast of miniature cream cakes and rich espresso coffee complimented with the morning papers.

Several weeks earlier we had discovered the most wonderful confectioners in Monforte. At the back of its sales floor stood a refrigerated glass counter that ran the width of the shop. Displayed inside was a tantalising range of mouth-watering miniature cream cakes, tarts, pastries and sticky buns.

The late morning sun was bright and warm as we headed into town to collect our weekly treats. Even though the time was approaching eleven, it came as no surprise to find the streets of Monforte almost deserted. With the previous day's celebrations lasting well into the early hours, and one day of festivities still to go, most people were still tucked-up in bed. Having parked the car we strolled across to the newsagent's kiosk on the edge of the square and bought a copy of the *Voz* newspaper. It wasn't quite The *Mail on Sunday* but it helped with the Spanish and if that proved too difficult, there was always the colour supplement to thumb through.

From the kiosk we strolled along narrow cobbled streets, across the *Romanesque* bridge and into the heart of the old town. We entered the confectioners and were greeted with a warm smile and a chirpy, *'Buenos dias'!* We replied courteously and headed for the chilled counter. Bright lighting brought these delicious miniatures to life. Brushed glazes glistened and sprinkled sugar sparkled like tiny diamonds. Like excited children in a candy store, we deliberated over our choices, a near impossible task. We limited ourselves to three each.

Back home I continued the ritual by preparing coffee: strong, black and sweet, the perfect Spanish espresso. By the time we finished munching on our treats and browsing through the papers, the morning had passed and there was still no sign of activity on the village green.

No sooner had the faint electronic notes of a distant church completed its two o'clock chimes than a large articulated lorry crept along the road leading to the green. Carefully and accurately the driver manoeuvred the 44-foot trailer into position. When he'd finished, the front half of the trailer was parked on the green while the back completely blocked the road. Happy with his parking the driver uncoupled the tractor unit and drove off. Moments later a gang of roadies appeared. There were eight in all. Two of them began erecting a shed-like structure in the middle of the green. The remaining six, set about working on the trailer.

The first task was to connect the power. Three of the gang began hauling a thick, heavy-looking cable from the trailer to the bright orange transformer. Step by strenuous step they marched backwards like a tug of war team, hauling the cable across the green. They connected it up and moved back to work on the trailer. The gang's organised discipline left me in no doubt that this daily summertime chore had become a well-oiled routine.

At one end of the trailer was a control panel of levers and switches. As five gang members unlocked bolted sections around the trailer, the sixth flicked switches and pushed and pulled at an array of levers. Slowly, a series of hydraulic legs, four at the front and four at the back, slid out several metres perpendicular to the trailer before sinking to the ground. Large lumps of wood were placed under the feet of the legs before another lever jerked the whole trailer into the air. Not too high, just enough to raise the wheels off the ground and level the vehicle. With the legs forming a safe and rigid platform the bed of the trailer then stretched out over the supporting legs. Hydraulic struts raised the roof of the trailer exposing an array of spot lights and mirror balls. Hydraulic lifting gear, folded inside the trailer, jolted into life. Loud speakers, the size of small bedrooms, were hoisted into the air, six either side.

Within two hours of its arrival, this motley crew of roadies had transformed a run of the mill articulated trailer into a fully functioning concert stage: 60-foot long by 20-foot wide and over 40-foot high. There were three different stage levels, an overhead gantry laden with spotlights and a sound system which looked capable of waking the dead. The shed like structure in the middle of the green became a mixing studio which, to my untrained eye, looked extremely sophisticated and very expensive. Just as this amazing spectacle was drawing to an end, a second articulated lorry pulled onto the green. Surely there wasn't enough room for two of these monsters.

It took the driver of this second vehicle over an hour to manoeuvre it into position: forward a bit, then back a bit, inching this way, then that. A similar transformation followed by another crew of roadies. By the time they had finished, one end of the green was completely enclosed. The sound system for the second stage was so close to the house that I could have stood on the wall and touched it. All those neighbourly jibes, their mischievous smirks and childish teasing were starting to make sense. Undoubtedly, our front terrace would have the best seats in the house but the sight of those enormous loud speakers hanging 15 feet from the front door, brought a whole new meaning to the phrase, 'wall to wall sound,' The stages were set and we were eager to see what the night would bring.

By eight o'clock, the heat of the summer sun was on the wane and the first few people drifted onto the green. The only remaining access road was closed to traffic.

Lining either side of the street were market stalls. There was no place here for those novelty items we'd seen in Monforte a few nights earlier. Rural village folk have no use for fake Zippo lighters and Che Guevara T-shirts. Country folk are more careful with their hard earned cash. Hardware stalls seemed the most popular. Old men bartered with stall holders over pitchforks and pickaxes. Weathered farmers gazed in envy at Ferrari-red, Honda-powered agricultural machinery. Traders from Portugal displayed a wide range of stainless steel wine vats. They were lined up on the pavement in order of descending size and resembled a giant set of open Matryoshka dolls. Alongside the vats were the hand-crafted, pot-bellied stills used to produce the local firewater – *aguardiente*.

At nine o'clock a surprise volley of aerial incendiaries exploded overhead. A ripple of nervous laughter and sheer fright permeated through the swelling crowds. The explosions were so loud that the windows rattled and Jazz scampered into the house, tail between her legs. I chased in after her. She had headed for the familiar safety of her bed and was curled into a tight ball, trembling with fear. I did my best to calm her down before returning.

The latest barrage of ordnance signalled the start of the musical extravaganza. As I closed the kitchen door a blast of sound echoed around the house. I walked down the side of the house and turned the corner to the front terrace. Another shockwave of sound hit me as I turned the corner. A skimpily-dressed, Spanish diva belted out popular tunes accompanied by a nine piece orchestra, which included a small brass section and three backing vocalists. The performance was well rehearsed and slick: very professional and highly entertaining. Before too long they had their excited audience dancing in the street.

Sitting on the elevated front terrace, overlooking the

massed crowds, felt as though we were occupying the Royal box. A bit later in the evening Elo, her daughter Carrie, and Antoniño turned up at the gate. We invited them in for a drink. Thankfully, the music was far too loud for anything other than the exchange of greetings. After an hour-long, non-stop performance their set came to an end, terminating with rapturous applause and shouts of bravo from the crowd. No sooner had the band members disappeared from view than the second stage burst into life.

Remote controlled, coloured spotlights created a kaleidoscope of flashing colours. Two overeager smoke machines filled the stage with man-made mist as the first musical notes erupted from the array of loud speakers hanging precariously from hydraulic arms. They bounced and twitched as the sound developed. I couldn't just hear the music, I could feel it. Every beat pulsated through my body like an invisible shockwave. Gradually the smoke drifted across the green, engulfing the crowd in a ghostly mist.

Although both bands were of the highest standards, their individual play-list had more than a hint of similarity. It didn't seem to bother the crowd though, young and old, male and female, they just kept dancing. Not so much soaking up the atmosphere as participating in its production. By 11 o'clock the second band had completed their set. They bathed in the audiences acclaim before exiting the stage.

Without warning another volley of explosions cracked overhead signalling a slow and orderly dispersal of the crowd. Within minutes the village green was almost empty. All that remained were a few small groups of adults chatting away while their excited kids chased one another. The late evening air was still and warm, the deafening

Latino beats were now replaced with the familiar, and intoxicating, sound of chirping cicadas. It was a perfect evening for nibbling on homemade *tapas* and opening another bottle of Spain's finest. All too soon the peace and tranquillity was smashed. The unmistakable *whoosh* of rockets, launching into the night sky was quickly followed by terrifying explosions. Like a revolutionary call to arms, the crowds reappeared and the music show commenced.

Another expertly conducted and masterly choreographed performance ensued. With the time approaching one in the morning, the group took their second bow of the evening and retired from the stage. Another volley of rockets took to the sky, exploding with a deafening bang, but unlike the previous fireworks these exploded into radiating balls of bright phosphorus colour: First green and then blue, one after another, reaching high into the dark heavens. Twisting tracers screeched into the blackness; pumping mortars ejected glowing balls of colour into the air, one after another. The finale was nothing short of a Monte Carlo-style harbour scene. An awesome display of pyrotechnics centred over our house – it was truly amazing.

By the time the second band began their second set, the crowd had thinned a little. After all, it was approaching two in the morning. We on the other hand had no alternative but to listen until the final note. The single-glazed window of our bedroom was less than 15 feet from the pounding sound system.

At half past three, the evening's entertainment finally came to an end. A round of tired applause rippled across the green. With our senses barely intact, Melanie and I hauled ourselves up from our seats and dragged our weary frames off to bed.

Before we'd climbed the stairs, a final volley of

explosions took to the sky signalling an end to the night's proceedings. It had been a marvellous experience but all we wanted to do now was rest our weary bones and slip away into dreamland. Unfortunately for us, this wasn't to be.

For us, the last series of aerial explosions were a double edged sword. Not only did they signal an end to the day's celebrations but they also served as a wake up call for the two gangs of roadies. The council had hired two different bands for each of the three nights of the fiesta. This meant that tonight's bands had to pack everything away and hit the road. By the time the two sets of roadies had banged and clattered their equipment back into an articulated trailer, the dark of the night had turned into the brightness of early morning. Melanie and I were exhausted.

The villagers weren't kidding when they had told us not to expect much sleep during the fiesta.

Oh well - one night down, only two more to go.

13

Boys and their Toys

It took us three days to recover from the sleep deprivation we had suffered during the fiesta. Once things had returned to normal our attention turned back to the house. Seven days had slipped by since we signed the contract. By now it should be ready to collect from the Notary.

After breakfast we drove to the bank in Ferreira. We needed some money to pay the *notario's* fees and the house purchase tax. We preferred using the local branch: a one-man operation with a personal touch. The only flaw to this otherwise quick and efficient service came when the manager took one of his numerous coffee breaks. During these regular time-outs, he would pin a notice on the door reading, 'Back Soon'. He took his refreshment breaks in the Bar Paris, two doors down. This morning we were in luck: no notice meant a quick visit; in no time at all we were heading for Monforte.

The air conditioning burst into life as we left the village, a good indication that today was going to be a scorcher. We parked in the car park next to the college. Less than a week earlier it had been bustling with people and crammed full of mechanical fairground rides. With the exception of two ageing camper vans and a grubby looking caravan, all traces of this travelling fair had vanished.

Yet again the Notary office was packed with people. A cacophony of sound greeted us as we entered the tiny waiting room. We shuffled across the floor to the reception counter and waited our turn. A busty receptionist greeted us with a cheery, 'Good morning. How can I help you?'

Before we had a chance to reply, she recognised us. 'Señor Bricks,' she said, with a broad smile.

'Yes that's right,' I replied, 'Craig Bricks.'

'Are you here to collect the contract?' she asked.

'Yes,' I replied.

She turned away, walked to the back of the office and pulled a pile of large manila envelopes off a shelf. Carefully she flicked through them and selected one.

Paper-clipped to the outside was an invoice detailing the *notario's* charges. From inside the envelope she pulled out a bound copy of the *escritura* or contract.

'Take this to the registry office within 10 days,' she instructed.

I glanced at the document to make sure everything was OK: unlike her pronunciation, our names were spelt correctly. We paid the fees and shuffled back out of the busy office.

Stepping from the dark, cool lobby onto the pavement outside was like walking through an invisible curtain of hot, dry air. Pilar had told us to call at her office once we had the *escritura* and she would take us to the registry office.

'Good morning,' said Pilar as we entered the office. 'Is that the *escritura*?' she asked, pointing at the manila envelope tucked tightly under my arm.

'Yes,' I replied.

'Olga will take you to the registry office.'

Hearing her name, Olga looked up from her desk-bound daydream. Reluctantly she rose to her feet and mooched across the office. Pilar explained her mission: we thanked her and left.

Olga set off up the road like a greyhound. Melanie and I were left trailing in her wake, bouncing off one person and mirror-dancing with another. Up ahead Olga stopped and glanced behind, waiting for us to catch up. She stood in the street, expressionless: her slouched body language said it all. Free from the crowds, Melanie and I picked up the pace; no matter how fast we walked we couldn't match Olga's canter. We sprinted past the stunningly beautiful college without so much as a by-your-leave. The midday heat and exhaustive pace were beginning to take their toll. A bead of sweat trickled down the back of my neck. We continued on, racing past the roadside cafes and bars, across the road and headed out of town. Surely it can't be much further? No sooner had I asked myself the question than Olga ground to a halt.

'Here it is,' she announced through a false smile. 'The registry office is on the first floor.'

The words had hardly left her lips when she spun around and shot off like a whippet.

'Gracias,' I mumbled under my breath as we entered the lobby and climbed the staircase.

A plastic plaque screwed to a door on the first floor landing read '*Registro*': I knocked and entered. We walked into a small waiting room. The floor was covered in rough carpet tiles and the wall colours were bland and uninviting.

Bright fluorescent ceiling lights were hidden behind squares of opaque plastic, and a square-panelled false ceiling sat uncomfortably in a white steel frame. To our left were two black, leatherette chairs separated by a low, square table. A smartly dressed woman in her early thirties was sitting opposite. Like me, she too was clutching a large manila envelope. At least we were in the right place. We wished her good morning and took a seat.

A fabric-covered panel separated the waiting area from the main office, behind which a reception counter ran parallel. An old man was leaning against it chatting with someone beyond. Due to the height of the counter and our low seating position, we had no idea who he was talking to. From time to time he would pause, arch onto his toes and peer over the counter. We hadn't been waiting long when the door opened and a portly gentleman walked in. He greeted everyone and took a seat. Moments later it opened again and a smartly dressed young lady entered. Time was drifting on and everyone was becoming restless. The large man shuffled uncomfortably in his seat and the woman to our right crossed her legs and then uncrossed them, only to cross them again.

Eventually the old man concluded his business. The first young lady rose swiftly and darted towards the counter. She wasn't taking a chance on anyone pushing in. I glanced around the room; we were next in line, but not everyone knew that. I edged forward on my seat, ready to pounce as soon as I could.

By the time we reached the counter we'd been waiting for almost an hour. I greeted the registrar and slid the manila envelope across to him. He reached up, pulled it off the counter and onto the desk in front of him. Holding open the gummed flap he tilted the envelope and slid the contents out. He thumbed through the *escritura* and asked if we were the title holders. We had taken our passports just in case, but our positive reply satisfied his question. He spun around on his chair to face a computer and began tapping the keyboard. He paused briefly to take a long pull on a cigarette that had been smouldering in an ashtray next to him, his nicotine-stained fingers evidence of his addiction. He stubbed it out and continued typing.

Before we knew it he'd finished. A laser printer hummed away as an invoice silently slipped through the machine. He picked it out of the tray, swivelled around on his chair and slid the bill towards us. Using a ballpoint pen he pointed at each item in turn, giving a short and swift explanation. He halted assertively at the final total.

'You don't have to pay it now,' blurted the registrar. 'The documents will be ready to collect in about six weeks. You can pay it then if you prefer,' he added.

'No, we'll pay now.'

Melanie handed me the cash. Carefully I counted it out onto the counter. The registrar recounted it and handed me a few loose coins in change. We thanked him, bid him good day, and left.

Registering the house and paying the taxes brought the buying process to an end. From start to finish it had taken less than two weeks to complete. We had found it easy to follow, completely transparent, inexpensive, and best of all, totally free of legal vultures. At last we could focus all our efforts on building a dream home.

The first task was to transfer Felipe's scaled drawings into a visible layout. I wanted to see exactly how the proposed changes to the house and gardens, looked in reality. Nothing fancy, a clutch of wooden pegs and a ball of string would do. We could mark out the main changes such as the extension and the swimming pool. This would give us a visible impression of how these new features fitted within the existing boundary. On previous visits to the house I'd noticed a decaying, oak barrel in the back garden. The old wooden staves would make ideal pegs.

After a good night's sleep we set off for the house. We'd spent so much time over the last few months carrying out mundane, yet necessary chores that we were both eager to get started on more practical hands-on work.

We decided to take Jazz with us to the house. The garden was fully enclosed so there was no chance of her running off. Over the last few months, she'd been left on her own for hours at a time and we were both feeling a little guilty. She was delighted at the prospect and leapt into the back of the car as soon as I had opened the door.

Our first task was to call at the local *ferretería* (hardware store) and buy an axe. Fashioning a sharp point on the wooden staves would be essential to hammering them into the sun-baked earth.

Stepping into a Spanish *ferretería* is like stepping back in time. The sales area begins on the pavement. All manner of items, from buckets to garden rakes, were piled up outside or leant precariously against the double-fronted windows. I eased past them and squeezed through the doorway, conscious of knocking something over. Visions of record breaking domino toppling flashed through my mind. Inside was an *Aladdin*'s cave of household goods, every nook and cranny stuffed with all sorts of bits-and-bobs. Hanging from the ceiling was an assortment of colanders and funnels, tied together like French onions. Every available space was filled with a seemingly unlimited collection of goods.

'Do you have an axe?' I asked, confident of a positive response.

A simple yes would have been ideal, but no such luck. She responded with an oral outpouring, none of which meant a thing to me. I waited patiently for her to finish and then smiled back with a vacant expression.

'*Espera*' (Wait) she announced.

This short command had become the standard response when actions spoke louder than words. She turned away and walked through a narrow doorway behind the sales counter. I waited patiently, peering through the doorway into a dark storeroom: Listening intently to the sound of rummaging. After a few moments she reappeared clutching an assortment of axes and dumped them on the counter.

'*Cual te gusta?*' (Which would you like?), she asked.

I'd never seen such a collection. The handles ranged in length from less than a foot, to over three; and the size and weight of the axe-heads increased in-line with the length of the handle.

That's the one for me, I thought, looking enviously at the biggest of the bunch.

Confidently, I pointed: my choice was a real monster, over 3-foot long and sporting a brightly painted, fire-engine red, axe head. Big toys for big boys!

'Anything else?' she asked.

Here we go again, I thought to myself.

'Have you got any string?'

She bent her head down under the counter and popped back up holding a large ball of string. It was a bit on the thick side but buying it seemed preferable to trying to ask for a thinner one.

Within minutes we were driving through the village of Canabal, location of our new home. The double gates were secured with a steel chain and weathered padlock. Melanie jumped out, unlocked the gates and pushed them open. Weeds had taken root in the cracked concrete of the driveway: it gave the entrance an air of abandoned neglect. The gardens were surrounded by unkempt grapevines; this hadn't always been the case. A series of equally spaced metal struts were secured to the top of fence posts with rusting bolts. Between the struts ran rusting training wires, sagging through years of neglect. Long vine shoots draped from the wires to the floor and bunches of ripening grapes hung from them like bags of pea-green marbles.

The tiny bungalow had a child-like symmetry centred on a wood-panelled front door. Its weathered varnish was peeling and flaking in the bright sunlight. Three steps, with wrought iron railings both sides and a corrugated plastic canopy overhead, led up to the door. Equally spaced, on both sides of the door, were two sets of sun-bleached, pale-blue window shutters.

I drove through the narrow entrance and parked. By now Jazz was whining with excitement. I hopped out of the car, raced to the back and opened the door. She jumped out in a flash, nose to the ground and tail curled high in the air. She darted excitedly, this way and that, sniffing at her new environment, before christening her new home.

I hauled a heavy toolbox out of the boot and on to the floor. Melanie picked up the axe and string.

'We'll start in the back garden,' I said, picking up the toolbox and marching off.

A narrow concrete path ran around the side of the house. The back garden was a sea of dry, straw-like grasses. Two rows of diseased fruit trees ran from front to back. Standing centrally, 10-feet from the house, was a thirsty looking willow, weeping in the hot morning sun. A few feet behind that was the largest yucca I'd ever seen. A huge, sprawling mass of green, sword-like spines mushroomed up through the gently swaying grasses. Three tall spires, of virgin-white flowers, jutted out from the prickly greenery and beyond that lay the collapsed remnants of the large oak barrel. I took the axe off Melanie and waded through the tall grasses towards it.

I couldn't imagine how long it had been lying there. The wooden staves were in a heap, held together by rusting metal bilge hoops. The staves were over 3-foot long: quite a sizeable barrel in its day. I picked one up off the top of the pile. Until this point, it hadn't crossed my mind that staves aren't straight. Hammering these curved lats into the baked earth was going to be more difficult than I'd thought.

'These are far too long,' I shouted across the garden to Melanie, who was entertaining the dog. 'I'll have to chop them in half,' I added.

Carefully I placed a stave on the ground, ensuring that nothing hard lay underneath. The last thing I wanted to do was chip the blade of my shiny new axe. I raised the axe and brought it crashing down: *Whack!* Not a mark, not even a minor indentation. This was going to be harder than I'd expected. I scoured the garden for a stone and leant the stave against it at an angle. This time I raised the axe higher and brought it crashing down with all the force I could muster. *Whack!* Crack! *Twang!*

'Look out!' I shouted, as one half of the broken stave catapulted through the air in Melanie's general direction, like the propeller from a downed *Spitfire*.

'*Be careful!* That nearly hit me,' snapped Melanie, rising from her crouched position.

Before long I'd smashed my way through a dozen or more staves. All I needed to do now was chop an angled point on one end. To achieve this I had to hold the broken stave in one hand while wielding the axe with the other. The limitations of a monster-sized axe quickly became apparent. To lift the axe with one hand, I needed to grasp the shaft very close to the axe head; and in order to hit the broken stave with enough force to chop a point, I needed to raise it as high as possible.

Raising the axe above head height meant sacrificing accuracy. Nightmarish visions of amputated fingers rushed through my mind.

'This isn't going to be as easy as I thought,' I murmured to Melanie.

'Do be careful,' she said, with a shiver of concern in her voice.

Slowly I raised the axe to head height, just to try it out. *Whoosh, clonk!* I managed to hit the right spot on the stave but the blow was so weak it simply ricocheted off. If I was ever going to fashion a point on these old oak staves I needed to throw caution to the wind. I raised the axe as high as possible, put my faith in Lady Luck and brought it crashing down with great force.

I spent the next hour or so chipping away at the staves in the midday heat, with sweat pouring out of me like a wet sponge. By the time I'd carved enough pegs, I was soaking wet, hot, and frustrated; but at least I still had all my fingers.

'Right, that's enough,' I called to Melanie who had brought a chair from the house and was lounging in the sun. 'You hold it and I'll hit it.'

Armed with Felipe's plan and a tape measure, we found the position for the first peg, this marked the far corner of the swimming pool.

'I'm not holding that,' said Melanie.

'Don't worry, I won't miss,' I replied, with more confidence in my voice than in my arm.

Even with a tapered end the sun-dried earth was more than a match for my bent staves.

'Do be careful,' said Melanie, now concerned for the welfare of her own fingers.

Before long we had the pool marked out and had started on the surrounding terrace.

'Watch what you're doing,' I sniped at Melanie.

She'd uprooted one of the pegs marking out the swimming pool and the string was now lying on the ground.

'I haven't touched it,' she snapped.

'Well it wasn't me.'

I waded through the long grass and hammered it back in.

'You've done it again,' I screeched in annoyance.

'I haven't been anywhere near that peg,' she replied.

'Well it's not me.'

No sooner had the words left my lips than I caught sight of Jazz tugging at the peg that I'd just hammered back into the ground.

'Jazz!' I screamed. 'Drop it!'

For her, this was just a game. She was yanking them out almost as quick as we were hammering them in. She sat on the long grass, head tilted to one side, chomping at a peg with a bemused look on her face. I picked up another stave.

'Come on,' I shouted.

Excitedly she dropped hers and came darting towards me. I threw it to the far end of the garden and turned to continue. In a flash she was back, waiting for me to throw it again. Once more I picked up the stick and turned to throw it.

'I don't believe it.'

On her return from the bottom of the garden she'd

walked straight through the proposed swimming pool, dragging the string and uprooting another two pegs. At this rate we would be here all day. Eventually we managed to calm her down. Before long she was lying in the warm sun, snoozing.

By early afternoon the task was complete. We had mapped out the swimming pool, the patio area, the house extension, and the new covered terraces, front and back. It turned out to be an extremely useful exercise. There were a number of minor changes we now wanted to make to the plans before proceeding with the alterations.

The following Monday we collected Sylvia and marched on to Felipe's office to explain the changes we wanted to make. His secretary greeted us with some annoying news.

'Felipe's on holiday.'

'Holiday,' enquired Sylvia, 'For how long?'

'He'll be back in a week.'

Just as it seemed we were making progress, everything would now be on hold. Of course, he was entitled to a holiday just like anyone else but he could have let us know.

We spent the rest of the week working at the house. We began by painting the ugly boundary walls. Several coats of white emulsion transformed the lifeless, grey breeze-blocks into a bright flowing border. The hard work and hot weather reminded me of a scene from Mark Twain's, *Huckleberry Finn*.

After a tiring morning, labouring under a baking sun, we would treat ourselves to lunch. Fortunately for us, Canabal has a small restaurant. It's called O Regata and serves *Menu del Dia* (Menu of the Day): a hearty, three course meal with refreshment, at a low fixed price. The car park outside the restaurant was always busy and the village green crowded with passing trucks: what better recommendation?

We pulled into the car park and wandered around the side of the bar into the garden. A leafy canopy of tall chestnut trees provides a cool and shaded environment. The centrepiece of the garden is a large wooden pergola, roofed with terracotta tiles. The restaurant was quite busy when we arrived: A number of lorry drivers were sitting alone, sipping wine and tucking into their meals. Others were grouped together, chatting and joking over lunch. We took a seat under the pergola and waited.

Before long a young waitress approached carrying a basket of freshly-cut, crusty bread in one hand and two wine glasses in the other. She placed them on the table and pulled a notepad and pen from the pocket of her apron. Without pausing to draw breath, she narrated the day's menu. Somewhere in the list I heard the word *filete* (steak) so opted for that; Melanie chose the same.

'Salad?' she enquired.

I nodded our approval.

'And to drink?' she asked

'Two beers.'

'And water?'

I glanced across at Melanie and nodded at the waitress. By now we were used to the brusque manner of Spanish service. Members of staff rarely use two words when one will do and find the English custom of adding please and thank you, to every reply, extremely nauseating.

The food is prepared in an open kitchen at the back of the bar. The seductive smell of wood smoke drifted through the garden from the open grill. Having given our order to the cook, the waitress returned with two icy-cold beers, dinner plates and a knife, fork and spoon, wrapped tightly in a paper serviette. No sooner had she turned her back, than we were both nibbling on a wedge of fresh, crusty bread. The rustic bread of the area is absolutely delicious but a real crown-tester. Large droplets of condensation dribbled down the glass of icy-cold beer, leaving a damp circle on the paper tablecloth. I raised my glass to Melanie with an offering of cheers! Vivid images of Sylvia Syms and John Mills in *Ice Cold in Alex*, flashed through my mind.

Plumes of smoke billowed from the stone chimney of the outdoor grill. Stomach-rumbling aromas of char-grilled steaks drifted across the patio. Before long the waitress returned, balancing our lunchtime order. She crashed it down on the table, with all the grace of a Tyneside welder.

'*Que aproveche*' (Enjoy your meal) she chirped, before rushing back to the kitchen.

'*Gracias,*' we replied.

We were both presented with a huge slice of barbecued beef and an ample serving of chips. The steak was so large that it drooped over the edge of the dinner plate. Accompanying this was a heaped plate of fresh, leafy salad with large chunks of tomatoes and slices of fresh onion, drizzled with olive oil and home-made red wine vinegar. We tucked in with gusto, pausing occasionally to sip our cold beer. All too soon we'd eaten up. With the miserly bill paid, it was back to the house and a short afternoon of work under the blazing sun. This became our leisurely work routine for the rest of the week.

The following Monday we were back at Felipe's with Sylvia.

'Is he in?' asked Sylvia, as his secretary opened the door.

A short conversation followed between the two.

'He's not here,' said Sylvia. 'He's decided to take another week's holiday.'

I couldn't believe it: one week's delay had been bad enough but a second week was really frustrating.

We spent the following week painting the walls and enjoying lazy lunches at O Regata. Apart from the delay, the long summer days were perfect: warm mornings, hot and sunny days and comfortable evenings: ideal for our alfresco lifestyle; exactly how we imagined a Spanish summer would be.

The week passed quickly and before we knew it we were standing outside Sylvia's apartment pressing the intercom.

'Come up,' she called.

The door buzzed open and we climbed the stairs to the first floor. Sylvia's door was slightly ajar.

'Come in!' bellowed Sylvia from the kitchen. 'I'll just ring Felipe to make sure he's there.'

That seems a strange thing for her to say, I thought.

Sylvia had always been the first to jump to her feet and barge into his office unannounced. She squeezed past us and into the hall. Minutes later she returned.

'He's not there,' she said hesitantly.

There was a short pause and then I asked, 'What time will he be back?'

Sylvia hesitated, before qualifying her statement, 'He's decided to stay for another week. Apparently the fishing is very good.'

I was speechless: I couldn't believe that we would have to wait another week. This unexpected and unwanted news was a step too far. One week had been understandable, two annoying but three, three weeks was down right unbelievable.

Sylvia broke the silence, 'You'll have to have another Spanish lesson,' she said, trying to make light of the news.

Her lack of concern tipped me over the edge, 'We haven't brought our bloody books!' I stormed. 'We were supposed to be having a meeting with *Felipe*.'

Thinking that I might live to regret my rage, Melanie stepped in. 'They're in the car. I'll go and get them.'

'*I'll get them*,' I snapped, fearing my temper might get the better of me.

The town had been quite busy when we arrived and we had to park someway off. The walk gave me the opportunity to calm down: after all, it wasn't Sylvia's fault. By the time I returned I felt much calmer, hugely disappointed, but much calmer.

Felipe was proving that urgency is definitely not a Spanish characteristic. However, we were English and I was determined to keep things moving along.

The only positive to come from this unscheduled delay was the opportunity to finish painting the boundary wall. We now had a flowing band of gleaming white breeze-blocks, running around our sun-dried patch of tall grasses, diseased fruit trees and unkempt grapevines. Our final job in the garden was to choose which diseased trees we would like to keep and nurse back to productive health. My imagination was stretched to its limit trying to visualise how this unkempt pasture might one day look.

Before too long, there would be a mindless excavator driver hacking great lumps of earth out of the place. We decided that a thick band of white paint, brushed around the trunk would clearly identify the trees we wanted to keep. Secretly I had my doubts but for the time being it seemed to pacify Melanie. Only time would tell if our action had merit.

14

I Hate Spiders

Felipe's decision to extend his holiday into a third week was a real setback. He knew we were keen to move things along. As well as securing tenders for the house, we also needed to find a swimming pool constructor. To make matters worse, Javier, the other architect, was also away, overseeing the birth of his first child.

That evening over a glass of wine my patience ran out.

'Bugger Felipe,' I announced, 'let's find a swimming pool supplier ourselves.'

Melanie was in agreement. When we first mentioned a swimming pool to Felipe he hadn't quite grasped the idea. He suggested an above ground plastic liner, filled annually from an outside tap. They're available from most large supermarkets and are one step up from an inflatable paddling pool; we had other ideas.

We wanted the focal point of our garden to be a large, concrete swimming pool lined with pastel blue tiles that would sparkle in the sun. At the shallow end, Roman steps would arc their way into the cool blue water. This would be our very own aquatic playground, a refreshing oasis to enjoy on lazy summer days or simply float away into dreamland. We couldn't blame Felipe: after all, this is Galicia, a place where gardens are used for grazing sheep or planting vegetables. All we had to do was find someone capable of building our dream centrepiece.

We were due a bit of luck and that's exactly what we got. By sheer coincidence, during a lunch break at O Regata, we saw a white van with the words 'Hentschel & Jones SL – *Piscinas*' emblazoned down the side. Melanie scribbled down the phone number off the side of the van.

That evening I managed to cajole her into giving them a ring. I successfully argued that with a company name like Jones, someone there would speak English.

'Well you can ring them then' she protested, unconvinced by my argument.

'It's probably better if you do,' I paused, trying to think of a plausible reason, 'just in case they don't speak English. But I'm sure they will,' I added quickly, terrified at the prospect of trying to decipher the rapid babble of incomprehensible Spanish over a crackling telephone line.

My reluctance proved well founded as Melanie stammered her way through the conversation. Bravely, she explained what we wanted and where we would like it to go.

The company was based in the nearby town of Ourense. The owner, a chap called Mariano, said he would meet us tomorrow morning at 10 o'clock in Canabal. Melanie was clearly pleased with her efforts, and rightly so. She had managed to communicate our wishes and understand Mariano's instructions. The only problem, in this otherwise perfect scenario, was that tomorrow would be Friday, and Friday is Gas day. Missing this important delivery would mean cold showers for the following week: butane gas was our only method of heating water.

Gas day had become an essential part of life since moving to Spain. Every Friday, without fail, Repsol delivers gas to Ferreira and the surrounding villages. The heavily laden truck dashes along country lanes with its cargo of highly-flammable butane gas. Once in Ferreira, it follows a predictable route. Gas cylinders can be heard clanking and rattling as it makes its way around the village and the blast of its distinctive horn alerts villagers of his arrival.

Every Friday morning by nine o'clock, the lanes and streets of Ferreira are lined with empty, bright-orange cylinders, waiting to be exchanged. The empties look like tiny steel spacemen waiting to catch a bus. At the sound of the horn, village folk scuttle out from darkened doorways, swap their empties for full ones and then struggle back inside with their much heavier replacements.

In her concentrated effort to communicate with Mariano, Melanie had forgotten all about this vitally important day. Just following the conversation had been difficult enough. Fortunately, our meeting wasn't until 10 o'clock; Repsol would have been and gone by then. There would be ample time to drive to the house in Canabal.

Changing an empty gas cylinder on the water heater had become the bane of my life. It was situated in the tiny boiler room in the basement: a room that measured no more than 10-foot by 4-foot. It also housed the central heating boiler and a 30 gallon oil drum, both of which were later additions. This fact turned the simple task of replacing an empty gas cylinder into a new art form. I can best describe it as a cross between weightlifting, yoga, and a game of blindfold Twister.

The central heating boiler was a free-standing, red-panelled, metal box, about the size of a double wardrobe. To the right of it was the 30 gallon oil drum. When installing the boiler, the plumber had cleverly welded a series of pipes and filters to the oil drum transforming it into the storage reservoir which fed the boiler. It resembled a clever piece of impromptu recycling that one might expect to see on the TV show *Scrapheap Challenge*. The only problem with this ingenious piece of self-build plumbing was that it had been installed after the water heater.

In comparison, the water heater is a relatively small piece of equipment. It's mounted on the wall in the far left hand corner of the room and hidden behind the huge, red boiler. Replacing an empty butane cylinder involved strength, balance, dexterity, and a large slice of luck. Most of all it meant overcoming one of my greatest fears – spiders.

In theory, the easiest part of the operation is removing the empty cylinder. The gap between the huge, red boiler to the left and the oil drum to the right is about a foot and a half, ample distance to squeeze through. Having said that, this straightforward manoeuvre is hindered by three feeder pipes connecting the oil drum to the boiler, two at ankle level and the third at chest height.

Once through this gap, the water heater and gas cylinder came into view; from here on in, things become even more difficult; both physically and mentally. The only light source in this dark, diesel-fumed grotto comes from a 40 watt bulb dangling from the centre of the ceiling on a short piece of flex.

For an arachnophobe like me, this is where the

operation becomes terrifying. The problem is the gap between the back of the central heating boiler and the wall. It's just over a foot, an incredibly short distance for those fearsome spiders to spin a maze of sticky traps. Matters are made worse by my lengthening shadow. The closer I inch towards the water heater the more I obscure the light from the centrally hanging light bulb. It always ends with a plethora of silky strands clinging to my face like fibrous threads of glue, I hate it.

The Repsol delivery driver has a predictable routine. He drives down through the village delivering on one side of the main street, at the taxi rank he turns left and drives past Elo's. After delivering to us, he continues to the end of the road, turns left and finishes the opposite side of the main street. Where he goes after leaving the village is anyone's guess.

As usual we had a couple of empties to exchange. One after the other I carried them up the drive and plonked them on the grass outside the gates. By nine o'clock we would usually hear the distant echo of the horn as the driver announces his arrival, but not this morning. I waited outside, pacing up and down. Five-past, ten-past and finally quarter-past nine, came and went. Melanie joined me on the green.

'Do you think we should set off for our meeting?' I asked, anxiously.

'Repsol should be here soon,' she replied. 'Perhaps we ought to just leave the money under the empties and hope he swaps them,' she added.

I felt a little uneasy with Melanie's suggestion. It wasn't a question of trust; I had no reservations on that score. My concern was over the driver's observation skills. Knowing our luck, he would miss the empties and drive straight past. The thought of cold showers for a week kept me firmly anchored to the spot.

'We'll wait a bit longer,' I said, 'just in case.'

By half-past we still hadn't heard a thing so I decided to walk to the end of the road. This served two purposes: first, it made me feel as though I was doing something positive; lord only knows what, and: second, I was starting to think that the rest of the village might know something I didn't. If the driver had told me last week that he might be late today, I wouldn't have had a clue. My conversation with him was limited to hello, good day, how much, and goodbye.

My communication fears were eased when I came across the first orange spaceman standing on the edge of the pavement. As I reached the main street, I looked both left and right. There were lots more of the little blighters waiting patiently at the roadside. I glanced at the time, 9:45. A decision had to be made. I turned and headed home.

'We'll have to leave the money under a cylinder and hope for the best,' I suggested to Melanie as I entered the gates.

Before Melanie had time to agree, the distant sound of a horn floated by on a breath of warm air. Thank heavens for that! We now faced an agonising wait until the heavily laden truck rattled up the hill and across the green. Hurriedly, I handed over the exact money and one at a time, manhandled the two heavy cylinders inside the gates.

'Right,' I said, with a bead of sweat trickling down my brow, 'let's go.'

We jumped in the car and sped off to Canabal.

On occasions such as this it's reassuring to know that Spaniards view time as we view the sea. To them, it's fluid and flexible: It bends and stretches with real life events. An hour late or an hour early, it really doesn't matter to most.

No sooner had we left home than the mobile phone rang. Melanie snatched her bag off the floor and scrambled around inside, searching for the source. Seconds before its final ring, she found it and pressed the answer button.

'Hello… No… No… Yes, we're on our way. Two minutes and we'll be there… Yes…. Yes… Bye.'

Her punctuated answers were in response to Mariano's questioning.

'Can you believe it?' exclaimed Melanie. 'The only occasion we've been late for anything over the last four months and it turns out to be an appointment with the best time keeper in the whole of Spain.'

Moments later I swerved off the main highway and raced down the slip road. Parked at the end was an old Mercedes-Benz 300D. The ageing, metallic-bronze paintwork was dull and scratched. We pulled alongside and lowered the window.

'Mariano?' enquired Melanie.

A deep, crusty, smoker's voice replied, *'Sí.'*

With a combination of single word exchanges and those all important hand gestures, he agreed to follow us to the house. We pulled off the lane and into the road-side driveway. Melanie leapt from the car and unlocked the gates enabling both of us to pull off the lane and into the drive. Mariano had other ideas. He parked at the side of the lane with two wheels in the drainage ditch and the other two on the edge of the tarmac. The ageing *Merc* rested at a precarious angle. To get out, he held the door open with one foot, grasped the door frame and hauled himself upright. With his weight missing, I half expected the car to roll into the ditch when he slammed the door closed. Thankfully, this wasn't the case.

Mariano was a ruggedly handsome man in his late 40's or early 50's with a deep brown tan. He was smartly dressed with a pair of dark slacks and a white shirt. Clutched under one arm were two plastic-bound, ring-files. After the initial pleasantries he wasted no time in telling us that he didn't speak a word of English. We ambled around to the back of the house to show him our proposed location. A bemused look rolled across his face as he gazed out over a sea of waist-high grasses and diseased fruit trees, some of which had a broad band of white emulsion daubed around the trunk. Then there were the pegs, fashioned from oak staves and sticking up like a family of meerkats in the African Savanna. This chaotic scene was finished off with a ball of string tied around the staves like a giant join-the-dots puzzle. After showing him the architects' plans and explaining about the white paint on the trees, which he thought was a brilliant idea, his mood changed from that of utter confusion to a man on a mission.

We explained what we wanted to achieve and waited for his response. He pulled one of the files from under his arm, opened it and slowly flicked through the glossy pages. We'd never seen so many different swimming pool designs: every shape and size imaginable. Cleverly created oases set against a backdrop of tropical gardens. Some were undoubtedly stunning, but not quite us. We wanted a pool for swimming in: a rectangular one, 10m long by 5m wide with semi-circular Roman steps descending into the shallow end. We were easy to please and had soon chosen the design.

While we decided on the design, Mariano wrestled to keep the second file tucked firmly under his arm. When he brought it out, it became apparent why. This file contained the tile samples and weighed a ton. Card after card of tiny one inch square, stained glass tiles mounted on a grid, six tiles across by six tiles deep.

The choice of pool design had been relatively easy: we had a clear vision of the size and shape before our meeting. The choice of tile colour was proving far more difficult. We narrowed it down to pale blue, dark blue, or a mixture of the two plus a splash of green. The problem was that we weren't talking about a seasonal splash of colour in the back garden, quite the contrary. This would be a 50 square metre, year-round display. If we weren't careful, it could become a permanent and annoying blight on our outdoor lives.

Mariano sensed our indecision and flicked to the middle section of the file. Here there were beautifully framed photos showing how each tile colour might look in a garden setting. At first we were drawn to the darker blue but eventually settled on the paler of the two.

With the tile colour decided upon, Mariano flipped to the final section in the file – borders and mosaics. The border would form a continuous pattern around the top of the pool. Once again the choices were quite staggering. Thankfully, one pattern jumped off the page at us. In one of those rare moments of marital synchronised harmony, we both pointed at the same border. The final few pages in the file contained an array of hideous mosaic patterns, designed to form a centrepiece on the floor of the pool. Such repulsive designs as a 10-foot wide turtle or a 15-foot dolphin, all made up from garish coloured tiles.

'No thanks Mariano, they're awful.'

A spontaneous laugh erupted.

'I know,' sniggered Mariano, 'but some people like them.'

With our decisions made, he dropped the heavy tile folder on the ground and began scribbling down our instructions. After each item he stopped, confirmed our approval before proceeding to the next item. With the details carefully recorded he tucked the paper inside one of the folders and we turned to leave.

'Lights!' he blurted.

'Lights,' I enquired.

'It's better with a pool this size to have lights,' he added 'It looks really nice at night with them on.'

Holiday memories of late night skinny-dipping sprang to mind.

'Yes, lights, that sounds like a good idea.'

We waited as he jotted it down; then turned to leave.

'A ladder,' he blurted.

'A ladder,' I enquired.

'Yes, you'll need a stainless steel ladder at the deep end of the pool. It's a safety feature.'

A safety feature, my foot, I'm sure he's more interested in bumping up the price than personal safety.

'OK,' I said, 'we'll have the steps and the lights.'

'And a shower,' he asked.

'A shower.'

'Yes, an outside shower to wash the sun cream off before going in, and the chemicals away when you get out.'

His brochures were packed full of useless accessories. Lights and steps seemed like a good idea but a shower was not on the agenda.

'No thank you,' I said firmly, 'they're always too cold to stand under.'

'We can plumb hot water to it,' he added quickly.

'No we don't want a shower.'

My firm response was enough to prevent him from pushing the matter further.

'What about the earth?' he asked.

Melanie and I looked at each other for inspiration.

Perhaps the word, *earth (tierra)* has more than one meaning in Spanish, I thought.

Our extended pause and bemused expression prompted Mariano to expand his statement.

'The earth from the hole,' he said.

With no discernable change in our facial expressions he continued, 'The earth from the hole that we'll have to dig to build the swimming pool.'

All of a sudden the penny dropped.

'Do you want it spread out over the rest of the garden, left in a pile somewhere, or taken away?'

Crikey! We hadn't realised that asking for a quote on a swimming pool would prove so complicated.

'Ah yes, the earth,' I said confidently. 'I think it's best if you take it away.'

We paused for a moment waiting to see if there were any more questions, but no. We turned and headed for the car. He agreed to have the quote prepared in about a week. I half expected to see his car resting on its roof when we walked back around to the front of the house. Fortunately, it was just as he had left it. We thanked him for his time, said our goodbyes and watched him disappear up the lane in a cloud of oily, blue smoke.

We wandered back into the garden, dreaming of our shiny new swimming pool; pleased as punch with our morning's work. Our architect might be on a never ending vacation but that didn't mean we had to be.

That weekend Sylvia rang to tell us Felipe would be back at work on Monday. We asked her to ring him first thing Monday morning and arrange a meeting for Wednesday. Having reached the midpoint in September we were eager to get the plans amended and the tenders submitted. Getting work started was our main priority.

15

The *Bodega* Run

'It sounds as if your sister is coming to see us,' announced Melanie, as she handed me the letter. 'Page three about halfway down.'

I flicked through the pages and scanned the hand written letter, scripted in her familiar school mistress style.

I've swapped my day off from Thursday to Friday so I'm going to come and see you Friday 20th September and return the following Monday. You'll have to pick me up and drop me off at the airport.

Organising events and then manoeuvring the participants into position, is one of my sister's favourite pastimes. She took it for granted that we would welcome her with open arms. Of course, this was the case but it wouldn't have harmed to ask.

Her regular letters to Melanie were packed with interesting information. She left us with the impression that every second of her family's leisure time, which is not inconsiderable, was planned and organised like a military operation. Julie is not one for lazing on a sun-drenched beach or relaxing around a hotel swimming pool: she likes to be doing.

'What are we going to do with her?' asked Melanie anxiously.

'I've no idea, but we'll have to think of something.' I replied

The thought of spending a long weekend in the company of my sister was quite daunting. Other than our parents, we don't really have that much in common. As the eldest, she proved a hard act to follow, in more ways than one. However, we do share one very important characteristic, our penchant for wine.

'I know what we can do,' I said, having had one of those eureka moments.

'What?' asked Melanie.

'We can take her on a tour of the local *bodegas*' (wineries).

'That's a great idea,' replied Melanie, 'she'll love that.'

The following week we spent a full day travelling around the area discovering a number of suitable *bodegas* to visit. We even gave our improvised excursion a name – The *Bodega* Run.

The following week we picked Julie up from the airport as instructed. We arrived back in Ferreira by late afternoon, and relaxed in the garden, sipping *Albariño* wine and watching the sun set over a neighbour's rooftop. Julie brought us up to speed with events in England while I lit the barbecue. After dinner I unveiled Felipe's plans for the house. She liked our ideas for converting the tiny bungalow into a Mediterranean-style villa: her positive comments were encouraging and reassuring. Before retiring we unveiled our tour plans for tomorrow which received a favourable response.

The weather the following morning was a little disappointing, bright but overcast. Immediately after lunch we set off on our tour – The *Bodega* Run. En route we stopped in Canabal to show Julie the house. We took a good look around and I did my best to explain the proposed changes. Julie found it far easier to look at Felipe's drawings and visualise the outcome, than look at the house and do the same.

From Canabal I drove up through the village of Sober heading out in the direction of the river Sil. After about 15 minutes we entered the sleepy village of Lobios. The road through the village was deserted. We passed the village church: a tiny old building made from local granite. On the left, a proud sign read, *Zona de* Amandi.

Amandi wines are the most prestigious of the Ribeira Sacra *denominacion*. Opposite this sign was another which read 'Adega San Cosmede', the first port of call on our wine tasting tour.

I pulled off the road and into the narrow entrance of the *bodega*. It felt warm and humid as we stepped from the air-conditioned car and made our way towards a small gate.

'It feels as if there's a storm in the air,' said Melanie as she pushed open the gate and entered.

A short pathway led to a small open courtyard in front of a traditional, stone-built farmhouse. Melanie marched down the path towards the farmhouse, unconcerned that a pack of hungry guard dogs might lay in wait, or worse still some dithering old guy with Parkinson's brandishing a shotgun. Julie and I followed gingerly, covering the rear.

'Hola!' shouted Melanie, as she walked down the path. 'Hola!'

If any dogs were sleeping, they wouldn't be anymore. To our surprise, a middle aged woman wearing a nylon working coat stepped into the courtyard from behind a stone water trough and returned Melanie's greeting. Cautiously we continued down the path. As we neared the woman we could see that we'd interrupted something: her overall sleeves were rolled up above her elbows and she was wringing a wet item of clothing. Droplets of water fell from the garment and splashed on the stone surface of the courtyard.

'She's doing her washing,' whispered Julie under her breath.

By the time we reached her, a small puddle had formed at her feet.

'Excuse me,' pleaded Melanie, 'we were wondering if we could visit the *bodega* and taste the wine.'

A broad smile beamed across the woman's face. 'Yes, yes, that's no problem. Just wait here one moment,' she turned quickly and scampered across to the stone trough.

The trough was about 3-foot square: A short section, on one side, angled into dirty grey water where patches of foamy suds floated in creamy swathes. Along this edge ran a series of equally spaced, parallel ridges. A pile of damp washing drained on one side and a large block of soap sat on the other.

The three of us glanced sheepishly at each other, guilty at our unannounced interruption. Unceremoniously the woman dumped the dripping garment on top of the damp pile and scurried off into the farmhouse.

'Wait there while I get the key,' she shouted from the bottom of the stone steps that led to the front door. A few moments later she reappeared, beaming from ear to ear. She dangled the keys in front of her face as she bounced down the steps.

The entrance to the *bodega* was directly opposite the stone trough. A huge door lintel, chiselled from a single slab of granite, formed an impressive portal. Less impressive were two large, wooden doors guarding the entrance, one of which had a smaller door built within it: all had seen better days. Keys jangling, the woman rushed to the doors and inserted a small Yale-like key into the lock of the smallest door. She stepped through and turned back, warning us to mind our heads and watch our feet on the high threshold. One by one we entered, picking our feet up high over the threshold and ducking our heads down low to avoid bumping them.

In contrast to outside, the air inside was cool and still. The light came from a long fluorescent tube suspended from the lofted ceiling on two lengths of rusting chain. The room was surprisingly small, about 12-foot by 15. The stone walls were painted with a lavish coat of whitewash. Above the fluorescent light, equally spaced wooden roof joists supported old irregular-shaped chestnut planks which carried the weight of the roof tiles. Resting on the floor, along one wall, was a single wooden pallet containing 15 or so, neatly stacked boxes of wine. Next to the pallet stood a quirky-looking, bottle labelling machine; it reminded me of an ancient piece of printing equipment.

Attached to a spindle at the back of the machine was a half-used roll of self-adhesive wine labels. To work the machine, the operator placed an unlabelled bottle horizontally on two rubber rollers. By turning a handle on the side, similar to that found on an old gramophone player, the bottle rotated. At the same time the labels passed through a series of other rollers, separating the label from the waxed backing sheet and applying it to the rotating bottle: very simple but extremely efficient.

Our host flicked on another light switch, drawing our

attention to a doorway in the far corner. She walked ahead and gestured us to follow. It led into another room of similar dimensions. Lined up along one wall were four identical stainless steel vats, about 7-foot tall. They were meticulously clean, as was the whole room; even the concrete floor was coated in a seamless, red glaze: everything ready for the forthcoming grape harvest.

'Our vineyards are down by the river Sil, in the Amandi zone,' she announced proudly.

In my pitifully inadequate Spanish, I tried to ask when the harvest would start. My incomprehensible babblings received an all too familiar response: firstly a vacant expression and a long pause closely followed by facial contortions, and a rolling of the eyes. At this point, Melanie would jump in and rescue the situation.

'My husband was asking, how soon will you harvest the grapes?'

I could have sworn that that was exactly what I had asked: don't these people speak the lingo?

'My husband is helping a neighbour to harvest his grapes and then the neighbour will help us with ours,' she replied.

This explained why the stock in the warehouse was so low and all the vats were empty. Our host moved across to a light switch on the wall and flicked it on. A beam of light fanned out across the concrete floor. We inched forward in search of the source. Hidden behind the vats was a narrow passageway carved through the wall. We followed the woman between the vats, down a number of stone steps leading through the wall, and into a room beyond.

'Wow! Look at that,' said Melanie, in astonishment.

Resting on wooden blocks, in this cool subterranean chamber, were two enormous wooden barrels. The circular ends were well over 6 feet in diameter and the barrel was at least 15-foot long: they almost filled the entire room. The woman explained that the barrels weren't used anymore: the wine was now made under much stricter controls in the new stainless steel vats. The only reason these old, wooden relics were still here was their size: to remove them would either mean smashing them into pieces or demolishing the *bodega*. This brought our guided tour to a fitting end. We scrambled back up the narrow stepped passage, through the new winery and into the stockroom.

'Can we have a taste?' whispered Julie under her breath. Melanie asked.

'Yes of course,' replied our host, with a broad smile.

In a seamlessly fluid movement, she grasped a bottle, trimmed the foil, effortlessly twisted a corkscrew into the cork and pulled it from the neck to a resounding *pop*! From a rickety old table close to the door she took three tumblers, checked each one against the light for cleanliness and handed them out. She poured each of us a full tumbler of the inky-purple wine and stared at us enquiringly. With all the skill of wine connoisseurs, we raised our glasses to our top lips, took a deep nasal inhalation and finished with a delicate sip. A murmur of contentment echoed around the room but unlike connoisseurs, none of us were foolish enough to spit it out.

'You like it?' asked the woman.

A unanimous chorus of approval rang out, resulting in an even broader smile from our host.

'Wait,' she said, before turning to leave.

Moments later she returned clutching a large bunch of pea-green grapes.

'Here, try these.'

She broke the bunch into three clusters and handed them out. With her hands free she whipped up the half-empty bottle and began topping up everyone's tumbler.

'Not for me thank you,' I said, desperately trying to cover the top of my tumbler with a handful of grapes. 'I have to drive.'

'You don't like?' she asked.

'Yes, I like it but I have to drive the car,' I said, rephrasing my answer in an attempt to be understood.

On this occasion, my inadequate Spanish wasn't the problem: our host was struggling with the concept of a designated driver. An uncomfortable silence followed. There were lots of questions we wanted to ask and comments we wanted to make but alas, the woman didn't speak any English and our holiday Spanish just wasn't up to the job. Conscious of the conspicuous silence, Julie glanced across at Melanie and whispered, 'Do you think we can buy some?'

With a hint of sibling sarcasm I quietly replied. 'That's the general idea.'

We decided to buy a three bottle, presentation pack. Melanie did the honours and asked our delighted host. Time was creeping on and the washing was still to do. Conscious that our impromptu visit had distracted her from her domestic duties, we drank up, placed our empty tumblers back on the rickety table, thanked our gracious host, and turned to leave.

'More wine?' she asked, with a hint of desperation in her voice.

Courteously, we declined and stepped back through the doorway, remembering to keep our feet up and head down.

Compared to inside, the air in the courtyard was warm and heavy. She followed us through the doorway and pulled the door shut. We turned to wish her one final goodbye and began making our way back to the car.

'Wait a moment,' she called, as we headed up the path.

She scampered off down the courtyard and disappeared around the side of the farmhouse. We stood on the path between the courtyard and the gate in the shade of a majestic chestnut tree. A light breeze gently rustled the thick leafed foliage. Its ancient roots bulged out of the ground creating gaping fissures in the concrete path. Before long her familiar figure reappeared; she walked towards us awkwardly, arms crossed in front of her. As she neared, we could see that her arms were full of freshly picked peaches.

'Here you are,' she said, thrusting the peaches at us.

Julie was overcome by her generosity and gracious nature but for Melanie and me, nonreciprocal generosity was becoming less extraordinary and more ordinary: it's a very Galician characteristic. Having thanked her again we wandered back to the car, stowed our newly gained booty in the back and continued on.

The car's warm interior quickly cooled as we meandered along the country lane. A weathered signpost marked our departure from the village of Lobios. Huge chestnut trees lined the roadside and bright sunlight splashed the car as we drifted in and out of their leafy shade. Before long we reached a fork in the road where we turned right, heading towards the village of Doade. On the left, 100 metres from the fork, was our next port of call – Adega Décima.

A short, dusty track leads from the road to a house in the middle of a field. It's nothing more than two dirt grooves, cut into the grassy meadow by vehicles driving to and from the house. I pulled the car off the track and parked in the meadow. Tall strands of late developing grasses swayed into the cabin as we opened the car doors and stepped into the warm afternoon sunshine. The area around the house was a hive of activity. As we wandered up, I spotted Carmen walking towards us. We'd met her last week while planning the excursion. She has the rare skill of being able to speak a little English.

'Hello! How are you?' I asked as we met at the edge of the track.

We exchanged pleasantries and I introduced Julie. She explained that everyone was very busy today, bottling last year's wine, and invited us to watch. As we strolled up the lane, a pick-up truck pulled off the road and bounced up the track towards us. We all stepped back as it carefully crept past.

Secured behind the driver's cab was a large plastic container measuring one cubic metre. Inside the container, a dark liquid swayed rhythmically to the contours of the lane and the motion of the rocking truck. It didn't take long for us to realise that its precious cargo was a cubic metre of red wine, the equivalent of over 1300 bottles. We followed the truck along the track until it pulled off onto the grass.

Opposite the house was a roughly constructed breeze-block shed with a corrugated tin roof. Inside the shed was a rather impressive, semi-automated bottling machine. Half a dozen workers surrounded the machine, frantically trying to keep pace with this mechanised monster. We stood and watched in awe as this wonderful contraption set about its business.

The machine was configured in a large U-shape. On one side of the U, two willing workers were busy loading empty bottles into a gently vibrating tray. The angle of the tray, combined with its gentle vibration, guided the bottles into a single line and then on to a narrow rolling lane. As the bottles moved along the lane they paused. A cap plunged down onto the neck and injected an exact measure of wine. I couldn't help thinking that it looked similar to a milking machine, except in reverse. With the bottle filled, the cap bounced off releasing the bottle to continue on its journey.

The cork came next. Once again the bottles paused. A clamp, tightly grasped the neck of each bottle and a mechanical arm shot a cork into it. With the cork secure, the bottle was released. They continued their journey, rattling along the guided course before being flipped on their side. As they rolled forward, a label was applied. After this they were righted again, just in time for the finishing touch: a metallic foil forced over the neck. At the end of this mechanised production line were two more workers frantically packing cases in an attempt to keep pace.

The whole process was fascinating, but time was moving on. All hands were needed to keep this bottle-eating, wine-drinking monster busy and our host Carmen was an integral part of the team. We'd distracted her for long enough.

The next stop on our tour was the quiet village of Doade, five minutes away. Before long we'd reached a crossroads in the centre of the village. Straight ahead the sign read Adegas Algueira; a few hundred metres further along sits this brand new *bodega*. From the outside it looks like a renovated building of the *Romanic* period; however, things aren't quite as they seem. On a previous visit to the *bodega* Fernando, the owner, had told us that it was built in 1996, from recycled stone. The building itself was designed in the *Romanic* style to fit in with its surroundings. Unlike the previous two *bodegas*, Fernando had made a significant investment in both premises and equipment and his award winning wines had justified his investment.

We pulled off the road and followed the concrete

driveway down the side of the building and into the car park at the rear. We parked and made our way towards a doorway at the side of the loading bay. The door was wedged open, so we entered.

'Hola!' I called, as we stepped from the overpowering heat of late afternoon into the cool subterranean air of the production area.

A reply echoed through an open door to the left, followed by footsteps. Fernando appeared at the doorway with a broad smile. He looked busy and seemed to be working alone.

'Do you have time to show us around?' asked Melanie, gingerly.

'I'm very busy at the moment, we're in the middle of *vendimia* (the grape harvest)' he paused mid-sentence 'but sure, I can spare you 10 minutes. Come and take a look at this.'

Proudly, he led us through the doorway and into the production area. This cavernous space was light and airy, and comfortably cool. Four stainless steel vats, standing 20-foot tall, occupied most of the floor space, and most of the roof space as well. Fernando explained that the red grapes were crushed at the upper level and pumped straight into the vats.

In the centre of the room stood a strange looking piece of equipment that resembled a clear plastic washing machine. It consisted of an electric motor mounted on a steel frame. Attached to the frame, above the motor, was an octagonal barrel. It was about 6-foot long, made of clear plastic and was agitating ferociously. Fernando flicked a switch at the side of the machine and the whole thing shuddered to a halt. On one of the Perspex panels was a small hatch with a lockable catch. It reminded me of a larger version of the barrels seen on TV game shows where a leggy blonde spins it and a cheesy host selects the winning postcards for this week's special prize. Fernando unlocked the catch and opened the panel.

'Come and smell,' he said, gesturing us closer.

We shuffled forward like three Japanese Geishas and stretched our necks towards the open hatch. A large nasal inhalation revealed a heady, alcoholic aroma of freshly-squeezed grapefruits. Surely we were mistaken! Indeed we were: although the sweet bouquet smelt like grapefruit, the actual fruits were white *Godello* grapes, harvested earlier in the day from the steep valley slopes of the river Sil.

'Would you like to taste the wine?' he asked, as we stepped back from the tombola-like wine making machine.

What a silly question: as reluctantly as *lotto* winners, we accepted.

'You can't taste the white but I have some of the award winning red in the warehouse. Follow me.'

We didn't mind if it was red, white or pink: having missed out on a tasting at Adega Décima, we were all parched. Following Fernando, we ambled lazily through into the warehouse.

This room was also light and airy with a high ceiling and a large, roller shutter door at one end. All the walls were bright-white which contrasted sharply with the pale grey floor. Along one wall were about ten, fifty-nine gallon, oak barrels and a further six, thirty gallon ones. All of them were beautifully clean, unblemished oak; a complete contrast to the massive barrels we'd seen at Adega San Cosmede. Fernando explained that his barrels were only ever used twice: once two vintages had matured in the barrels they were sold to Scotland for use in the whiskey distilling industry. In addition to the barrels, there were several pallets of boxed wine, bound in clingfilm and ready for despatch.

Fernando walked over to a workbench on the opposite side of the warehouse, pulled a bottle from an open box and opened it. Next to the box were several rows of clean glasses, he handed one to each of us and poured. A deep, cherry-red wine flowed into the glasses. I took a sip and rolled my tongue over the front of my teeth. The fruity flavours of the *Mencia* grape are quite unique. We nodded our heads in appreciation and before long, we'd emptied the bottle. Fernando's wine was undoubtedly the best wine we'd tasted so far, but it was also the most expensive. Undeterred by the price, we bought a couple of bottles and headed off to our final *bodega* of the day.

The tiny village of Doade is blessed with two of the finest *bodgeas* in the area; fittingly I'd saved the best until last. Perched majestically on the edge of the river Sil gorge is the Regina Viarum winery. Even the name conjures up images of Imperial Roman legions marching towards Rome with their precious cargo of fruity red wines. The winery itself is a modern interpretation of a palatial Roman villa. It has a long, arched façade and sits perfectly within manicured grounds of lush, green lawns and purposefully positioned flora. We parked the car and crunched along the gravel pathway to the entrance.

Having stepped inside we were warmly greeted by a middle aged gentleman who introduced himself as the winery manager. After reciprocating his greeting he guided us on a private tour of the facilities.

On the ground floor was the production area. Large stainless steel vats towered above us. Pieces of ancillary equipment were ergonomically positioned around the edges of this vast, temperature-controlled area. To Julie's relief, our lack of communication skills cut short this part of the tour.

Leaving the production facility we climbed a wide staircase to the first floor. The manager guided us into a large rectangular room lined on two sides with granite worktops, inlaid with stainless steel sinks. We didn't know if it was a tasting room or a laboratory for testing and analysing the wine, and lacked the vocabulary to ask. By now Julie was becoming restless: her attention span is about as long as her nose.

'Ask him if we can taste some,' she whispered impatiently to Melanie.

Melanie popped the question: the manager smiled, partly in acknowledgment of our patient participation in his tour and partly at our brazen cheek. He led us from the tasting, or testing room, and into a vast lounge spanning the width of the building. This room was themed on minimalism and decorated to impress. One end of the room featured a large open fireplace. Widely spaced shelves rested comfortably both sides of the grand chimney breast. Replica, antique ornaments were thoughtfully positioned for maximum effect. In front of the fireplace was an enormous coffee table, at least 6-foot square and flanked by two sumptuous pastel-yellow sofas. At the opposite end of the room was a large wooden desk, topped in green leather and embossed with gold stencilling around the edge. A reading lamp sat on one corner and an antique-style, leather upholstered bankers-chair complemented this impressive design feature.

The manager asked us to take a seat and left. He returned a few minutes later with a bottle of their finest *Mencia* red and three large wine glasses. Without ceremony he opened the wine and poured. Each of us took a small sip and through a series of nods, smiles, and limited Spanish, conveyed our satisfaction of the subtle flavours and delicious fruitiness. We relaxed into the deep cushioning of the yellow settees and chatted about the day's events. To our surprise and delight, our gracious host continued topping up our glasses until the bottle was empty, and then left the room.

'Do you think he's gone to get us another bottle?' joked Julie.

A few minutes later he returned, not with one more bottle but with three. We stared at each other in amazement.

'What are they?' asked Julie.

'They're liqueurs,' replied Melanie,

The first was colourless *aguardiente*, the second, a dark, chocolatey-brown, was *licor café* (coffee liqueur) and the third, a rather off-putting yellowy-green, was *licor con hierbas* (liqueur with herbs).

Melanie and I chose the syrupy *licor café*. A good inch in a whisky tumbler is a fine measure. Julie decided to try all three, one after the other. By now the girls were getting a bit giddy. I on the other hand, as the designated driver, had been far more sensible with my afternoon's tasting.

'Does anyone fancy a nibble?' I suggested.

We thanked our host for his hospitality and treated ourselves to two of the most expensive bottles of the day.

We left the Regina Viarum winery and headed down the very steep, very narrow, and extremely winding road from the village of Doade to the river below. Built into the valley side, and sandwiched between the road on one side and the river on the other, is the Doade Fluvial Café: a perfect place to enjoy a glass of wine and a few *tapas* before heading back home.

No sooner had we picked Julie up from the airport, than we were dropping her off. We'd all enjoyed a great weekend and we were looking forward to her next visit.

16

Lessons in Bricklaying

The sound of the phone ringing sent a shiver of fear rippling through my entire body. Communicating face to face with someone in Spanish is difficult enough but remove facial expressions, hand gestures and body language, add in a crackling and fuzzy phone line and it becomes nigh on impossible. Thankfully, I had a backup plan.

'Mel, the phone's ringing,'

'Why don't you answer it?' she snarled.

'It's bound to be for you, I don't know anyone,' I replied cheekily.

She rushed to the phone and lifted the receiver.

'Hello,' a short pause followed, 'oh hello Sylvia! How are you?'

She glanced in my direction and stuck her tongue out in a show of contempt. Sylvia was ringing to tell us that she'd arranged a meeting with Felipe on Wednesday morning as we'd requested. We were desperate to see him and keep things moving along. Thanks to his extended holiday, he still hadn't made the alterations to the plans. Remaining calm, when progress is slow, was mentally draining but stern demands were often met with stubborn resistance. Coaxing and cajoling were far more effective methods of getting things done but such tactics were alien to me.

The meeting with Felipe went well, he agreed to make the necessary changes, prepare a full set of plans and build specifications, and submit them to the Spanish School of Architects for approval. Without their approval, Felipe would not be allowed to supervise the project. Along with submission to the School of Architects, he would also send the plans out to tender. As soon as he'd received the quotes he would let us know. We left his office feeling more positive than we had done for weeks.

With Felipe back on track, we could turn our attentions back to the swimming pool. At the moment, the heavy plant and equipment needed for the pool could easily access the back garden but once work started on the house extension, that route would be closed. Any delays could bring the whole project to a standstill.

As we anticipated, Mariano's 'about a week', ended up being 10 days. He rang to arrange a meeting at the house. It seemed that every time a decision needed making, it had to be made there. Giving a quote over the phone or popping it in the post is just not the Spanish way of doing things: everything is done face to face. As frustrating as we were finding it, if we wanted things to progress we had to flow with the status quo.

The next morning we were up and ready in good time, excited by the prospect of finally making a decision. In readiness for our meeting, we'd discussed a few possible scenarios. One overriding conclusion emerged: whatever the price, we needed to negotiate a better one. We were embarking on a journey that would significantly lighten our bank balance. Even a small saving on every purchase would result in a considerable saving overall. The prospect of haggling made Melanie feel a bit uncomfortable, I on the other hand couldn't wait to get started.

In contrast to our previous meeting, this time Mariano kept us waiting. A plume of blue smoke, billowing from the exhaust pipe of his ageing Mercedes, announced his arrival: we shook hands and exchanged pleasantries. Tucked tightly under his arm were two white folders printed with his company name and logo. It all looked very professional, not what I expected. He placed the folders on the bonnet of his car and opened the top one. Inside was a comprehensive quotation, several pages long, detailing the exact specification of the pool and listing all the ancillary equipment. Line by line, he explained everything in great detail: a thorough and polished presentation. The final page revealed that all important detail: the price.

I'd primed Melanie beforehand: whatever the price, don't let your facial expression give away your mood. This was one game of high-stakes poker we couldn't afford to lose. Mind you, having read the price, even I found it difficult not to seem a little pleased. Setting my emotion to one side for a moment, I began to haggle, much to Melanie's embarrassment. It's surprising how swift negotiations are when neither party can understand what the other is saying. Mariano took out a ballpoint pen, drew a line through the price and penned in a new one. Very quickly an agreement was reached: we were delighted that work could finally begin.

'I'll amend the contracts and then we can sign them,' said Mariano.

We shook hands on the deal and Mariano left, agreeing to return next Monday at 9:00 a.m. to survey the back garden and prepare the site.

All of a sudden, time seemed to leap forward; the weekend passed in the blink of an eye. Imagine our surprise when, at 8:45 on Monday morning the phone rang and Mariano's crusty tones echoed down the line.

'I'm here in Canabal at the house. Where are you?' he asked.

'We're just leaving,' replied Melanie. 'We'll be there in 10 minutes.

Despite the early hour, the air was thick and hot. Today looked like being another cloudless day with a pastel-blue sky and bright sunshine. As we zipped through the village and up the lane towards the house, we could see Mariano's Mercedes parked at an awkward angle with two wheels in the drainage ditch. I pulled into the drive and we hopped from the car. Three men stepped from the Mercedes, Mariano and two younger, fitter-looking men. Mariano headed straight for us, while the two young men opened the boot. With great care they hauled out a weighty looking tripod and a black plastic case the size of a briefcase.

He introduced the two young lads as '*los trabajadores*', or workmen. They acknowledged their introduction with a courteous smile and a nod of the head. Before long the five of us were standing in the back garden. Under instruction from *el jefe* (the boss) one lad positioned the tripod while the other opened the case and lifted out a set of professional-looking laser surveying equipment. Melanie and I glanced at each other in astonishment: if it was designed to impress, it had done the trick.

Like a pair of well practiced and beautifully choreographed dancers, they set about surveying the garden and plotting the location of the swimming pool. These lads certainly knew their stuff. The only blot on their otherwise professional copybook was that after each precise measurement, they marked out the area with the same bits of old, broken wine barrel that we had used weeks earlier. To make matters worse they hammered the staves into the parched ground with the back of an enormous monkey wrench.

Within the hour the survey was complete. Before leaving, Mariano explained that he was going to sub-contract the excavation to a local firm. Doing so would reduce the cost of transporting an excavator from outside the area. He seemed confident of securing the services of a local firm by the end of the week.

Mariano had fulfilled his commitments, unlike Felipe. We'd waited patiently for him to ring regarding the tenders without success: a more direct approach was called for. The following morning we decided to turn up on his doorstep and demand some answers.

The morning was warm and sunny as we drove into Monforte. The influx of summer tourists, mostly from within Spain, had long since departed. The roads were once again quiet and virtually traffic-free, even the town centre was quieter. We quickly found a parking space and headed for Felipe's. For the first time this summer we noticed a distinct temperature change as we walked through the town. We were warm and cosy in the sunlight but in the shadows we were decidedly chilly, the first indication that the long, hot summer was drawing to a close.

Before long we were at the entrance to Felipe's. We

climbed the steps to his first floor office and rang the doorbell. All thoughts of the weather were forgotten. We were here for answers and were determined not to leave without them. The door opened and his secretary ushered us inside.

'Is Felipe here?' we enquired.

'Just a moment,' she gestured for us to take a seat and disappeared around the corner in the direction of his office.

A few moments later she returned, accompanied by an apprehensive looking Felipe. As always he greeted us with a warm and sincere handshake. At times, Felipe's manner was like that of a naughty schoolboy, caught with his fingers in the biscuit barrel. His innocent expression made it very difficult to be stern with him. We trusted that he had our best interests at heart but at times his casual, laidback approach was infuriating. Putting aside the fact that we liked and trusted him, we were determined to get some answers and move the project along.

'Have you received the tenders back?' I asked, in my woefully inadequate Spanish.

He stared back at me with a familiar vacant expression that I'd seen many times before. It meant that I'd just spoken complete gibberish and he couldn't make any sense of my linguistic ramblings, as usual Melanie intervened.

'The prices for the house, do you have them?' she asked.

His facial expression changed. I couldn't believe that she'd done it again: or had she?

'Come with me,' he said, turning and heading into his office.

At last we were getting somewhere. As he rounded his desk and fell back into his leather-clad, swivel chair he gestured for us to take a seat. We sat down, eager to see the results of the tenders. Seconds later our hopes were dashed as he picked up the phone and rang Sylvia.

'The English are here in the office and I haven't a clue what they're saying. Come quickly.'

So much for my plan to catch him off-guard.

After a few minutes Sylvia arrived, breezing into the office as if it were hers. By now we were all pleased to see her.

'What do you want?' demanded Sylvia.

She wasn't being rude, just Spanish.

'We want to know if Felipe has received the quotes back from the tenders he sent out,' I replied.

It always amazes me how two short questions can extend into minutes of rapid Spanish narrative. It's a bit like trying to get a politician to answer yes or no.

'Yes he's had them back,' said Sylvia after a while, 'there are three of them'.

The three quotations were very similar but Felipe felt that we should reject the most expensive, and the cheapest, and plump for the one in the middle. He knew the constructor well and there was the added benefit of him living in the village of Canabal. We were happy to go along with his recommendation.

'Does the price quoted include the alterations to the original plans?' I asked.

'No,' Felipe's cheeky smile said it all.

My facial expression conveyed our frustration. His response hinted at the fact that he was finally beginning to understand me. Without any persuasion, he picked up the phone and began dialling.

'He's ringing the builder, Pepe,' whispered Sylvia.

A short conversation followed.

'Felipe's arranged to meet Pepe at the house,' she paused while Felipe finished explaining. 'In 10 minutes.'

It had taken us two months to get to this stage and now we had just 10 minutes to get to Canabal. We weren't complaining but I couldn't help thinking that we should have barged into Felipe's office and demanded some action months ago. The four of us ran down the stairs and out onto the road. Sylvia hitched a ride in Felipe's ageing Suzuki Rhino while we hurried off to our car.

As we approached the house I could see Felipe and Sylvia standing in the lane chatting to a small-framed chap. Sylvia introduced him as Pepe the builder. He greeted us with a firm handshake, a cautious smile and a single nod of the head. He and Felipe set about discussing the issues. Serious conversations followed interspersed with graphic arm movements and the occasional stamping of the ground. At one point Pepe scrambled up onto the roof and started lifting the roof tiles. Melanie and I hadn't a clue what was going on.

'Sylvia, what are they doing?' I asked as they disappeared around the corner of the house.

'They're discussing what needs to be done, but I don't know why it's taking so long,' she added impatiently

Her frustration was clear to see: time was ticking on. First one hour and then two and still the discussions continued. The three of us were tired and bored but this was the first time since we'd instructed Felipe that I felt he was earning his keep.

As time ticked by Sylvia became more and more animated. It's surprising how many expletives foreign language students learn, as Sylvia was adequately proving. Although aimed at Felipe, her tirade of swearing fell on deaf ears. Melanie and I tried not to laugh but our smiles only served to encourage her. Sylvia was genuinely concerned that her husband, Francisco, might return from work before she had time to prepare his dinner: for Galician men, this would be unthinkable. Thankfully, after two and a half hours, Felipe brought the meeting to a close.

'Sylvia can you tell Felipe that we must have the final quote this week. We're going back to England for 10 days to sort a few things out and we want to get this matter resolved before then.'

Sylvia relayed my request, and to our surprise Pepe agreed to have the final quote ready by Friday. If we approved it, he could start work by the middle of the month: a more than satisfactory conclusion to a very long day.

The reason for the trip back to England was to prepare our house for letting. Since leaving home in May, we'd tried unsuccessfully to sell. Rather than leave it lying empty, we'd decided to try letting it: a bit of rental income would offset some of our costs here in Spain. The idea was to drive back to England, empty the house of all our remaining personal items, and prepare it for renting. Despite the long and torturous drive here, I was confident that we could make the return trip to England without stopping.

All our hopes now rested on Pepe having the final quote ready in time. We were desperate not to delay the start of building work by one day, never mind the 10 days we would be away. Pepe had solemnly promised to have it ready on Friday, the day before we set off.

Readying the car for the journey went some way to taking our minds off the wait. Inevitably Friday seemed to drag-on forever. Pepe wouldn't finish work until 7:00 p.m, if he hadn't done the quote by then, it wouldn't get done. The short drive to Pepe's passed in silence, neither of us wanted to contemplate the possibility of being let down. We pulled off the road and climbed the stone steps to his front door and rang the bell. After a short wait it opened slowly and Pepe's son answered.

'Is your father in?' I asked.

'Wait here,' he replied, before gently closing the door.

Moments later it opened again, this time Pepe appeared holding a sheet of paper.

This looks promising, I thought to myself.

Pepe had a very reserved personality, most uncommon amongst the Spanish we had met so far. He handed us the quote and did his best to explain the breakdown. We thanked him for his time and returned home to dissect it in more detail.

Our initial impressions were good. The total price was well within budget. The swimming pool would increase the total cost and Pepe hadn't included any outside work, but overall we were very pleased. At the very least, it meant we could both get a good night's sleep before embarking on our long trip to England.

The following morning we were abruptly woken by the high pitched tone of Melanie's alarm clock: the dimly lit dial read 07:00. By 7:50 we were on the road and heading towards Madrid. The October morning was warm and sunny, it felt as though the summer was reluctant to end. Strangely enough, our journey began by travelling 300 km in the wrong direction. Although not the most direct route, the excellent roads gave the big V6 a chance to do her stuff. The quality of the roads and constant high speed soon compensated for the detour. Within seven hours, and after three thirsty fuel stops, we had crossed the French border. We took a quick lunch break before heading toward Bordeaux and then on to Paris.

The French border marked a shift in the weather. It was still clear but the clouds had thickened and the temperatures were heading north as quickly as we were. By 11:30 p.m. we had reached the outskirts of Calais and were following signs for the Eurotunnel. Unfortunately, we had just missed the last train of the day and the next wasn't until 1:30 the following morning.

Up to this point, I'd coped pretty well with the long drive. Behind the wheel I was focused and alert but as soon as we stopped, my eyelids felt like lead weights and my head like an atlas stone. Once through the tunnel we continued north, reaching our house in Huddersfield at 5:20 on Sunday morning. Taking into account the time difference, our mammoth drive had taken 23½ hours. I knew it could be done in less than a day.

First thing Monday morning, I rang Sylvia.

'Hello Sylvia, this is Craig'

After a brief pause she replied, 'Hello Craig! How are you?'

She seemed quite surprised to hear from me. I explained that we were happy with Pepe's quote.

'Can you ask Felipe to instruct Pepe to start work as soon as possible?' I asked.

'Sure,' replied Sylvia, 'I'll ring him straight away.'

We spent the next week clearing the house. Essentials would go back to Spain; the remainder was divided between my dad's loft and Melanie's mum's. We'd been so busy that before we knew it, we were once again being rudely awoken by Melanie's alarm clock. A tearful goodbye followed between mother and daughter.

The journey back to Galicia took longer than I'd expected. I knew we would lose an hour crossing the

Channel but the miles dragged by. One thing was certain: we weren't going to make it home without an overnight stop. Dusk crept up on us as we reached the outskirts of Bordeaux. By the time we'd negotiated our way around the city it was dark. We continued south through the densely forested area along the unlit E70 looking for a place to stay. Strangely enough, this near pitch blackness helped our search.

Fluorescent road signs take on a life of their own on unlit highways. Luminous signs jumped over the brows of approaching hills and stepped out from behind darkened bends. We continued on, passing the remote French villages of Salles and Belin-Beliet. We'd almost given up hope of finding a hotel when two more signs appeared in the distance, the village of Saugnacq-et-Muret but more importantly the hotel Le Grand Gousier.

We slowed and left the main carriageway. The road leading to the village was even darker than the E70. A mechanical failure now would leave us well and truly stranded. No sooner had this horrific thought flashed through my mind than a beacon of light appeared in the distance. At last we'd found our overnight retreat – Hotel Le Grand Gousier.

I pulled into the car park and stopped. The old girl could finally take a well earned rest. She had performed flawlessly, a little thirsty at times but quick, smooth and comfortable – the perfect travelling companion.

From outside, the hotel looked warm and inviting; less so from the inside. The rates were reasonable and perhaps more importantly they were still serving dinner: although the less said about that the better. At least the local *Bordeaux* wine hit the spot and slipped down without touching the sides. The hotel, and its clientele, reminded me of a 1950's, Hitchcock movie-set: I half expected one of the guests to be murdered during the night. Needless to say, the night passed without incident and we both had a good night's sleep.

The following morning was a leisurely affair. We skipped breakfast in favour of an extended lie-in and a long, hot shower. Eight hours after leaving the hotel we were turning off the road into Ferreira. We were both excited to find out what, if anything, had happened at the house; but the day had been long and tiring and the sun had disappeared over the rooftops. We decided instead to unpack the car and start afresh in the morning.

After an early night and a long sleep, we woke refreshed and ready for action. During yesterday's long drive home we had joked about what might, or might not have happened during our absence. Expectations were low: we'd had so many disappointments that we found it far less stressful to demand everything, hope for something, and expect nothing. We trundled slowly along the narrow road running through the village of Canabal and up the lane towards the house.

From the bottom of the lane we could clearly see three vehicles parked outside. All three were tipped at an angle with two wheels in the drainage ditch and the other two on the tarmac. As we neared, it became clear that they were all LAV's or Leisure Activity Vehicles. They're favoured by workers throughout Spain and provide a very flexible mode of transport. These cleverly designed, multi-purpose vans have the valuable advantage of falling outside Spain's commercial vehicle legislation. They combine all the benefits of a small truck with that of a family saloon. Champion amongst LAV's is the highly prized Renault Express. Bearing in mind that Renault ceased production of this model in 1993, they are fast becoming an endangered species.

We manoeuvred carefully past the parked vehicles and pulled into the drive. Attached to the fence in the entrance was a large sheet of pre-printed plastic. Printed in bold blue lettering across the top of the sheet was, *Obras – Salud y Seguridad* (Works – Health and Safety). We were stunned that work had actually started, but absolutely delighted: it was unbelievable.

All that remained of the garage was one outside wall. The garage doors were leant against the garden wall and the back of the garage had been completely demolished giving a clear view of the garden beyond. The roof tiles had been taken off and stacked neatly in one corner of the garden, and the roof joists and timbers removed and stacked purposefully next to the tiles.

Pepe and his two brothers were busy digging out the foundations for the reinforced concrete columns that would support the roof of the new kitchen and dining room. We walked across the driveway to make a closer inspection. The plans indicated six reinforced concrete pillars, one on each corner and two in the centre. The three brothers were all busy, each one working on a different foundation hole and each at a different depth of excavation.

Pepe was wrestling with a large electric drill, breaking through the concrete floor of the garage. His youngest brother was hacking away with a pickaxe at the earth beneath and his other brother was standing in another hole up to his waist, thrusting a post spade into the compacted earth. The finished hole was about 2-foot square and 3-foot deep. Noticing us looking on, Pepe stopped for a moment, looked up and using his customary greeting, smiled and nodded his head.

During earlier conversations with Felipe and Pepe, a completion deadline of Christmas had been hinted at.

Considering all the delays, we'd almost lost sight of this. Dare we start to dream of being in by Christmas!

With all but the outer wall of the garage demolished, we had an unobstructed view of the back garden. Standing at the front of the house we could clearly see that work was underway on the pool. Excited by the prospect of even more progress, we made our way through the garage. Taking care not to disturb Pepe and his brothers we stepped into the back garden.

Two weeks earlier this enclosed garden was nothing more than a patch of scorched grasses and diseased fruit trees: the contrast now was unbelievable. All the rotting and infected trees had disappeared; unfortunately all the healthy ones had gone as well. Our idea of branding them with a band of white emulsion ended as I'd expected. They'd been ripped up by a mechanical excavator and an overenthusiastic operator.

Marking the pool area with pegs had given us a one dimensional view of its size. Seeing the hole in 3D was mind-blowing. It reminded me of the type of crater one might see on the news after a car bombing: absolutely enormous. Around the edges of the garden were mounds of earth, presumably these would be used to level the area once the pool was constructed. The cavernous hole was lined with red bricks. From their uneven appearance they looked to have been laid by a one armed blind man with one leg shorter than the other. Ripples of dried cement oozed out from the joints like fresh cream from a squashed *Victoria* sponge cake. The inclined base was covered with bulky gravel.

Mariano was nowhere to be seen but his two lads were beavering away. One of them was hauling sturdy looking grey tubes from the far end. The other was standing inside the pool tying steel reinforcing mesh to the brick walls.

They seemed surprised to see us but both stopped to wish us good morning. After returning their greeting I felt compelled to question them about the quality of their brickwork.

'Erm *ladrillo's...*'

Fortunately for me, no sooner had I mentioned the word bricks and pointed at them, than they knew exactly what I wanted to know.

Through a combination of words, hand gestures, and amateur dramatics, they managed to explain that the bricks were absolutely irrelevant to the structure of the pool. They provided a mould, or backdrop, on which the reinforcing mesh could be attached. The strength of the pool was formed by spraying concrete onto the mesh. It all seemed fairly obvious once they'd explained.

We spent the rest of the day wandering around with broad grins on our faces, in a state of euphoria. It seemed ironic, having spent months working tirelessly to get the project underway that no sooner were we out of the country than everyone had suddenly become available and miraculously started work.

17

Military Exercise

Rain, rain and more rain: Since we returned from England, hardly a day had passed without there being a cloud burst. Not for the first time, we both had a disturbed night's sleep. Several nights ago I discovered that the guttering above our bedroom window was missing an end cap. As a consequence, every time it rained, water flowed over the end of the gutter and dropped 30 feet onto the concrete below. It felt as though we were sleeping next to Niagra Falls. To make matters worse the gutter inclined ever so slightly away from the direction of the fall pipe and towards the missing cap. Every drop of water that fell on the roof ended up cascading off the gutter. Unfortunately, this wasn't the only cause of our broken night's sleep. Adjacent to the bedroom window is an outside light. It's a huge coach-style lamp that hangs from a rusty chain. The slightest breeze causes it to sway, and the weathered chain to squeak like an un-oiled barn door, blowing in the wind.

We were sitting up in bed contemplating a second mug

of coffee when the phone rang. We stared at each other with nervous trepidation.

'Go on love, you answer it. You're much better on the phone than I am.'

Melanie heeded my plea and ran to answer the phone.

A few minutes later she returned.

'That was Mariano. He wants us to meet him at the house next week to sign the new contract and make the first payment.'

'It didn't take him long to find out we were back,' I remarked.

His urgency was understandable. We'd agreed to make the first of three payments prior to work commencing. Having started work without us even being in the country, the least we could do was repay his trust with some hard cash.

The weekend passed uneventfully. More rain and more interrupted sleep. By Monday we were happy to be able to do something useful.

'Let's get the money out of the bank to pay Mariano,' I suggested. 'That'll be one job out of the way.'

Later that morning, during a break in the showers, we strolled into the village.

'I'd like to make a withdrawal,' I said to the bank manger.

I told him the amount and slid my bankbook over the counter.

'No,' the manager's reply was short and to the point.

I stared back at him, quizzically. The bankbook hadn't been updated recently but I knew that we had ample in the account. Besides which, he hadn't even checked the balance on the computer.

'I don't have enough money,' he added.

Not enough money. I couldn't believe it: I only wanted a few thousand euros.

'If you order the money now it should be here tomorrow,' he said.

I was still in shock: a bank that didn't have any money. I paused trying to rationalise a moneyless bank. I doubt it will ever catch on.

Confused by my silence, and thinking that I hadn't understood, he repeated his statement. The repetition jolted a response, 'Yes, yes I'd like to order the money.'

The manager scribbled a note on a scrap of paper and handed the bankbook back to me. I turned to leave and then remembered one vital piece of information, 'What time tomorrow?'

'*Que?*' (What?)

My blank expression had traded places.

'The money: what time tomorrow?'

Now he understood.

'In the morning, about 10 or 11,' he replied.

I thanked him and left.

The following morning I returned, and true to his word the money was there.

Since returning from England, time seemed to be passing at an alarming rate. The week had flown by since Mariano rang asking for a payment, but the weather remained unchanged: wet, miserable, and cold. This morning had started off dry but as we made our way to the house for our meeting with Mariano, we could see from the menacing clouds that it wouldn't remain so. Mariano was waiting for us as we drove up the lane and pulled into the drive.

In just a few weeks, the whole appearance of the property had changed; everywhere was filthy. A lorry load of sand and an equally large pile of aggregate had been tipped on the driveway. Surrounding an old cement mixer was a damp, dirty area of watery-cement, washed out from the mixer. Tyre tracks from a wheelbarrow ran in all directions like a child's scribble. Mud and building rubble lay everywhere: a thoroughly depressing sight. The lane outside didn't look much better. The daily comings and goings of cars, vans and heavy goods vehicles had left the grassy drainage ditches looking as if a brigade of tanks had driven through them. Lines of mud ran up and down the lane, fading into the distance.

Mariano greeted us with a warm smile and a resigned shrug of his shoulders as he stared up at the heavens. With some urgency, he led us around the side of the house and into the back garden. We hadn't visited the place since last week and were stunned by the sight that greeted us. The huge, brick-lined template of the swimming pool was literally swimming in water. It must have been at least 3-foot deep at the deep end and covered the entire base of the pool. This huge volume of water highlighted exactly how wet the weather had been.

He explained that they'd been unable to do any work for a week. The next part of the construction involved spraying concrete onto the framework of the reinforcing mesh. He was hoping for a break in the weather, long enough to pump out the standing water and concrete the pool. Nothing could be done until it improved. Disappointed, we walked back to the car: eyes firmly fixed on the ground in a vain attempt to avoid stepping in the mud.

'I have the contracts in the car,' said Mariano, as we stepped from the driveway into the lane.

After trudging through all the mud, we'd almost forgotten the reason for our visit. He pointed out the changes and resting on the bonnet of his Mercedes we both signed each copy. He kept one for himself and handed me the other. In turn, I handed him a white envelope containing the first instalment. To our surprise he opened it, pulled out the notes and started counting them. Did he think we were going to leave him short! After counting the money he stuffed it back inside the envelope, we shook hands and he left.

As Mariano disappeared down the lane we thought it only polite to go and say hello to Pepe and his brothers. They were cracking on regardless of the weather.

Pepe is a complicated character, very difficult to read. He was always pleasant but never seemed happy. His brothers on the other hand were a right pair of jokers, hard working and conscientious but with a sense of fun. Where Pepe's glass was always half empty, his brothers glasses were definitely half full.

Inside the house they'd erected a makeshift clothes stand made from three pieces of timber in the shape of a door frame. They'd nailed several, four inch nails into the cross beam to act as hooks. Hanging on three of them were three brand new, brilliant-white hard hats. I assumed that owning the hard hats, rather than wearing them, was part of an EU health and safety regulation; they hadn't moved off the clothes stand since the first day.

Every morning they would arrive for work in their civvies and change into work clothes: matching blue overalls with the words Hermanos Quiroga (Quiroga Brothers) emblazoned across the shoulders in white. I couldn't help thinking that the name sounded more like a circus high-wire act than a building company. Instead of hard hats, each one wore a green, floppy sun hat, the style made popular by '70s cricketers. Every day at exactly 1:00 p.m., regardless of what they were doing or what stage a task was at, they would down tools, change back into their civvies, and drive off home for lunch. Exactly two hours later they returned, changed back into their overalls and worked through until 7:00 p.m. We said hello, had a quick look around and left them to it.

The following morning Melanie woke with stomach pains. At first I thought it might be a reaction to paying Mariano but as the day wore on the pain became worse. Since moving here, neither of us had needed medical assistance. By lunchtime I was becoming concerned.

Although we weren't registered with a local GP, we'd taken out private health insurance when we moved here. By mid-afternoon, Melanie was doubled-up in pain.

'We'll have to phone the insurance company for help,' I said. 'There's an emergency telephone number in the paperwork.'

'No. Don't worry I'll be fine.'

Melanie isn't prone to seeking sympathy but she clearly wasn't fine, so I insisted.

'I'll get the number and you tell them what's wrong.'

I shot off upstairs in search of the policy.

'Here you are,' I said handing her the hotline number.

She rang and a short conversation followed.

'They say I have to go to the hospital in Ourense.'

'Ourense, we don't even know where the hospital is in Ourense,' my protestations weren't helping and Melanie was obviously feeling worse.

'I can't go all that way. I feel terrible. Let's just throw ourselves at the mercy of A&E in Monforte,' she pleaded.

That was all I needed to hear. Before long I was pulling into the hospital car park in Monforte. If the worst came to the worst we had her E111 certificate to fall back on. Surely she was entitled to emergency treatment using that.

Externally, the building looked like any other modern hospital but inside the decor was tired and dated. It reminded me of how the Huddersfield Royal Infirmary looked back in the late '70s.

The A&E department is at the rear of the hospital. We walked across the car park and pushed open the reception door. The room was dark and uninviting, lit only by the daylight filtering through the opaque glass panels in the double doors we entered through. I began to wonder whether we were in the right place. The area was completely abandoned; devoid of people or furniture. To our left were two reception windows. They looked more like the ticket office of an old railway station than anything you would expect to find in a modern hospital. We moved closer to take a look.

Around the edges of the glass were old information notices printed on yellowing copier paper and stuck to the glass with rippled, browning Sellotape, a telltale sign of their age. One of the notes, stuck adjacent to a white plastic doorbell read, 'Ring for attention'. Melanie pushed the buzzer and we waited. Without an audible sound, we didn't know if it was working or not.

'Perhaps it's not working.' I said after a while.

No sooner had I whispered the words than a young woman appeared. She was in her late twenties and smartly dressed in a white medical uniform. Apprehensively, Melanie slid the insurance card through a gap in the glass, desperately hoping it would be accepted. The nurse studied it carefully before asking for her NIE. Melanie slipped her national identity number through the glass. From under the counter she pulled out a form and began copying the details

'What's the matter?' asked the nurse in a typically direct manner.

Melanie did her best to explain and the nurse made a note on the form.

'Through the door and wait,' she said, pointing at a door in the corner.

Relieved at being admitted, we walked across the reception area and pushed open the door.

The waiting room was large and square. There were metal-framed, moulded-plastic chairs around every wall, leaving the centre of the room totally unused. Including ourselves, there were about 10 people waiting: evenly spaced around the room. We took a seat and prepared for a lengthy wait.

After a few moments my eyes were drawn to the centre of the room and a large, black bug, limping across the floor. The creature had four legs, two large ones at the back and two smaller at the front; and from tip to toe must have been at least two inches long. The size of it took me by surprise: and in a hospital as well.

Where are all the cleaning staff when you need them? I thought to myself: mind you, if its leg is broken at least it's in the right place.

Without appearing too obvious, I glanced around the room. Everyone's gaze was focused on the hobbling insect. Like the players on a Ouija board, we were all willing the creature to limp away from us. For a few minutes it limped around in circles, unable to compensate for its broken leg. However, after a while it got the hang of moving in straight lines. Unfortunately for us, it was heading in our direction. The sense of relief among the others in the room was almost tangible.

Turn you bugger, turn: my telepathic pleading fell on deaf ears. As it made steady progress across the floor, I raised my eyes to take another shifty glance around the room. Suddenly and without warning, Melanie sprang to her feet, took one step forward, and stamped her foot on the floor, crushing our brave visitor. A squirm of disgust ran around the waiting room followed by a deathly silence.

I hope the treatment Melanie receives is a little more sympathetic, I thought to myself.

Patient turnover was slow but steady, eventually the duty nurse reappeared and stammered through her pronunciation of Melanie Briggs. I watched as both Melanie and the nurse disappeared through a door in the corner. I waited and waited as people came and went, each one disappearing through the same door. After almost an hour Melanie returned. She explained that she'd had a thorough examination followed by an x-ray. They'd even found someone to help explain her condition in English. The diagnosis led to an immediate visit to the pharmacy for the prescribed cure. Within moments of inserting the remedy, the offending problem was flushed away and harmony was once again restored.

This medical resolution was in stark contrast to the goings on at the building site. Work started on a wave of optimistic enthusiasm but had soon deteriorated into a chaotic mud-bath. Day after day of miserable rain dampened everyone's spirits. For the first time since work began, the long-range weather forecast was good. Work could start on spraying concrete into the swimming pool.

Before they could begin, all the standing water needed to be pumped out. The water was now over 4-foot deep at the deep-end and covered the first of the Roman steps at the other: over five cubic metres of muddy water. Mariano's lads had brought what looked like a fairly light-weight, electric pump to drain the water but at a capacity of 250 litres per minute, the pool was emptied in less than an hour. Spirits were lifted, but not for long.

In the right conditions, spray concreting a swimming pool is quite straight forward. A dry mix of cement and sand called Gunite, is pumped through an agitator to ensure there are no large lumps in the mix and then on into a spraying unit. Immediately before application, the dry Gunite is mixed with water and a thick layer is sprayed onto the reinforcing mesh. The rough Gunite surface is then smoothed with a trowel and left for about a week to dry. Once dry, another smooth coat is applied before it can be tiled and grouted. In theory it all sounds very simple but in practice it turned out to be a nightmare.

The plant required to do the job is colossal. Firstly there's the cement mixer – laden weight approaching 20 tons. Then there's the concrete pumping truck, weighing in at about half that. Finally there's an agitator, a relatively small piece of equipment. The latter had been on site for some time. I'd often wondered what it was but never felt the need to ask. They'd parked it down the side of the house, restricting access to the back garden. Not that it mattered: neither the pumping truck nor the cement mixer was small enough to squeeze through. Therein lay the problem.

There is a finite distance over which the pumping truck can effectively pump Gunite, this is restricted by the pressure required to force the dry mixture through the 15cm diameter hose, and the length of the hose. Somehow the pumping truck had to be positioned no further than 75 feet from the furthest point to be sprayed, and the cement mixer needed to be in close proximity to that. Unfortunately, the distance from the lane outside the house, to the furthest point of the area to be sprayed, was well over 90 feet.

This problem had manifested itself in a stationary convoy of heavy plant vehicles, partially blocking the lane.

Curiosity had brought Jose, a neighbour and senior village figure, out to investigate. A typically Spanish discussion ensued, with lots of umming and arring, raised voices and thumping of machinery, the odd expletive and plenty of flailing arms and pointing fingers. Eventually the pump truck driver came up with a suggestion.

'Who owns this land?' he said, pointing at the attached field on the right hand side of the house.

'Pepino owns that,' replied Jose. 'Why do you want to know that?' he added

'If I drive the truck across the field, past the house and adjacent to the boundary wall, we can throw the pumping tubes over the fence and be less than 36 feet away,' he said, 'That would be perfect.'

The lane fell quiet. Everyone turned and stared at Jose, willing a positive response. A long, silent pause followed. The pressure mounting on Jose was almost palpable. Eventually he replied.

'I don't suppose Pepino will mind, he hasn't done anything with the field for years.'

Jose's reply was followed by a unified sigh of relief. Everyone was eager to proceed, despite the fact that Pepino hadn't even been consulted. The drivers mounted their respective vehicles and Mariano's two lads began directing proceedings. Jose, Melanie and I took up station at a safe distance.

Jose told us that many years ago Pepino had used the field for grazing his sheep. All that now remained were a few patches of straw-like grass scattered among the overgrown gorse bushes and tangled masses of wild blackberries.

Because the field had only ever been used for grazing, Pepino had never gone to the trouble, or expense, of building a proper entrance. Consequently, to access the field, the pumping truck and cement mixer would have to drive across the drainage ditch at the side of the road.

To avoid getting the trucks stuck in the drainage ditch the drivers would cross it at an angle. Approaching the problem this way meant that as one of the front wheels went down the ditch, the other would still be on the road. As the second wheel began its descent into the ditch the first wheel would drive up the other side and into the field. The twin-axle rear wheels would then follow at the same angle. Cautiously the pumping truck neared the ditch.

As the first of the front wheels rolled down the ditch, the whole vehicle lurched forward at an acute angle. We held our breath as this commercial monster inched forward, rolling viciously from side-to-side.

Having negotiated the ditch the driver edged steadily forward. The heavily waterlogged field seemed to suck at the tyres, pulling it deeper into the muddy earth with every inch covered. The deep drainage ditch was one thing but this unforeseen hazard was creating an even bigger problem. The truck pitched forward as the rear wheels struggled for traction, spinning uncontrollably. Finally, with less than half the distance covered, all forward motion stopped. The front wheels had sunk so far into the mud that the cab was caught fast in the earth. Not to be defeated by a boggy field, the driver slipped the truck into reverse and hit the gas pedal. Plumes of blue smoke shot from the exhaust pipe. As the truck bounced backwards and forwards, lumps of mud sprayed up from the rear wheels, flying into the air like muck from a farmyard spreader. Eventually it hauled itself free of the quagmire and back onto the asphalt lane.

Undeterred, the driver drove up the lane to the cemetery car park, turned around and reversed back down the lane: 'If at first you don't succeed...'

Rather than pushing the lorry through the mud by driving in forwards, he decided that reversing would be a far better option. Logically, this approach made much more sense. In reality the result was the same: except that this time, when he tried driving out, the front wheels sank into the mire and no amount of engine revving and wheel spinning would free it. The only option now was to tow the pumping truck out of the field using the cement mixer.

The cement mixer reversed slowly to the edge of the drainage ditch and stopped. Between them, the two drivers hauled a heavy chain across the muddy field to attach the two vehicles. The mixer inched forward to tension the chain, before effortlessly dragging the pumping truck across the field and out. Unfortunately the angle of extraction was not the same as entry. By the time the two vehicles were back on terra firma, the field looked as though a tank battalion had rolled through on military exercise.

The whole morning had been wasted. What seemed like the perfect solution had ended in disaster. They needed a rethink, but not before their obligatory lunch break.

Later that afternoon we returned to check on progress. To our astonishment the cement mixer had reversed into the driveway and parked, leaving the cab of the mixer blocking the lane. More amazing was the position of the pumping truck. The driver had managed to squeeze the entire vehicle through the gates. Its front wheels were in the garden, sunk up to their axle in waterlogged mud, and the rear of the truck was just inside the gates.

Both vehicles were noisily revving their engines. The huge steel bucket on the bed of the cement mixer revolved slowly at a constant pace, forcing the dry-mix Gunite into the pumping truck. A dusty black tube, attached to the back of the pumping truck, snaked across the garden like that of a fire engine. It disappeared around the side of the house and on into the agitator. Plumes of grey dust erupted from the vigorously vibrating agitator as the dry mix passed through and on into the back garden.

We quickly forgot the disappointment of this morning's fiasco and excitedly squeezed past the cement mixer and on into the back garden. The thick hose appeared from the far side of the house and disappeared into the pool. We scrambled up a mound of earth to get a better view.

Standing in the middle of the pool, grappling awkwardly with the large diameter hose, and covered in grey cement dust, was one of Mariano's lads. He was dressed in an all-in-one, dark blue, rubberized suit with an attached hood. He wore Wellington boots on his feet, rubber gloves on his hands, and a gasmask-style dust mask covering his face. There wasn't an inch of exposed flesh on his entire body. He looked more like a mad scientist preparing for biological warfare than a swimming pool constructor.

Strapped to the top of the thick hose was a much smaller diameter pipe. As the dry mix Gunite gushed from the large hose, a directed jet of water wet the mixture tenths of a second before it splattered into the reinforced meshing and bonded with the brick-built retaining wall behind. The cavernous hole in the middle of the back garden was finally beginning to look a little more like a swimming pool. Delighted with the progress but feeling surplus to requirement, we decided to leave them to it: After all, there was nothing we could contribute to proceedings.

Driving back to Ferreira, I couldn't help thinking that

extricating the pumping truck from the front garden was going to pose far more of a problem than driving it in. I had an uneasy feeling but decided to keep my thoughts to myself.

The following day, just before lunch, we decided to check on progress. As we drove up the lane towards the house I could see that my darkest fears had been realised. The good news was that neither the cement mixer nor the pumping truck was anywhere to be seen. Surely, this would mean that the job was complete. The bad news was that the driveway entrance looked like a mortar shell had exploded in it.

Access to the driveway from the lane was over a concrete pad, about 10-foot long by 6-foot wide. Underneath the pad was a concrete drainage pipe. This allowed rainwater to flow unobstructed under the entrance and down the drainage ditch at the side of the lane. Somehow, a 6-foot section of this pad had been crushed, no doubt under the weight of the pumping truck and cement mixer. All that remained were chunks of broken concrete and pieces of smashed pipe: squashed into the muddy base of the drainage ditch.

Access to the house by vehicle was now impossible. To make matters worse, the two lorries had knocked down the left hand gatepost and also managed to demolish a 6-foot section of boundary wall, the remnants of which were now scattered over what remained of the front garden. I couldn't believe that only 10 weeks earlier I'd mowed the lawn here. The whole area was now covered in mud and rubble: a scene more reminiscent of a war zone than a building site.

'Is that Felipe?' I remarked as we stood in the lane surveying the damage.

Felipe was standing at the front of the house staring up at the roof. We tiptoed through the devastation, trying to find some firm ground to walk on, and headed for our studious site manager.

'What's happened here?' I asked.

Felipe shrugged his shoulders in an air of resignation and began to explain. The pumping truck had become stuck in the garden and the only way to get it out was for the cement mixer to tow it. Unfortunately, the lane was too narrow for the cement mixer to pull it out at the same angle as it had entered. In the pushing and pulling that ensued, the gatepost had been knocked over, the wall demolished and the entrance crushed.

There seemed little point in dragging Felipe over the coals for the mess. At least the Gunite coating in the pool was finished. All we had to do now was wait a week for it to dry and then it could be tiled.

Every passing day brought with it a new set of problems. The house looked more like a demolition site than a building site. Surely we were due a bit of good luck.

18

A Floating Pool

A break in the weather was the only excuse we needed to hop in the car and go exploring. Visiting new places and discovering new wonders was a welcome distraction from the constant delays and disappointments of our house reconstruction. We decided to drive to Ourense and follow the old road, heading east along the course of the River Miño. We weren't exactly sure where we would end up but hoped it might lead to Northern Portugal.

The drive down to Ourense is always a pleasure. Keeping the river on our right, we drove through the city and continued along the old OU-402 heading downstream. From here the road narrows to little more than a single track. It winds its way through tiny hamlets nestling in the Ribeiro wine growing region. The scenery here is one of rolling fields and sculptured terraces. Orderly rows of grapevines had long since surrendered their annual harvest. Now it's the turn of their leaves to provide a spectacular display of autumnal colours: deep cherry reds and rusty browns. We meandered through the villages of Freixendo, Astariz and Oleiros, after which the river widens into a shimmering lake. A hydroelectric dam, built below the village of Santa Marina has created this marine playground. From this point on the driving challenge begins.

The narrow road snakes its way through thick forests. This tight, winding track provides fleeting glimpses of the river below. So severe are the bends that weave and pitch their way from one ravine to the next that, finding a long enough straight to get into third gear is a rare treat. At the village of Cortegada the road merges into the OU-801 signalling the end of our motoring test. From here, the going is much easier and it wasn't long before we reached the border town of Pontebarxas.

Sitting on the Spanish/Portuguese border, like a relic from the Cold War, is an abandoned checkpoint: a pleasant reminder that not all EU regulations impair individual rights and personal freedoms. Effortlessly we slipped into Portugal. The roads here are far less taxing: straight and wide. Before long we were on the outskirts of Melgaço: an historic town, centred on a medieval castle. Although we'd only travelled 100 km, our choice of route had taken us over 2 hours to complete. In a few more hours we would lose the light. With this in mind, we turned around and headed home: our exploration of Melgaço would wait for another day.

Not for the first time the old Rover had done us proud, effortlessly negotiating the twists and turns of Galicia's narrow lanes. However, we knew her days were numbered. We made enquiries about insuring her in Spain but none of the insurance companies were interested. To get insurance, we would have to re-register her: a complicated, lengthy and expensive process. We did consider it but finally decided on replacing her: the old girl was getting on a bit and we couldn't escape the fact that she would always be an English, right-hand drive car.

We'd been looking at various options for a few weeks and finally decided on the new Renault Megane. Renault has a long and respected history of producing economical and powerful diesel engines. The new Megane was quirky and fun-looking, in a stylish sort of way: At least we thought so, and the dealership in Monforte meant servicing would be convenient.

Negotiations over the price, with the likeable salesman Ricardo, were long and drawn out but we managed to get there in the end. Unfortunately, the dealership wouldn't take the Rover in part exchange: we couldn't even give her away. With our minds made up, and the terms agreed, we signed the paperwork and placed the order. Delivery would take approximately six weeks. That would take us upto the middle of January. It's amazing how this little bit of retail therapy lifted our spirits; however, this temporary high was short lived.

The following day we received a phone call from Sylvia. She explained that Pepe had rung Felipe, Felipe had then rung her; and now she was ringing us.

'Can you meet Pepe at the house tomorrow morning at 10?' she asked.

We didn't really have a choice. The question was asked politely enough but it was a summons rather than a request.

'No problem Sylvia, we'll be there.'

It wasn't until Melanie had put the receiver down that she realised tomorrow was Friday – Gas Day.

On a Friday, we could almost set our watches by the Repsol gasman – almost. The only times he was late, seemed to coincide with us making arrangements to be elsewhere. True to form, the streets and lanes of Ferreira were deathly silent at his allotted time. A few months ago such a delay would have been infuriating; now it was just a minor inconvenience. So easily had we slipped into the Spanish way of life. Pepe would be at the house at 10 o'clock whether we were there or not, so what was the point in getting upset? The gasman finally arrived just after ten. With our week's supply of butane safely stored, we hopped in the car and headed for Canabal.

The weather over the last few weeks had been the worst so far this year; today was no exception. Menacing, grey clouds rolled over the landscape; light showers were interspersed with torrential downpours: all-in-all a thoroughly damp, miserable, and depressing start to the day. As we expected, Pepe was already at the house when we arrived. More surprising was the presence of his wife, Emily. Pepe ushered us into the house and through into the back bedroom.

The roof tiles still hadn't been replaced and the house was leaking like a sieve. Small droplets of water dripped from the bedroom ceiling onto the dirty, tiled floor forming muddy puddles. The room felt cold, damp, miserable and thoroughly uninviting. However, we were out of earshot of his brothers who were busy working in the new extension.

Pepe and Emily are an odd couple. He's quite short and very lean: Emily on the other hand is much taller with a big, motherly frame. She had spent most of her childhood in England. Her parents were migrant workers, which enabled her to take advantage of the UK education system. Pepe had asked her to accompany him to interpret. We apologised for our lateness: not a particularly Spanish thing to do, but old habits die hard.

'It is not necessary to apologise,' insisted Emily. 'Time is not so important as for the English,' she added, in her broken English.

She explained that Pepe, who throughout the conversation was referred to as *mi marido* (my husband) had asked her along to translate.

'You haven't made a payment,' said Emily. 'The first payment was due when my husband started work.'

We were well aware of the payment arrangements and happy enough with them. We expected Pepe to either ask for the money, or at least provide us with an interim invoice when payment was due.

'That's not a problem Emily.' I said, 'We'll make the arrangements with the bank tomorrow and settle the first payment by this time next week, if that's alright with you?'

Emily explained our proposal to Pepe whose solemn face momentarily lit up: a rare sight indeed. We did sympathise with him and his brothers, since starting the job the weather conditions had been dreadful. Hardly a day went by without the heavens opening and torrential rain flooding the site. To add to their misery, the temperatures had been dropping steadily since the middle of October. Through it all they'd managed to keep busy, even resorting to burning garden rubbish in an attempt to stay dry and warm. Hopefully our payment would lift their spirits.

'Look at this,' said Pepe, guiding us to the window.

We tiptoed across the wet, slippery floor to the window and stared out. Things were finally starting to improve in the garden. The mounds of earth from the pool excavation had vanished, used partly to backfill around the sides of the pool and partly to level the plot. The edging flags, circling the top of the pool, had been cemented in place.

'That looks much better,' I said, acknowledging the improvement.

'No not that,' replied Pepe 'that!' he pointed into the garden.

We stared out across the garden to the boundary walls. They were caked with muddy earth. Hours of back-breaking painting, in the blazing heat of summer, had all gone to waste.

'That doesn't matter,' I said, trying to put on a brave face, 'we can paint them again when the weather improves.'

'No not that,' he said, in an increasingly frustrated manner. 'That!'

What on earth was Pepe trying to show us? I stared out of the window, trying to find something out of place: then I noticed it.

The pool was full to the brim with muddy water. I knew we'd had a lot of rain over the last few weeks but surely not enough to fill it: but that wasn't all. My eyes were drawn across the muddy water, rippled by a constant barrage of raindrops, to the boundary wall behind.

Why is there a section of the wall missing, I thought to myself; and what on earth is that trench for?

A deep trench gouged its way across the garden from the back of the pool, sliced through the section of missing boundary wall, and vanished into a deep ravine at the far end of the garden.

'Pepe, what's happened? Why is the pool full of dirty water and what's that trench doing ripping through the back of the garden?'

Through Emily's splintered English, Pepe explained. Yesterday morning, he and his brothers had turned up for work as usual. Shortly after that, Mariano's two lads arrived to continue working on the pool. The two of them spotted it immediately. The whole pool had risen out of the ground by over a foot.

"Risen out of the ground"? I asked: confused by what I was hearing.

'Yes,' said Pepe, 'risen out of the ground like a wet bar of soap being squeezed in your hand.'

"Risen out of the ground… wet bar of soap"? This wasn't making any sense at all.

Undaunted by my bewildered repetition and bemused look, Pepe continued. The ground underneath the swimming pool was undisturbed and compact but the newly backfilled area around the pool wasn't: the soil in this area was far more porous. Rainwater, seeping through the porous earth, had accumulated underneath the swimming pool like an enormous underground puddle. Unable to drain away, this mass of accumulated water had eventually created enough pressure to lift the pool out of the ground.

All of a sudden his explanation began to make perfect sense. I knew from experience that hydraulics are a very powerful technology. Pepe could tell from my expression that we were finally reading from the same page and continued.

After speaking with Mariano, they decided that the best course of action was to try and alleviate the mounting water pressure. They asked the excavator driver to return – post-haste. Upon his return, a trench was dug along the back of the pool: it ran the full width and to a depth of just below the base. After that they excavated a second trench, perpendicular to the first. This one ran across the garden, through the broken section of boundary wall and vanished into the ravine. A constant stream of water flowed along the excavated channels and into the valley below. In an attempt to speed up the draining process, they had filled the concrete pool with water to make it as heavy as possible.

After digesting Pepe's explanation, one question remained, 'What happens now?'

'Now, we wait,' he said nonchalantly, 'eventually the water should drain away and the pool should go back down.'

That didn't sound too bad, although I sensed there was more to come. After a short pause he continued.

'The only problem will be if the pool doesn't go back down straight.'

He raised his hands to waist-height and tilted them at an angle to demonstrate.

Hesitantly I asked 'And what happens if it doesn't go back down straight?'

'I don't know: you'll have to ask Felipe.'

Just as it seemed things couldn't get any worse, we were left in limbo, with more questions than answers.

Would the pool go back down? If it did, would it go down straight? Could the reinforced concrete withstand all this turmoil? What would happen if it broke? Would the 10 year guarantee cover an unfinished pool? More importantly, how much was all this going to cost?

The weekend passed slowly, I couldn't think of anything other than the pool. No longer a swimming pool, but a pool that was swimming: swimming in a sea of claggy, waterlogged mud.

Eventually Monday arrived. Impatient for answers, we turned up early at Sylvia's. We explained the situation to her and asked if she would take us to see Felipe. We were quite nervous. As site manager, his responsibility was to oversee the planning, execution and quality control of the house construction. In our eagerness to get things moving, and without Felipe's knowledge, Melanie and I had instructed Mariano to design and build the swimming pool.

None of this catastrophic mess was his responsibility. We were hoping that he would be able to give us some advice on how we should proceed. As much as anything, we were looking for some reassurance that everything would turn out fine.

As usual, he greeted us warmly and showed us straight into his office. As soon as Sylvia mentioned the word *piscina* (swimming pool), we could tell from his reaction that Pepe had already spoken to him. He sensed our concern and set about reassuring us that everything would be alright. He even joked that it wasn't all bad news. The fact that the pool floated, instead of breaking, meant that its construction was very strong.

Felipe left us in no doubt that he was happy to take control of the situation and ensure that the pool was finished to the standards we'd agreed.

He began by ringing Mariano and arranging for us all to meet in Canabal on Thursday afternoon: we would discuss the problem and try and find a solution. We were mightily relieved: the problems hadn't changed but we were no longer facing them alone. After a rocky start to our professional relationship, Felipe was fast becoming our knight in shining armour.

We kept ourselves busy over the next few days, despite the continuing bad weather. We spent some of the time visiting furniture warehouses and looking for interior furnishings. It's incredible how easy it is to choose things when you don't need them and how difficult it is to find the right things when you do.

Even knowing that Felipe was working towards finding a solution, we found it difficult to mentally switch off. For the last three days my mind had been churning over the problems and their possible financial consequences. By

Thursday, we were eager to hear some news: be it good, or bad.

As arranged, we arrived at the house at 4:30 in the afternoon. We had considered being early but knew that Felipe would be late: he always was. Hanging around in damp, cold conditions with fading light was not our idea of fun, regardless of how impatient we were for news. Entering the drive by car was now impossible; repairing the drainage pipe, shattered by the cement mixer, was the least of our problems. We parked on the lane and made our way towards the house. Pepe and his brothers were busy at the front, building the arches that would support the roof over the covered terrace.

Access to the back garden was limited to walking through what was originally, the garage but would become the new kitchen and dining room. Work on this part of the project had progressed reasonably well. The walls were built and the concrete for the roof had been poured. There was a large hole in the front wall, where the French doors would go, and two holes in the back wall: one for the kitchen window and the other for the kitchen door.

The interior space was congested with acro props. These supported the planked shuttering which in turn supported the weight of the concrete roof. When it had dried, the props and shuttering would be removed. Access to the back garden from the opposite side of the house was virtually impossible. The ground was a quagmire, made so by tons of materials and the heavy machinery that had passed through to build the pool.

We weaved our way through the kitchen-diner trying to avoid rubbing up against the acro props, while attempting to dodge droplets of dirty water seeping through the roof shuttering. As I edged closer to the back garden, I was so astonished by the developing imagery that I tripped over a brick lying on the floor, stumbled out of the door opening and into the garden. Quickly I turned to Melanie and shouted, 'Watch that brick!'

Melanie stepped carefully over the brick and out into the garden. What greeted us was a scene of utter mayhem and destruction.

In the middle of the garden, half way between the house and the front edge of the pool, was an ageing JCB. All four wheels had sunk into the mud. It was so deeply embedded that the body of the excavator was resting on the muddy ground. The 10-foot deep trench, which had been dug across the back of the pool to help drain the water, had been extended. It now ran down the entire length of both sides of the pool, exposing its outer red-brick skin. Tons of oozing wet mud, excavated from the trench, were piled high around the sides of the garden obscuring the once bright-white walls. The only recognisable features in this chaotic landscape were the speckled-cream flagstones around the top of the pool, creating a vivid outline of its shape.

Surely, even in the darkest days of the *Great War*, the fields of Flanders could not have looked so wretched.

Mariano, his two workers, and the excavator driver were huddled together in discussions when he spotted Melanie and me surveying the damage. Avoiding the deepest of the muddy puddles, he trudged across to greet us. He began by trying to explain what had happened, and what they were doing to remedy the situation. In an effort to help us understand, he began by speaking very slowly and clearly, but after a few sentences reverted to his customary high speed and broad Galician accent. We tried to nod in the right places and smile when he did but in truth we hardly understood a word. After one extended pause I managed to ask a question, 'Is the excavator stuck?'

I was hoping for a simple yes or no, but nothing ever turns out as you would hope. After another barrage of Spanish prose and dramatic hand gestures, he seemed to be saying that the excavator wasn't stuck but it had sunk very close to the swimming pool. If it slipped any closer, it might crack the Gunite. This would be an irreversible catastrophe.

Where is Felipe?

By five o'clock, he still hadn't arrived. The light was fading and the temperature dropping. By half past we were both feeling terribly fed up and bloody freezing.

'I'm going to wait in the car,' said Melanie impatiently.

'I'd better wait here – just in case.'

In case of what, I'd no idea. I had nothing to contribute and couldn't understand them, even if they did decide to include me.

By the time Felipe arrived, it had gone six o'clock and I was frozen stiff. With the addition of Pepe and his brothers, there were now nine of us trying to figure out what to do.

At least if the JCB did smash into the swimming pool there would be a piece for everyone.

Intense discussions followed. Everyone had an opinion and everyone wanted to be heard. After half an hour or so of brainstorming, they had agreed to do nothing: nothing but wait. The subsiding water had been placed in the hands of God, and extricating the JCB in the hands of its driver.

As he hauled himself out of the mud and into the cab, the rest of us stood well back holding our breath and crossing our fingers. A plume of thick, black smoke billowed up into the air as he brought the monster to life. Pushing and pulling on levers, the mechanised beast lurched this way then that. Skilfully, he used the powerful hydraulics of the large bucket on the front, to lift the digger free of the mud: At the same time, he used the hydraulic arm on the back with the smaller bucket, to push it forwards and away from the swimming pool. By repeating this, up, forward, down motion, the monster was completely free in less than 10 minutes. We all breathed a collective sigh of relief. We weren't out of the woods yet but for the time being the pool was still in one piece. As the excavator headed off up the lane, I said goodbye to everyone and we set off home. Disaster avoided, we were looking forward to a warm fire and a relaxing glass of wine.　.

19

Breaking Point

The weeks were flying by and the only let up in the wet, miserable weather seemed to coincide with the weekends. For our team of contractors, the mere suggestion of working weekends to catch up for lost time was unthinkable. No amount of persuasion, or financial incentive, could encourage any of them to swap family time for work time. Although we found their attitude frustrating, a relaxed and balanced attitude to life was one of the reasons we'd moved to this remote corner of Spain. We continued to fill our weekends with journeys of discovery: long and interesting road trips to familiarise ourselves with our new home. This weekend was no exception.

With all thoughts of house building, floating swimming pools and muddy quagmires put aside, we took advantage of the good weather and headed off into the mountains. The *Carretera Nacional* 120, known locally as the N-120, is the main highway through the area. It runs for over 662 km in total, from Logroño in the east to Vigo in the west.

Leaving Ferreira we headed east in the direction of Ponferrada. After skirting past Monforte the road follows the course of the river Lor. As we headed upstream the swollen river rushed through the narrow valley, cascading through fast flowing rapids. The route snakes its way through some of the most dramatic scenery in Galicia. Rocky, weathered outcrops, twisted and contorted over millennia, rise hundreds of metres from the valley floor. We drove through the small towns of Quiroga, A Rua and O Barco. From here we headed upward into the snow capped mountains. We continued on, through a series of poorly lit tunnels, joined together by long bridges suspended high above deep gorges: Gorges so deep that from the car, it's impossible to see the river below. This series of tunnels signals the border between Galicia and the province of Castile and Leon.

The scenery is an inspirational reminder of why we are here, an uplifting tonic to sooth the stresses and strains of house building. Unfortunately, this scenic escapism was not without cost. As we drove over the crest of a hill the bright, winter sunlight momentarily blinded me and before I could react, we had hit a pot-hole in the road.

The impact was incredible, a shockwave shot up my spine, making the ends of my fingers tingle. Whatever we'd hit was no ordinary pot-hole, no minor pitting of the tarmac surface. This highway crater was more like a small sink-hole or tiny mineshaft. We continued on for a while, hoping to avoid any lasting damage. Everything seemed fine, the steering felt crisp and precise; and there were no abnormal vibrations or unusual noises. Fearing the worst, I thought it prudent to turn around and head back home.

By the time we arrived back in Ferreira, there seemed

to be a strange noise coming from the front wheel. I couldn't be sure, so chose to ignore it and hope for the best. We could certainly do without adding to our lengthening list of problems. Surely nothing else could go wrong.

I'd spoken too soon: that evening another catastrophe struck; the computer died. It had been playing-up for quite a while. The problem was switching the damn thing on. It was either taking an eternity to boot up, or failing to boot at all. Tonight; however, it finally gave up the ghost and refused to obey any of my increasingly frustrated commands. Panic set in. I'd been meaning to do a backup since our move to Spain but somehow, never quite got around to it. All the documents I'd written and all those irreplaceable photos were now at risk – my heart sank.

Since moving to Spain the computer had become indispensable. An invaluable tool that helped us keep in touch with family and friends, gave us the opportunity to conduct important research into anything and everything, and even allowed us to listen to UK radio stations. We had to get the problem diagnosed and repaired as quickly as possible.

First thing Monday morning we were out of the house and speeding our way to Sylvia's. My suspicion about the car was proving correct. The noise from the front wheel was getting worse, particularly when driving around left hand bends. Monday mornings were normally spent discussing important issues with Felipe, today; however, our pseudo Spanish lesson would be conducted in the computer shop.

'But I don't know anything about computers,' insisted Sylvia.

'Don't worry Sylvia. You don't need to know anything

about them. Just explain what I tell you, to the shop owner.'

I tried to reassure her that knowledge of computers was not a prerequisite to helping us out. Reassured, we set off on the 10 minute walk to the computer shop.

The morning was damp and cold but at least it wasn't raining. Once at the shop, and with the help of Sylvia, I explained the problem to the owner Jesus, and my backup dilemma. Jesus seemed quietly confident that he would be able to recover most, if not all of the data once he had diagnosed the start-up problem. It had been a very encouraging visit: after all, if Jesus couldn't fix it, who on earth could.

A few days later Jesus rang us with mixed news. He'd diagnosed the problem as a faulty hard drive that would need replacing. Unfortunately, he wouldn't be able to make the repairs before Christmas; but we were relieved to hear that he'd managed to recover all the files from the faulty drive: at long last, a tiny piece of good news!

December was drifting by like a passing thunderstorm and Christmas was fast approaching. We were delighted to see that people, and businesses, still valued Christmas as a religious festival and not just an excuse to max-out their plastic. Being English, we thought it would be a nice gesture to buy Pepe, his brothers, and Felipe a gift for Christmas. It certainly couldn't do any harm.

As the main contractor, we decided that Pepe merited the best gift and decided on a food hamper, as for his two brothers and Felipe, a bottle of whisky each would suffice. In Spain, the traditional time for giving gifts is the night of the 5th of January, but even sleepy Galicia is not immune to the marketing powers of the West. With this in mind we waited until Christmas Eve to deliver our festive cheer.

The progress that Pepe and his brothers had made over the last couple of weeks was astonishing. The extensions on both sides of the original house were up to roof level. The arched covered terrace at the front of the house just needed roof tiles. They'd even found time to re-set a new concrete gatepost, the original of which was demolished by the cement mixer. The house and grounds were once again safe and secure. The only things missing, when we turned up on Christmas Eve, were Pepe and his two brothers. Even they had fallen victim to the seasonal madness. Fortunately, Pepe lived nearby, so we trotted off to see if he was at home.

Pepe's house is typical of many homes in the area. He lives with his wife, two children and his wife's parents: An equally typical arrangement. The ground floor is reserved for livestock and winemaking. Pepe's father-in-law has a small flock of sheep and an ageing donkey for working the land. The ground floor or *bodega* is a traditional, stone-built construction. Above this is the living accommodation: a later and more modern addition.

On our approach to the house we could see Pepe's van parked in the gravel driveway, an encouraging sign that he was probably at home. We parked on the roadside verge and climbed the steps to his front door, knocked and waited. I was just about to knock again when the handle lowered and the door slowly opened. Pepe peered out from the dark interior. We could tell from his body language that he had no intention of inviting us in: on the contrary, he looked very uneasy. Given that all we wanted to do was wish him and his family a happy Christmas, his demeanour was a little off-putting.

'*Hola – Feliz Navidad!*' we wished him Merry Christmas and handed him the gifts.

With his right foot holding the door partially open he

leant forward, took the gifts from us and slid them surreptitiously inside the house.

What curious behaviour, I thought.

'*Gracias,*' he said, before calling his wife.

Perhaps she would be a bit friendlier. Pepe edged the door open slightly to allow the much larger frame of his wife to stand besides him.

'Hello,' chirped Emily: a short but warm greeting, delivered with a broad smile. Quickly she continued, 'There is a problem and my husband has stopped work. He will not return after the holidays and cannot continue working at the house.'

We were stunned into silence: we hadn't seen this coming. I couldn't understand what sort of problem could bring about such a devastating decision. We'd made the first payment as requested: admittedly we were a little overdue but nonetheless, he now had the money. The building work had progressed at a much faster pace over the last month, particularly considering the atrocious weather conditions, and once the roof was finished we would be making the next stage payment. Emily could see that we were totally crushed by her news and after a short pause continued.

'You need to speak with Felipe,' she said, 'but I don't think you should worry,' she added.

That was easy for her to say, she had a roof over her head. We were so shocked we couldn't even utter a response. We said goodbye and trudged forlornly back to the car.

'We need to speak to Felipe, right now.' I barked, as I slumped into the car and turned the key.

Melanie was very upset and I felt powerless to reassure her. Control was slipping away and everything and everyone seemed to be against us. We headed straight to

Sylvia's. Christmas Eve or not, we needed some answers and we needed them now.

Within minutes we were standing in Sylvia's kitchen explaining the afternoon's events and asking for her help. Without hesitation, she scooped up her coat and the three of us marched off towards Felipe's. We rang the office doorbell and waited. Moments later it opened and his secretary greeted us.

'Is Felipe in?' asked Sylvia.

'No.'

Direct and to the point, like a dagger to the heart. He'd left earlier in the day and wouldn't be returning. Downtrodden and dejected, we trudged off back to Sylvia's.

'There he is,' blurted Sylvia as we plodded past the Bar Castillion close to her apartment.

We pushed open the door and made a b-line for our elusive project manager. Felipe was standing at the bar enjoying a glass of festive cheer when he noticed the three of us heading his way. He greeted us warmly, apparently oblivious to our mounting rage. He ushered us towards a table in a quiet corner of the bar and Sylvia began to explain. Felipe's face said it all: he was shocked by the news. For the first time since we'd made his acquaintance, he was obviously annoyed.

'Leave it with me. I'll ring him and we'll all meet up next week to sort out the problem,' he said.

Our muted response clearly signalled our desperate disappointment.

'Don't worry,' he said, 'we'll sort it out,' he added, in a vain attempt to reassure us.

We thanked him for his time, wished him a Merry Christmas and left. Any lingering doubts I had that Felipe was not wholly behind us were extinguished.

Christmas Day was a fairly muted affair. At the time, hauling boxes of trimmings and an artificial Christmas tree from England to Spain didn't seem like the best use of our limited space. This year we had to content ourselves with buying a small, living tree from the agricultural store in the village. We decorated it with home-made trimmings: Aluminium foil, sections of egg boxes, wine corks, of which we had plenty; anything that either shone or sparkled ended up hanging from our little tree.

For gifts, we performed our customary ritual. A few days before Christmas we drove into Monforte. Armed with 20 euros each, we separated and set about buying each other as many gifts as possible. It always surprised me how many things can be bought with such a small amount of money. It turned the stresses and strains of Christmas shopping into a fun event and always gave us a giggle opening them on Christmas morning. We tried to make the best of things but it proved impossible to think about anything other than our mounting problems.

The following morning the phone rang.

'Hola!' Sylvia's familiar tone echoed down the line; she seemed as bright and breezy as ever. 'Felipe has just rung me. He has arranged for Pepe to meet us at his office this Friday evening at seven o'clock to sort out the problem. Is that alright with you?'

We knew that Boxing Day wasn't a public holiday in Spain but were nonetheless surprised by Felipe's urgency in the matter. He was obviously as keen as us to resolve the problem.

'That's fine,' I replied.

'OK. I'll meet you there,' said Sylvia.

'At least we might have something positive to tell Dad,' I said to Melanie after putting the phone down.

He and his lady-friend Claire, had arranged to come

and visit us for 10 days over New Year, arriving on the 30th of December. We were hoping that they would cheer us up and take our minds off things.

They were flying into Porto in Portugal. Given the deteriorating condition of the car, and the fact that the new Megane wouldn't be delivered until the middle of January, we decided to hire a car for the duration of their stay. The last thing we wanted was to breakdown on the way to the airport or worse still, on the way back. Their flight arrived early on Monday morning so we'd arranged to collect the hire car from Europcar in Ourense on Friday. Picking it up would only take two to three hours so we would be back in plenty of time for our seven o'clock rendezvous with Felipe, Pepe and Sylvia.

We woke early on Friday morning. Over the last few weeks, neither of us had been sleeping very well. The thought of our Spanish adventure ending in a European disaster, was not conducive to a peaceful night's sleep. The dripping gutters didn't help either. Since Christmas day the weather had improved and the forecast was good. With a bit of luck, we might have some decent weather during Dad's stay. For the time being, Lady Luck had other ideas.

'Are you ready?' I called to Melanie. The last thing we wanted was to be late back from picking up the hire car.

'Ready when you are.'

The stairway from the hall down to the large garage was cold and uninviting. Once downstairs Melanie unlocked and opened the garage door. I slipped into the driver's seat, pushed the key into the ignition and turned it. The dashboard lit up as usual but nothing else. I turned the key back and forth, back and forth but still nothing, not a murmur. By this time Melanie had walked to the top of the drive, unlocked the gates and opened them.

'What's the matter?' she shouted from the end of the drive.

I screamed back at her, 'The fucking thing won't start!'

I'd lost it, lost control: I'd been pushed to the limit and beyond. Everything that could go wrong had gone wrong and I was struggling to cope. For the first time since we'd left home at the beginning of May, I was starting to question what we were doing. Had we made the right move? Was this the right part of Spain for us? Should we be here at all? Should I have sold the business? Where do we go from here?

I took a deep breath and tried to calm down. There was only one place to go – Ourense. What had happened had happened; no amount of analysis, worry, or self-pity was going to change that. The only people that could turn this almighty catastrophe into the Spanish dream we'd planned, was us – Melanie and me.

First things first, stop shouting at Melanie, go to Ourense and pick up the hire car. Having calmed down and re-directed my thought process in a more positive direction, I slammed the car door shut and called to Melanie. She was holding open the gates at the end of the driveway.

'The car's knackered, it won't start: we'll have to get a taxi to Ourense.'

The taxi rank, if I can call it that, was at the end of our road. It's more an unofficial waiting area than a regulated taxi rank. The drivers use the public phone opposite as their private telecommunications service. The system seems to work fine and everyone concerned appears happy with the arrangement. We marched down the road and jumped in the taxi.

'Where to?' asked the driver.

'The train station in Ourense,' even I could manage that piece of Spanish.

'I don't know where that is. Do you?'

I couldn't believe it: how could a local taxi driver not know where the train station was in Ourense. Fortunately, we'd been before; with a series of simple verbal instructions, and plenty of pointing, we finally arrived at our destination. Within half an hour we were heading back to Ferreira in our VW Polo.

We spent the rest of the day mooching around the house, killing time until our high-stakes meeting with Pepe. Focusing on anything else was difficult. We couldn't prepare for the meeting; we had no idea what to expect. The delay was tortuous, watching seconds become minutes and minutes turn into hours. Eventually the moment arrived. We hopped in the car and before we knew it, were climbing the stairs to Felipe's office.

We rang the bell and waited on the landing. Moments later the door opened and Felipe's secretary ushered us inside. Sylvia and Pepe were already waiting in reception. Pepe was standing in the corner, smartly dressed with a folder tucked tightly under his arm. He forced a smile and dipped his head in acknowledgement. In complete contrast to Pepe, Sylvia jumped to her feet and greeted us both with a broad smile and a kiss to each cheek. We sat next to her and waited in silence.

The wait was quite uncomfortable: Pepe, the villain of the piece, stood in the corner like a naughty schoolboy. Sylvia, Melanie, and I, sat opposite him like the three wise monkeys. Thankfully, it wasn't long before Felipe popped his head around the corner and called us into his office. Unusually for Felipe, he was ready for us all. He'd managed to borrow the correct number of chairs and position them around his desk. We each took a seat and got straight down to business. I couldn't help thinking that the outcome of this meeting might well decide our future here in Galicia or even Spain itself.

Felipe opened the discussions by asking Pepe to explain why he wasn't prepared to continue working on the house. From the start, Pepe's demeanour was very defensive in an arrogant sort of way. The crux of the problem hinged on a combination of bad weather and design problems. He claimed that he was already one million pesetas over budget and not yet halfway through the build.

While Sylvia translated, Pepe and Felipe continued their discussion. I couldn't believe Pepe's excuses, or his simplistic reasoning. The responsibility for being behind schedule and out of pocket was his, not mine. From the outset, we asked all those tendering to submit a fixed price quote. The clue is in the title – fixed price! He should have allowed for any unforeseen cost increases in his original quote, and as for the weather, if anyone should know what to expect from a Galician winter it was him. We were the newcomers to the area: he was born and bred here: I was absolutely furious. Inside, my blood was boiling but now was not the time to vent my anger. We sat patiently, waiting to find out what, if anything, Pepe was proposing. After a few minutes the conversation stopped and Sylvia turned to us.

'Pepe said that he will only start work again if you agree to pay any future increases in the price of labour or materials.'

I paused for a few moments, absorbing this ridiculous suggestion. In principle, Pepe was asking for a blank cheque. Surely he couldn't be serious. Hell would freeze over before I would agree to such an unquantifiable proposal. I turned to Sylvia, looked her straight in the eyes and in a quiet and calm voice said, 'No, no chance.'

My reply needed no translation and the office fell eerily quiet. Internally I was ready to explode with rage and struggled to remain calm. A drawback of having a long fuse is that once it's burnt and the charge ignited, the explosion is uncontrollable and the fall-out severe. After a short pause I turned to Felipe, looked him straight in the eyes and in a calm and controlled manner added, 'It's very important that we find another solution.'

The discussions had reached a critical point. The seriousness of my tone left no one in any doubt. Since moving to Spain, I'd made a conscious effort to leave my tough, businessman alter-ego back in England. There had been a few occasions when he'd tried to reunite us but I resisted his calls in favour of a more passive approach. Such was the importance of this meeting that a brief reunion was called for.

The next person to speak was going to lose this encounter and I was determined that it wouldn't be me.

My facial expression remained unchanged and my gaze stayed focused, staring straight at Felipe. His eyes dropped to a blank piece of paper on the desk in front of him and then across at Pepe but the silence continued. After what felt like an eternity, but was probably less than a few minutes, Felipe looked across at Sylvia and spoke.

'Of course, there are always other options.'

My relief was enormous: the content of Felipe's response was unimportant; victory was ours. These few simple words shattered Pepe's confidence. He wriggled uneasily in his chair, knowing that his opportunity had passed. A line had been drawn in the sand and all but Pepe were standing on my side. From now on, we would be driving this project forward and he would be a passenger.

Felipe directed his proposals at us: a small but significant change in the course of the meeting. Pepe was no longer contributing to the discussions. He sat quietly on the sidelines a dejected and forlorn figure.

'We could put the remainder of the project back out to tender,' said Felipe, before adding, 'of course Pepe will have to complete the roof first.' he stared across at Pepe, 'You agree to that – don't you?'

Sheepishly, Pepe agreed. His general lack of enthusiasm for anything made it difficult to judge his mood. One part of me thought that he wanted to see the project through to the end and another that he really didn't care. Despite the problems, we didn't want to lose him. His failure to keep within budget was partially due to his high standards and determination not to compromise.

Felipe diverted his gaze back to us. 'Another option would be to place Pepe into administration.'

My eyes widened at the thought: administrators, bankruptcy, solicitors, accountants, it all sounded very messy, very expensive, and very time consuming. Perhaps I'd missed something in translation.

'Administration,' I asked.

Sylvia looked at Felipe for an explanation. A lengthy and instructive conversation followed about the meaning and mechanics of administration. Although Sylvia could understand Spanish perfectly, we couldn't automatically assume that she could understand technical issues. Confident with her newly acquired knowledge, she turned to us and explained.

Spanish administration is nothing like the legal process of its namesake in the UK. Felipe and I would be the administrators. Pepe would remain as the main contractor on the project. Once the roof was completed we would agree a fixed daily rate for him and his brothers. As the main contractor, his responsibilities would extend to organising the subcontractors; however, all quotes had to be approved by Felipe and me. In turn, we could seek alternative tenders and instruct different subcontractors if we deemed it financially beneficial. It sounded like a win-win situation. My only concern was that Pepe would no longer be on a fixed price for the job. This meant that we would be responsible for any future delays. It would also mean a lot more work for Felipe, Melanie and me.

The room fell silent again as everyone considered the proposals. I had a fourth option mulling around in my head but this wasn't the time to voice it; I needed clarification out of earshot of Pepe.

This time I broke the silence. For the first time since we'd marched into Felipe's office, I turned to Pepe and looked him straight in the eye.

'Before we finish I want to make it perfectly clear. If anyone has any other proposals then now is the time to air them. Once we conclude this meeting Melanie and I will consider the options and make our decision.'

Sylvia translated and Pepe listened, his eyes drifting between her and me. I stared at him continually: it was the only weapon I had to emphasise the importance of this final opportunity. His failure to grasp this opportunity brought the meeting to a close. Felipe thanked him for his time and said he would be in touch with him as soon as we had decided. With Pepe gone, I could reveal my option.

'What about taking legal action against Pepe for breach of contract?' I posed the question directly to Felipe.

'I don't think that's a good idea,' he replied in his usual sedate manner.

Felipe was calmness personified. He had a casual, laidback, unflappable approach to almost everything: it could be quite infuriating at times.

'Why is that?' I pushed him for a better explanation.

'You don't have a written contract.'

We don't have a written contract. I couldn't believe it. The very first thing we'd asked him to do was ensure that whoever won the tender should sign a contract.

He continued, 'Even if we had one it wouldn't do any good. I have a client at the moment that has been in dispute with his constructor for over two and a half years. The best thing to do is talk things through, and move on.'

He had a point. The last thing we wanted was to involve solicitors. There's only one winner when those vultures get involved. Although his argument was sound, the fact that we didn't have a contract was rather annoying.

We bounced the three remaining options around for a while, deciding on the best one for us. The general consensus was erring toward administration. A course made that bit more attractive by Felipe's suggestion that after re-tendering the subcontractors jobs, electrician, plumber, etc, the total cost might be less than Pepe's original quote.

'OK,' I said after a while, 'we'll go down the administration route.'

The decision was made. Felipe would let Pepe know in a few days and work would begin again in the New Year. At the very least we had some positive news to tell Dad on his arrival.

20

Gobbling the Grapes

Despite resolving Pepe's tantrums, we were still feeling pretty low. The building work was way behind schedule. The entire plot looked worse now than at anytime since we'd bought it. The swimming pool was still floating. There was no indication of a let-up in the wet weather. The car was knackered and the death of the computer had severed our links to the outside world.

We kept ourselves busy by preparing for Dad's visit. This would be his first trip to mainland Spain. Although a Galician winter wouldn't be everyone's first choice, I was fairly sure that he would prefer the panorama of snow-capped mountains bathed in crisp winter sun, to the stereotypical images of sea, sand and sunbathing. All we needed was a break in the weather, surely we were due that.

On Monday morning we were up with the larks. Dad and Claire were flying into Porto in Portugal, arriving midmorning. We needed to be up and off in good time: Porto is a 2½ hour drive from us. The journey there went without incident and the frugal VW made a pleasant change to the gas-guzzling V6 Rover.

The wait in arrivals was short. Before long, Dad's tall figure, topped with his trademark flat cap, appeared over the heads of the arriving hordes.

For years, airport arrivals have been a regular source of personal embarrassment. The kind of embarrassment suffered by children worldwide who are forced to endure the shameless behaviour of their tactless and humiliating parents. True to form, the moment Dad clapped eyes on us the antics began.

They started with him raising one arm high above the crowds and waving frantically in our direction. Oblivious of other travellers he made a b-line straight for us. The location of the actual exit seemed unimportant. He waded through the crowd, stepping in front of people, crashing his case into others and trampling old dears underfoot. I was forced to respond. Reluctantly I smiled back and pointed the way to the exit, desperately trying to avoid drawing attention to myself. Who on earth would want to claim responsibility for this crazed old Englishman flapping his way through the crowd. Claire on the other hand is a delight, a Yorkshire lass through and through with a big heart, a broad smile and a good sense of direction. She tugged at his flailing arm, guiding him to the exit. Thank God for that.

The drive back home flew by, as did the rest of the day. One thing about Claire is that she's never short of conversation: on the contrary, Claire could talk for England.

The following day was New Year's Eve. We woke to

find Dad and Claire already slurping their second mug of tea. Claire was standing outside on the covered terrace. She was wearing a calf-length, quilted dressing gown over a floral-patterned, flannelette nightie and pink, fur-lined slippers.

'Good morning,' I called, as I stepped from the kitchen juggling a mug of hot coffee.

'Good morning,' she replied, in a bright a bubbly voice, 'How are you this morning?'

Before I could even consider a reply she continued.

'I can't believe how warm it is, I just can't believe it.' a statement that ended with her waltzing uncontrollably around the terrace like Deborah Kerr in a scene from, *The King and I*.

Claire radiated a childlike fun and an infectious positivity: just the tonic we needed. We'd become really depressed over the last month or so, a spiralling mood that, like falling into quicksand, was dragging us under. Unwittingly, Dad and Claire's arrival had thrown us a lifeline; slowly but surely they were dragging us out.

A week earlier we'd booked the venue for New Year's Eve. Bar Carabelos in the village. It's a typical rural eatery that had become a weekend favourite of ours. From the street, one enters a scruffy, smoke filled bar that leads through to a plain but clean restaurant at the back of the premises. Like the restaurant, the menu is plain and simple: traditional country fare at its most average. Our favourite was fried chicken and chips, washed down with a bottle of the house red and finished off with a small jug of *Licor café*: a thick, syrupy liqueur straight from the owner's *bodega*. More often than not, we would watch a *La Liga* football match on the widescreen telly perched high in one corner of the room. The tables were arranged at such an angle that it didn't matter where Melanie sat; I always had an excellent view of the game. Good food and great entertainment, what more could a man ask for?

When asked what we would like to eat on New Year's Eve, we'd chosen our favourite, chicken and chips. It hadn't crossed our minds that there might be a special New Year's menu.

The table was booked for nine o'clock. To ensure that we were all ready on time, the showering relay began at 6:30 that evening. Although there were two bathrooms, using both showers at the same time was impossible at this time of year. From the gas water-boiler in the basement, a copper pipe wormed its way through the cavernous chalet to the bathrooms on the second floor. The pipe lagging consisted of a watery coat of white emulsion. It hadn't really mattered in the baking heat of summer but with the passing of autumn into the icy chill of winter, showering had become a whole new experience.

In order to heat the water sufficiently for bathing, I had reduced the water flow through the boiler. As a result, the water pressure at the showerhead was now little more than a series of gravity-fed droplets. Attempting to use both bathrooms at the same time resulted in nothing more than a single watery-drizzle dripping from each of them. Compared to spring and summer, it now took twice as much gas to heat half the amount of water.

The most unpleasant side-effect of this excessive gas consumption was the body-numbing frequency at which the gas ran out whilst showering. There's nothing worse than standing in a lovely warm shower, covered in suds, when the gas cuts out unexpectedly. Icy needles of freezing-cold water shoot from the showerhead and while the unfortunate victim stands there stark naked covered in creamy suds, dripping wet and shivering with cold, the other person has to negotiate the obstacle course of a boiler room and change the gas bottle as speedily as possible. To avoid this unforgettably unpleasant experience, I had changed the gas the day before. With a bit of luck it would last for the duration of their stay.

The staggered showering worked a treat. By nine o'clock we were all washed, dressed and ready to party. Since Dad and Claire arrived, the weather had been great: patchy cloud with sunny intervals, warm during the day, but bitingly cold after sunset; best of all, no rain. We wrapped up well for the short walk down the hill into the village and on to Bar Carabelos.

Melanie led the way into the bar followed by Claire then Dad and I brought up the rear. The place was busier than normal, hardly surprising given the date. A line of men stood at the bar, some staring at the giant, flat-screen TV angled across the corner of the opposite wall. Others were leant against the counter, chatting together in clandestine whispers. In the far corner, a group of teenagers sat quietly at a partitioned desk, home to three coin-operated computers. They sat silently, staring at dimly lit screens, hypnotised by their online gaming. The rest of the bar area was filled with families enjoying the festivities, and regulars: Most of which were old men, playing cards. Not even New Year's Eve was going to distract them from their daily gambling. Rarely did money change hands but accounts were meticulously kept.

Melanie caught Pili's eye, daughter of the owner, Señor Carabelos; she called us to the end of the bar. Double doors and an opaque glass partition, separated diners from the melee of the bar area. We jostled our way through the crowd, pushed open the doors and entered the calm oasis of the restaurant. To my surprise there were only two unoccupied tables, the place was heaving. This volume of customers was usually reserved for nights of the *El Clasico* – the nation-splitting football match between Real Madrid and FC Barcelona.

We sauntered across to one of the remaining tables and took a seat. In front of each guest was a sealed, foil-type bag, brightly printed with an animated scene of festive fun. A glance around the room hinted at its contents. First to rip it open, with childlike excitement, was Claire. Within seconds she'd tipped the contents onto the table, unfolded a tissue-paper crown and squeezed it onto her head.

'Come on,' she urged, 'get into the spirit of things.'

Not wanting to disappoint, we ripped open our bags and donned the paper headgear: Much to the satisfaction of Claire, and our fellow diners. The table was covered with an assortment of different coloured balloons, tightly-wound bundles of paper streamers, and a handful of exploding party poppers, all waiting to welcome in the New Year. Before long Ana, Pili's sister, emerged from the kitchen, skipped across and welcomed us to the night's events.

'What would you like to drink?' she asked with a beaming smile.

As well as the bar and restaurant, Ana's father also owns a modest winery. Sometime ago he'd embraced modern wine making methods which gave his bar a distinct advantage over his numerous village rivals. The house red was pretty good and at a quid a bottle, ridiculously cheap: our decision was simple.

'*Vino tinto de la casa,*' I replied.

'And you've ordered chicken?' she asked, with a wry smile.

'Yes that's right.' I replied.

I could tell from her cheeky grin that she found the thought of serving fried chicken on New Year's Eve slightly eccentric. Perhaps so, but chicken was the only dish we'd ever ordered here and we loved it. More importantly, we were confident that it would prove a sure-fire winner with Dad and Claire.

Before very long Ana returned from the kitchen carrying a small wicker basket piled high with thick-cut chunks of crusty bread, and clutching an unlabeled bottle of red wine. She set the basket down in the centre of the table. With her free hand she whipped a corkscrew out of her pocket. A smooth flick of the wrist twisted the screw deep into the cork; effortlessly she levered it out. She placed it on the table, spun around and headed back to the kitchen. Self-service suited us down to the ground.

Free from pomp and ceremony, I grasped the bottle and poured. The wine is made from a local grape variety, *Mencia*. At its best, it's a deep purple colour, bursting with rich, fruity flavours and characterised by a velvety-smooth finish that glides over the tongue and kisses the back of the throat. At its worst, it makes a great salad dressing. Señor Carabelos' wine fell somewhere in between. We raised our glasses and chinked them together to a chorus of, *'cheers!'*

The restaurant was now full. Earlier murmurs had escalated into a boisterous and disorderly party atmosphere. Ana was rushing in and out of the kitchen with dishes of paella, and plates overloaded with langoustines and crayfish. We quickly realised that these exotic dishes were pre-ordered from a special New Year's Eve menu. No wonder Ana had smiled at us when she asked about our chicken and chips.

We waited patiently, nibbling on chunks of crusty bread and sipping wine. The room fell eerily quiet as everyone tucked into their exotic starters.

What must they think of the four of us, nibbling on bread and sipping wine?

Thankfully, the starters were soon devoured and the raucous party atmosphere resumed. We were next to be served. I moved the half-empty basket of bread to one side as Ana placed two stainless steel platters in the centre of the table. The first was piled high with chunks of jointed, roast chicken and stacks of homemade chips. The second was heaped with fresh, green, salad leaves and thickly sliced, beef tomatoes coated in olive oil, red-wine vinegar, and finished with a sprinkling of rock-salt and herbs.

Hungrily, we tucked in as the service continued around us. The food was worth the wait and our unconventional choice, justified. A second bottle of wine soon followed. Time flew by and the year was quickly drawing to a close. With a few minutes remaining until the midnight chimes, Ana emerged from the kitchen carrying a tray of small, freezer bags, filled with grapes.

Systematically she handed them out, one bag for every diner. Each bag contained 12 grapes. Spanish tradition dictates that one grape must be eaten on each of the twelve chimes prior to midnight. It's called *Las doce uvas de la suerte*, (The twelve grapes of luck). Luck had been one ingredient in short supply over the last few months, so this was one tradition I was intent on participating in.

As if by magic, the TV in the corner burst into life a few minutes shy of midnight. A feverish excitement filled the room. Bag in hand, everyone prepared to devour their lucky grapes.

Dong! – I popped in the first one.
Dong! – A second later, I thrust in another.
Dong! – Followed by a third.
In the space of one second, my stubby fingers fumbled

through the tiny opening of the sticky freezer bag, grabbing at the fleshy fruits. Once caught, I quickly whipped one out, taking care not to lose any of the remaining lucky charms, and thrust it into my overloaded mouth. Frantically, I chewed the seedy mush in a vain attempt to reduce the volume.

Twelve good-sized grapes in twelve seconds is no mean feat and the final dong came as a great relief. Melanie had given up after about three: seeded grapes aren't really her thing. Claire had done a little better with five and whoever had counted out Dad's bag needed to go back to school: he had run out of grapes after just 10. Hopefully, my successful attempt would be sufficient to appease the gods of good luck.

The final chime signalled the start of the festive love-in: an annual outpouring of peace on earth and goodwill to everyone. Ushering in the New Year without an incoherent rendition of *Auld Lang Syne* seemed very strange.

After the seasonal good wishes came the dancing; the locals like nothing more than a good dance. To my ear, none of the melodies appeared to have been penned in this century so Dad and Claire were in their element. Waltzing, Fox Trotting and whatever other body-hugging, fancy-stepping movements they could think of. Melanie and I sat quietly at the table watching this group of ageing pensioners thrashing around on the dance-floor, swapping partners whenever it took their fancy and generally running amok – they loved it.

By three o'clock, the festivities were drawing to a close. People had been quietly drifting away for the last hour or so; even Dad and Claire were starting to feel the pace. We said goodbye to the remaining die-hards, settled the bill, and wandered off towards the house. Claire was still buzzing with excitement, dancing up the road and recounting the evening's events.

'This is the best New Year's Eve ever,' she declared. 'I think he wants to marry me,' she added jokingly.

'Who wants to marry you?' asked Dad.

'That nice man with the yellow waistcoat: the one who asked me to dance. I bet he's got a big house, and lots of land, with sheep and cattle.'

'Well if he gives me two sheep and a donkey, he can have you,' joked Dad.

A night of drinking and dancing had put us all in a good mood. We laughed our way home, dreaming up ever more outrageous dowries for the promise of Claire's hand.

By lunchtime the following day we'd all surfaced. Unsurprisingly, we were feeling a little worse for wear: a small price to pay for such an excellent evening.

Their 10 days with us passed regrettably quickly. We filled the days with sightseeing. Our repertoire of tourist destinations ranged from a trip to the coastal town of Baiona, to a long drive into the mountains and the medieval castle at Castro Caldelas. We even took them down to our building site, trying desperately to put a positive spin on the progress. Most evenings were spent laughing and joking over games of Scrabble, fuelled by copious amounts of red wine. The only disappointment during their stay was the eve of *El dia de los Reyes* (Three Kings Day) on the 5th of January.

For Spanish people, this is the day when children receive their Christmas gifts, brought to them by the Three Kings from the East: Better known to us as The Three Wise Men. I can't understand why this idea hasn't caught on globally. It's a far more plausible fairytale than the one about some fat bloke from the North Pole, dressed in red, tumbling down chimneys with a sackful of presents: and travelling around the world on an aerial sled pulled by a herd of flying reindeer.

A few years ago, Melanie and I were fortunate enough to be staying on the island of Lanzarote for this important religious festival. Arriving back in England we recounted wondrous tales of a magical procession through the streets of Arrecife, the island's capital. Imperially dressed kings mounted high atop native camels, bounced through the town. Colourfully themed floats carrying traditionally dressed children followed them. The kids hurled handfuls of candies into the excited crowds that lined the route. Accompanying the parade were energetic marching bands, blasting-out Latino rhythms and upbeat tunes of African origin.

The scene in Monforte was a complete contrast. The Kings arrived from the west, not the east as tradition suggests, on the 19:45 train from Ourense. The four of us had waited on the icy-cold, windswept station platform for over half an hour. By the time the train arrived the crowd had swollen to almost fifty. This small crowd, of mainly excited children, managed a muted cheer as the train squealed to a halt. No noble camels for these kings, just a few bales of straw on the bed of a farm trailer hitched to a rusting 1950s Massey Ferguson tractor. Rather than follow this pitiful procession into the town we decided to head off home and thaw out.

Driving them back to the airport was tinged with sadness. Their visit was just the tonic we needed. Unwittingly, Dad and Claire had woken us from our depressing nightmare and given us renewed impetus to realise our dream.

21

What's the Balance?

As a result of the demise of the Rover, the costs of hiring the VW were escalating on a daily basis. We decided to call and see Ricardo at the Renault dealership: hopefully he could give us an update on the Megane's delivery date.

Through the glass-fronted showroom we could see Ricardo sitting at his desk. We walked across the car park, pushed open the glass door and entered. As we did, Ricardo looked up.

'I'm glad you've called in,' he shouted from behind his sales desk. 'I've got some good news about the car.'

Excitedly, we marched across the highly-polished, marble floor towards him. As we approached he hurriedly flicked through a pile of papers perched precariously on the edge of his desk.

'Yes, here we are,' with a broad smile he gleefully waved a computer printout high above his head. 'Look,' he said enthusiastically, 'it's the delivery date from the factory in Valencia.' pointing at the flimsy sheet he continued.

'This is the chassis number, and the colour, and here is the delivery date – anytime between the 7th and 14th of January.'

Great news: maybe those lucky grapes were already starting to work their magic.

'I'll ring you as soon as it's been delivered.'

With an official delivery date and the promise of a phone call we left, thrilled with the news. Surely an official factory printout must be accurate.

Patiently, we waited for his call, a call that never came. On the morning of the 15th we went back to the dealership, demanding to know what was going on.

'Ricardo, where's the car? You promised delivery last week,' without pausing I continued, 'The Rover's knackered and the rental car is costing us a fortune.'

I'd spent the previous evening referencing our Spanish dictionaries and rehearsing my lines. I was determined not to let him get a word in before I finished my well rehearsed prose.

Ricardo's response was pathetic. We knew it wasn't his fault. He was just selling the car, not building it. Trying to apportion blame was futile. All we wanted was the bloody car.

'Wait here a moment,' said Ricardo, trying his best to appease us, 'I'll contact the factory for a new delivery date.'

We took a seat as Ricardo scuttled off towards the main admin office. A few minutes later he returned, looking rather uncomfortable.

'The factory said that they should be able to deliver your car to us by the 22nd.'

We could tell from his demeanour, and the tone of his voice, that even he didn't believe that.

'Ricardo we've been renting a car for almost three

weeks and it's costing us a fortune. We only decided to rent it when you told us that the Megane would be here no later than the 14th.'

That wasn't strictly true, but it was costing us a fortune and we were desperate to take it back.

'Just wait another moment,' he said, before rushing back to the main office.

Melanie and I waited patiently, racking our brains to find a solution to our current predicament. Before long Ricardo returned.

'Good news!' he announced enthusiastically, 'My boss said that we can lend you a courtesy car until your new one is delivered.'

'Lend us a courtesy car?' I asked enquiringly

'Yes, we give you a car for free and you use it. All you have to do is put petrol in it.'

Thanks for the explanation Ricardo but I am familiar with the concept of a courtesy car.

My response was more in surprise than anything else. Officially, we weren't yet a customer but they were still prepared to lend us a car. Not that we were complaining, on the contrary, this was great news; a real result.

Without further ado, Ricardo whipped out the relevant paperwork and within a few minutes he'd completed the forms and I'd signed on the dotted line.

'Just follow me,' he said, handing me a copy and leaping to his feet.

The earlier disappointment over delivery dates was soon forgotten as we followed Ricardo towards the maintenance bays.

The maintenance area was much cleaner and tidier than I'd expected. To the left, mechanics were busy working on several vehicles. Some were leant over engine compartments and others knelt at open doors with their heads tucked awkwardly under the steering wheel. A couple of vehicles were held aloft on hydraulic lifts as mechanics worked underneath them. The only thing missing from this automotive scene was a courtesy car.

'Here you are,' announced Ricardo, with outstretched arms.

Although I'm familiar with the concept of offering clients a courtesy car, offering them a discourtesy car was a new one on me.

The dealership's idea of a courtesy car was a 15 year old Renault Laguna, in varying shades of matt white paint. The lustre had long since left this tired looking wreck. However, beggars can't be choosers and needs must. With a curious smirk, Ricardo handed me the keys. I couldn't work out whether he was pleased at securing us this questionable vehicle or simply taking the piss. Either way, it didn't really matter; as long as it ran we really didn't care.

Politely, I thanked him for the keys and wandered around to the driver's door. I lifted the handle and pulled. The whole door dropped about an inch and let out a long, agonising creak as I tugged it wide open. The interior reminded me of an old Ford I once owned. Lots of poorly-fitting, moulded plastic, worn to a glossy shine and curvaceously warped through years of exposure to bright sunlight. I put one foot inside, half expecting it to go through the floor, and slumped into the driver's seat. Whatever support it once provided had long since given up the ghost. It felt more like sitting on the springs of a burnt-out mattress than a supportive car seat. I pushed the key into the worn ignition and turned. To my surprise it started first time, and for an aged diesel engine sounded OK. I pulled the door shut with a double bump, once to crank it over the door sill and the other to slam it into the frame. I was ready for off.

Engaging the clutch felt like a workout at the gym. I wedged myself into the back of the seat and forced the heavy clutch pedal to the floor.

A few more weeks of this and my left leg is going to look like a tree trunk.

My next challenge was selecting a gear. The gear lever had so much play that trying to select one was like chasing a knob of melting butter around a saucepan with the wrong end of a wooden spoon. Eventually I found first and cautiously set off. Incredibly, the steering wheel had a full quarter turn of play before the front wheels moved – just like my old Ford. It was a bloody miracle I managed to get out of the dealership in one piece, never mind back home. In the meantime, Melanie had jumped in the VW and followed me back, oblivious to my motoring challenge. As she wouldn't be driving this death-trap, I decided to keep its short comings to myself.

The following day we were up early, keen to return the hire car as soon as the rental office opened. We'd already rented it for a week longer than expected, and every extra day was costing us. If we could return it as soon as the office opened, we would avoid an extra day's rental fee. Officially, I was the only person insured to drive either the rental or the discourtesy car. Rather than risk the 70 km round trip with both cars, we decided to get a taxi back home from Ourense.

'We'll have to get some money out of the bank before we go,' I said, as we readied to leave.

'We can call at the ATM in the village on the way,' suggested Melanie.

We drove around to the bank and Melanie withdrew the necessary funds.

'Did you get a receipt slip?' I asked.

'Yes, it's in my bag,' she said, as I pulled away and set off for Ourense.

'What's the balance?' I asked.

'Wait a minute.'

She fumbled around in her handbag looking for the elusive slip of paper.

'Here it is…' a short pause followed while she flattened out the creased receipt. 'There's 8,348 euros and 27 cents.'

'That's not right,' I snapped, knowing full-well that she'd misread it. 'It's the balance I'm after not the account number,' I added sarcastically.

'That is the balance,' she replied in an angry tone, '8,348 euros and 27 cents.'

I knew she was wrong, so it wasn't worth arguing over.

'Just leave it.,' I said, I'll have a look when we get to Ourense.'

Annoyed at my dismissive tone she pushed it back into her handbag. I knew for a fact that we had 10 times that in the account. In mid-November we had transferred sufficient funds to cover all the building costs and more besides. Unconcerned I continued on, heading down the valley and on to Ourense.

As luck would have it, a member of staff had just started to unlock the office door as we pulled into the Europcar car park. We rushed into the office, handed over the keys and settled the account, relieved at avoiding an extra day's rental charge.

The taxi rank at the far end of the car park was full of waiting cabs. We hopped into the back of the first one and instructed the driver.

'Ferreira de Panton.'

'Ferreira de Panton,' he replied quizzically.

Anyone would have thought that I'd asked him to take us to Timbuktu as opposed to half an hour up the road.

'Yes, Ferreira de Panton,' I thought it wise to confirm our destination.

'OK,' he said, 'but that's quite a long way. It will cost 30 euros,' he added.

'That's fine,' I replied.

I couldn't help thinking how reluctant he seemed to take the fare. When it came to work, I doubted that I would ever understand the Spanish mentality. What could be better for a driver than to take an hour-long, stress-free journey through spectacular countryside, along traffic-free roads, and at the end of it all, receive a fat fee for the privilege.

Before long we were through the busy city streets of Ourense and out on the open road.

'Let's have a look at that ATM receipt now.'

In our rush to the office, I'd almost forgotten about Melanie's dodgy interpretation of the bank balance. She rifled through her bag and handed me the slip. I unfolded it carefully and stared at the printed figures. I couldn't believe my eyes.

'That's not right,' I whispered in disbelief.

'I told you,' said Melanie with a hint of satisfaction.

'But this can't be right.'

My stomach tightened and my heart raced. I felt a lump forming in the back of my throat and began feeling a little nauseous. My brain went into overdrive as I tried to make sense of this bizarre situation. Perhaps it's not our account, perhaps this slip is from the previous customer and our slip pushed this one out of the ATM. There had to be an explanation.

'Have you got the bankbook in your handbag?' I asked nervously.

'I think so,' said Melanie, with an air of concern in her voice.

She delved back into her handbag and pulled out the bankbook.

'Here it is,' she said.

I snatched it impulsively, anxious to prove my implausible theory correct.

'Here, look,' I held the bankbook out and pointed at the balance, 'more than eighty thousand euros not *eight*.'

We hadn't updated the book for nearly a month but I was sure that we hadn't had any major expenses since then, certainly nothing over seventy thousand euros.

'There haven't been any major expenses since we last updated the book, have there?'

Melanie racked her brains for a moment before answering.

'No, definitely not, that receipt *must* be wrong.'

Quickly, I flicked to the front of the book to check the account number against that printed on the receipt. They were the same, identical. My out-of-the-box theory had fallen at the first hurdle.

'It must be a mistake, it must be.'

Tabloid headlines, of fraud in foreign climes, flashed through my mind.

'It must be a mistake,' I repeated in disbelief.

All I could think to do was go back to the bank in Ferreira and get the bankbook updated. That would settle the matter once and for all.

Thankfully, our reluctant taxi driver wasn't hanging around; before long we were exiting the slip road in Ferreira.

'Where do you want dropping?' enquired the driver.

'Outside the bank on the main street,' I replied tensely.

Within seconds we were parked outside the bank. I gave the driver the exact fare. Unfortunately for him, our missing funds dictated my lack of generosity. I pressed the entrance switch to gain access to the bank and waited impatiently for the release buzzer. We could see through the glass-panelled door that a wait was imminent.

Banking in Spain is tortuous. The service is deathly slow and many of the customers treat their banking business as a social experience. The couple in front of us were a case in point. Melanie and I were on tenterhooks, suffering heart palpitations and nervous convulsions. The elderly couple in front were laughing and joking with the bank manager about vegetable growing and pest control – For Gods sake hurry-up!

Eventually the elderly couple concluded their business and turned to leave. Before they had reached the door, we were standing at the counter facing the manager. I smiled nervously and slid the bankbook towards him.

'Will you update this please?' I asked politely.

He smiled back at us, oblivious of our mounting tension, and lifted the book off the counter. He opened it at the last entry and, face down, fed it into a desktop printer. The printer sucked the book into the heart of the machine, holding it firmly as the printer-head slid back and forth before finally spitting it back out. The manager pulled it from the printer, closed it and slid it carefully back across the counter. Hurriedly, I snatched the book up and opened it at the newly printed page. I scanned it carefully, looking for any anomalies. One entry stood out like a sore thumb: a withdrawal for exactly seventy thousand euros.

'What's this?' I asked, pointing at the relevant entry and sliding the book back to him.

Studiously, he stared at the transaction and grinned insightfully.

'Do you have another account?' he asked.

His assured tone gave me the impression that he knew the answer before he'd asked.

'No,' I said forcefully.

That certainly wiped the smirk off his face but did nothing to calm my nerves. Once again he picked the book up and stared at the pages, flicking back and forth through the entries, desperately seeking an answer. With nothing jumping off the page at him, he rested the book back on the counter and began tapping away on his computer keyboard.

The wait was agonising. If he couldn't find the answer in the bankbook, what good would the computer be? Suddenly the smile returned to his face.

'Yes you do have another account.'

His insistence that we had another account was starting to become annoying. I felt like leaping over the counter and punching him in the face.

'No we don't, this is the only account we have,' I replied, doing my best to remain calm.

'Yes, this was the only account you had but it doesn't pay any interest.'

What on earth is he bleating on about?

Convinced that the language barrier had once again defeated me I turned to Melanie, looking for inspiration.

Noting my dejected frustration the manager continued. 'The main branch in Monforte, has opened another account for you.'

'Another account?' I asked enquiringly.

'Yes, another account. One that pays interest,' he said.

Spontaneous laughter filled the room as his explanation sank in. It was a combination of released nervous energy and relief.

Quickly, he pulled a new bankbook from a drawer in his desk, folded it open and inserted it into the printer. A few seconds later he slid the open book across the counter.

'Look! Seventy thousand euros,' he said gleefully.

I stared down at the open book and smiled, the missing money had returned. Printed in fresh black ink was the number seven followed by five lovely zeros. I looked back at the manager and grinned.

'You thought that I had taken the money,' remarked the bank manager jokingly.

We could both see the funny side of things now, but if truth be known he's damn right I did.

22

A Pleasant Surprise

Since their festive break, Pepe and his brothers had returned to work with renewed vigour and enthusiasm. The weather had been relatively kind: icy-cold but for the most part dry. By mid-January they'd completed the new roof: row upon row of brand new terracotta tiles. It looked out of place atop the old, white-washed walls of the original house and the bare red-bricked extensions on both sides. By the end of the month all the external and internal walls were complete, and both the plumber and the electrician had started work. Felipe had managed to secure improved quotes from both of these important subcontractors, so the overall budget was looking pretty healthy as well. Even the swimming pool had finally sunk back into the ground.

Unfortunately, it hadn't settled back level. Felipe was determined to resolve this problem once and for all and summoned Mariano back to the house for crisis talks. It turned out that Felipe had a plan, a very ingenious plan. It combined scientific theories with modern construction methods to harness the forces of nature and get them working for us, rather than against.

The primary problem was rainwater seeping through the surrounding earth and accumulating under the pool. This created strong hydraulic pressure which had lifted it out of the ground. In order to divert the water and relieve the pressure, Felipe proposed digging a drainage trench. This would be deeper than the pool, encircle it completely, and extend to a well at the far end of the garden. The trench would be lined with a waterproof membrane and packed to a depth of half a metre with hardcore.

In theory, the water would follow the path of least resistance: Through the hardcore and into the well. Hindered only by gravity, it would rise in the well rather than raise a heavy concrete swimming pool. To make doubly sure that it would never rise again, a concrete step would be cast along the outside edge of the base of the pool. Once the trench was backfilled, this step would provide an anchor to prevent it from sliding upward.

I was very impressed by Felipe's ingenuity and lateral thinking, and so was Mariano. I had no idea if it would work or not, but it sounded brilliant. The only flaw in this ingenious plan was the lack of access to the back garden. Now the new extension was built, the gap between the house and the boundary wall was only six foot: far too narrow for an excavator to drive through.

How would they get the digger into the back garden to excavate the trench? Surely they weren't thinking of digging it by hand.

The solution was simple: without further discussions, or anyone's permission, the excavator ploughed through the neighbour's field, smashed through three sections of the boundary wall and began work in earnest. Felipe remained on site to oversee his ingenious plan.

With the pool secured, Mariano and his team could set about levelling it. They would raise the sides of the pool and level the floor with a new skim of concrete.

We were relieved to know that the problem had finally been remedied and any repetition was virtually impossible. It provided us with an emotional lift, coming days before our second trip back to England.

On the 13th of February, Melanie's granny would be 90 years old. Missing this milestone was unthinkable.

'Will you take a video of the house so that I can show granny?' asked Melanie.

'Are you sure?' I replied, 'I know things have moved on a bit but it still looks pretty grim,' I added.

'Oh please,' pleaded Melanie, 'I want to show her how it's going.'

'OK, but I'm not sure it's such a good idea.'

On this return trip to England, we decided to split the long drive into two equal parts. We reserved a hotel room in Saintes, France: a mere 1000 km from Ferreira. We were hoping that the new car would be delivered before we set off, but it wasn't. At least the dealership was happy to let us drive the discourtesy car all that way. Arriving back in England driving a knackered old Renault Laguna, was not the return we were hoping for. At least the 5000 km round trip would be done in someone else's car.

Unsure how long it would take us to drive to Saintes we made an early start. We left Ferreira at 7:00 a.m.; it felt like the middle of the night as we trundled through the abandoned streets. A thick frost sparkled in the headlights like a carpet of tiny diamonds. Within a couple of hours, daybreak had brightened the night sky revealing an icy, sugar-coated landscape. This coincided with our climb into the mountains.

Without warning, a fine drizzle began falling on the windscreen. Within seconds it had turned to rain, then sleet and moments later into thumbnail sized snowflakes. The higher we drove the thicker it became. Before long the carriageway was covered with a fresh white carpet of snow. Initial excitement quickly turned to concern.

Just as we were starting to worry, a series of flashing amber lights appeared up ahead, piercing through the heavy snowfall. The closer we came to them, the clearer the road became. A freshly ploughed track signalled our approach to a convoy of four snowploughs. We were relieved to reach the summit and begin our descent. As quickly as it had started the snow stopped. Before long the clouds lifted, revealing bright, wintry sunshine.

By lunchtime we were approaching the Pyrenees. The road meandered its way through lush, green valleys of pine forests and pastures. Spectacular, snow-capped mountains rose dramatically from the valleys and glistened in the midday sun. We crossed the French border at Biarritz. After a quick lunch break we continued north, and on to Bordeaux. After 10 hours of driving, through dramatic and beautiful countryside, we reached our overnight destination: the French market town of Saintes.

An enjoyable meal and a good night's sleep left us refreshed and ready for another day's drive. By late afternoon on the second day we were driving off the ferry in Dover and heading towards London. We spent a few days with my sister, before continuing on to Huddersfield.

Melanie's granny was in good spirits for her birthday. I couldn't help thinking how difficult it must be to celebrate reaching the grand old age of 90 when almost all the people you grew up with, including your husband, were no longer alive to enjoy it with you.

'Can you set the video up?' asked Melanie, as family members and friends gathered around the TV in the lounge of the nursing home.

I hadn't realised there would be such a large audience. The response to my cinematographic masterpiece was at best muted. I could understand why: Melanie and I were the only people who had seen the site at its worst, and the only ones to know how it would look in the future. No one else could see beyond the unfinished shell of a house, sat in the middle of a muddy field, and surrounded by a smashed and broken boundary wall. Even the swimming pool looked like an upturned concrete garage, buried in the middle of a boggy meadow. It didn't surprise me that most people stared silently at the screen, wide-eyed and dumbfounded. Melanie did her best to explain but one picture speaks a thousand words.

Before we knew it, the visit was over and we were once again saying goodbye. Melanie left England with a heavy heart. She was excited to be returning to Galicia but Granny wasn't getting any younger; one day soon her heartfelt farewell, would be her last.

The drive back to Ferreira passed without incident. We saw a smattering of snow around Burgos but nothing like we'd experienced travelling in the opposite direction. By late afternoon we had pulled off the main highway and were driving down through the village.

Excited by the prospect of further progress, we thought of driving straight to Canabal but my back was having none of it. The old Laguna had done us proud but the seats were incredibly uncomfortable. On the journey back I brought a couple of cushions with me but even they hadn't helped. By the time we were within striking distance of Ferreira, there was only one place I wanted to go, straight home for a well earned rest.

After being away for 19 days, just one message had been left on the telephone answering machine, but it was the one we'd been hoping for. Our three month wait had finally come to an end.

'Please leave a message after the tone,'...*Beep!*

'Hello. This is Ricardo, Ricardo from the Renault garage. Your car is here.'

After a very long and very uncomfortable drive, we couldn't have wished for better news. The message had been recorded earlier that day. It finished with Ricardo asking us to call into the dealership tomorrow. We were delighted; first thing in the morning we would call and see him. Visiting the house could wait until later in the day. There had been times when we thought that the car would never be delivered. Now it was here, we could hardly believe it.

The following morning we woke early, eager to meet Ricardo. All thoughts of an aching back, and stiff shoulders were quickly forgotten as we sped off to Monforte and on to the Renault dealership. No sooner had we entered the showroom than Ricardo came striding towards us, beaming from ear to ear.

'Hello! Good morning! How are you?' he seemed as happy to see us as we were to see him.

'Come this way,' he said, gesturing us towards the back of the showroom. 'Look, here it is: your new car.'

The car looked fantastic, not a mark or blemish anywhere. The deep-blue, pearlescent paint sparkled and glittered under the bright spotlights of the showroom ceiling.

'Come, sit inside,' urged Ricardo as he pulled open the door.

With the grace of a ballroom dancer, he skipped around the car and pulled open the passenger door.

'Come Melanie, sit inside.'

That unique, new-car smell filled my nostrils as I relaxed into the driver's seat. Everything was spotlessly clean, not a speck of dust anywhere.

'Here Craig, the key: start her up.'

Ricardo handed me the key and I duly obliged. I tapped the accelerator pedal a few times to hear the engine rev. All I wanted to do was drive it out of the showroom and hit the open road: no such luck.

'As soon as we've registered the car you can drive it away,' said Ricardo.

I couldn't believe it. Why they hadn't registered it before telling us was anyone's guess? One thing was certain: I wouldn't be driving off into the sunset this morning.

With our hopes so cruelly dashed, all we could do was wait – 101 days and counting. I'm sure I could have built the bloody thing quicker. Getting annoyed was pointless; shouting at Ricardo, or anyone else for that matter, wouldn't do a blind bit of good. I took a few deep breaths and calmly asked, 'How much longer do we have to wait?'

'Just a few more days,' said Ricardo, consolingly.

We'd waited this long, a few more days wouldn't make any difference. Ricardo promised to ring us as soon as they'd completed the registration. We were getting used to having our hopes raised, only to have them dashed.

We left the dealership and headed for Canabal. The morning had developed into quite a nice day. Grey-white clouds drifted above us, punctuated with patches of blue, and warm rays of sunlight. We turned off the main road and drove slowly past the church and up through the village. A burst of sunlight bathed the house as we neared. This angelic glow illuminated an unbelievable sight. In our wildest, and most optimistic, dreams we could not have imagined such staggering progress.

'Look at it!' said Melanie enthusiastically, 'I can't believe it. They've even repaired the driveway.'

For the first time since November, we were able to drive the car off the lane and into the driveway. The concrete drainage pipe, crushed by the giant cement mixer, had finally been replaced and topped with a new concrete pad. The rate of progress in just 19 days was unbelievable. From the driveway the house looked finished. The only thing missing was a fresh coat of white paint. All the shuttering had been removed and the new exterior walls rendered. The new double glazed windows, and French doors for the dining room, were all fitted and looked great. Without the shuttering, the three brickwork arches supporting the roof over the front covered terrace gave the house a real Mediterranean feel.

We leapt out of the car itching to see more. I pushed open the gates and we marched excitedly up to the front door. I thought it prudent to give a quick tap before pushing it open, just in case anyone was behind.

'Wow! Look at that.'

This time it was my turn to rave over the work. We'd chosen a very contemporary floor tile for the entrance hall. It has a very high-gloss sheen, almost like glass. After all, first impressions count and my first impression was – *WOW!*

We stepped across the threshold and peered into the lounge. All the internal doors were being replaced so these had long since been removed. Angel, Pepe's brother, was kneeling on the floor, laying tiles.

'Hola!' my bouncy tone mirrored my feelings.

He looked up and returned my greeting with a cheeky smile. Across the hallway, opposite the lounge, was the first of the three bedrooms. Here too the floor tiling was complete, finished off with matching skirting tiles. Then I noticed the bright-white, electrical switches mounted on the walls and the plug sockets above the skirting.

'Look Melanie,' I said, pointing at the new switches. 'It looks as if the electrician might have finished.'

We drifted through the bedroom, passed the dressing room and towards the en-suite bathroom. The bathroom was tiled floor to ceiling, and all the new furniture was fitted. We popped our heads around the door to see Pepe kneeling over the corner-bath, finishing off the intricate tiling around the arced edge.

'Hola,'

Pepe responded in his usual muted manner with a forced smile and nod of the head.

'You've been very busy since we left,' I said, expecting a response.

Trying to chat with Pepe was like having a tooth pulled – difficult and painful. We left him to his work and turned around to explore the rest of the house. Not even Pepe was going to dampen our enthusiasm.

The other two bedrooms and bathrooms were the same: all the walls plastered and the bathrooms tiled. Melanie and I could hardly contain our excitement. Everywhere we looked was exactly as we'd hoped it would be. We made our way back to the lounge and asked Angel if we could walk through.

'Keep to this side and try and stand in the centre of the tile,' he replied.

Carefully we tiptoed across the lounge, through the newly opened archway into the kitchen/diner. Without the kitchen units and dividing breakfast bar, the room looked huge. With French doors at one end and a glass-panelled door and kitchen window at the other, it felt light and airy. Here too the electrics were finished and the walls newly plastered. Even the false ceilings were finished and the plaster coving. The only thing left to do was tile the floors: pastel-blue in the kitchen and a rustic tile in the dining room. Melanie wandered over to what would soon be her new kitchen.

'Oh my God, look at this!' exclaimed Melanie, staring out of the kitchen window.

My heart sank. Surely the pool hadn't risen again. I rushed across to the window and peered out.

The last time we'd seen the swimming pool it looked like an enormous concrete bath, surrounded by a sea of claggy mud. The scene was so depressing we couldn't possibly have imagined how it might one day look. In the time it had taken us to drive to England and back, imagination was no longer necessary.

Stretched out before us, in the middle of the garden, was a brand new swimming pool. Greenie-blue tiles sparkled in the patchy sunlight. They looked like tiny square emeralds, held together with a criss-cross pattern of virgin-white grout. After months of catastrophic problems, and agonising delays, we finally had our finished pool: an unimaginable sight that made the long wait worthwhile.

After a long, reflective pause, I managed a quiet response. 'It looks fantastic.'

We unlocked the kitchen door and hurried outside for a closer look. We scarcely noticed the rest of the muddy garden. Our eyes were trained on this beautiful sight. We stood for a while staring in awe.

Melanie was the first to speak. 'It looks great, really great.'

'Yes,' I said. 'All we need now is some water.'

The irony of my statement made us both laugh. For months we'd been cursing the constant deluge of rainwater, and now we actually needed some, the weather had improved. We were in excellent spirits as we drove back to Ferreira. For the first time in five months, the end was in sight, the new car had arrived, the house was nearing completion, and even the weather was improving.

23

Farming Hierarchy

Telephonophobia: I wonder if such a thing really exists. The sound of the phone ringing sent a nervous shockwave rippling through my entire body.

'Melanie,' I shouted from the kitchen, 'that'll be for you.'

The thought of answering the phone still chilled me to the bone.

'Hola,' said Melanie as she picked up the receiver.

I crept quietly to the kitchen doorway to eavesdrop.

'Hola Ricardo, this is Melanie.'

At last the car is ready to pick up, I thought to myself.

'I see.'

That didn't sound very encouraging.

'OK, thanks for ringing. Bye.'

Unable to restrain my curiosity, I stepped into the hall, 'Is the car ready to pick up?' I asked.

'No,' replied Melanie.

Ricardo had rung to tell us that due to yet another

fiesta, the *Trafico* department in Lugo was closed. Until it reopened, they wouldn't be able to register the car.

On this occasion the fiesta was Carnival: a national holiday adopted by most Hispanic countries. It's better known to us as Ash Wednesday and always falls 40 days before Easter.

'He could have told us that the other day,' I said disappointedly.

At least we still had the discourtesy car to run around in and having seen the new Megane, we knew it wouldn't be long before we finally got our hands on it.

'I wonder if there's a Carnival procession in the village,' remarked Melanie, 'like the one we saw in Lanzarote,' she added.

'If the Three Kings procession is anything to go by, it certainly won't be like Lanzarote.' I replied sarcastically.

That afternoon we bumped into one of our neighbours and asked. It turned out that there were two Carnival processions. The main one was in Monforte, on Tuesday the 11th and a smaller one through the village this Sunday.

Drawing back the curtains on Sunday morning revealed a damp and dreary start to the day. Rather disappointing given that the weather had improved significantly over the last few days. However, the day's activities weren't scheduled to begin until noon. Hopefully it might improve by then.

No such luck, by lunchtime the conditions were even worse. We wrapped up warm, pulled on our raincoats and wandered along the street to the junction with Ferreira high street. I'd taken a brolly to provide a bit of protection from the rain but fearing the wind would whip it inside-out, I rolled it up and tapped it along the pavement like Charlie Chaplin. Undeterred by the blustery conditions, a number of villagers had gathered along the route. They were huddled together in small groups, no doubt indulging in their favourite pastime: moaning about the weather.

Before long the distant sound of music faded in and out on the strengthening wind. With each passing minute the tune became louder until we finally caught sight of the village orchestra.

The band was made up of a strange assortment of players. There were all shapes and sizes: ranging in age from ten years through to those in their seventies. A smart uniform failed to hide their comical appearance. I would like to think that the weather conditions played a part in the band's apparent lack of musical ability but perhaps I'm being too kind. Regardless of their limited talent, siblings, parents, and grandparents were thrilled to see these young musicians at the head of the Carnival procession.

Following the orchestra were a rag-tag group of children accompanied by their parents. Most were dressed in colourful, if somewhat damp, home-made costumes: an eclectic mix of designs: from a delicate fairy to a windswept Spanish galleon. Flitting in and out of the bedraggled troop were more sinister figures, witches and crows, clad head to toe in black. They rushed at watching bystanders and dragged them into the street to dance.

Without warning, a blackened crow dashed out of the crowd, grabbed Melanie and tugged at her arm. She responded with a frightened shriek and pleaded for her freedom while clinging tightly to my arm. Sensitive to her sheer terror, he released her arm and moved on to a more willing participant. Melanie quickly recovered, releasing most of her startled fear with nervous laughter. As the music faded into the distance and the last remnants of the rain sodden procession disappeared down the high street, Melanie and I headed for home, smiling at the comical events. If nothing else, the villagers enthusiasm to have a good time had certainly brightened up what had been a thoroughly miserable day; and whet our appetite for the main event in Monforte.

The weather over the next few days was excellent, clear blue skies and bright sunshine. Sunset brought a nip to the air but during the day the temperatures were definitely T-shirt weather.

The main Carnival event in Monforte was a procession through the town, scheduled for six in the evening. The route of the procession followed the river Cabe through the town and finished with everyone congregating in the main square in front of the Jesuit College. Eager to find a parking space close to the college, we set off in good time. Not good enough however.

The sunny weather had brought the residents of Monforte, and the surrounding villages, out in force. Eventually, we found a parking space and made our way along the busy streets towards the college. The whole town was buzzing with excitement. Young and old alike were revelling in the party atmosphere. Many wore colourful costumes, some were shop-bought but most had been painstakingly created using any number of different materials.

'Hola! How are you?'

We'd been approached by a smartly dressed man wearing a warm looking overcoat. We could tell from his greeting that we'd met before but both Melanie and I stood there dumbfounded, racking our brains for a name, a place, or an encounter, anything that would trigger our grey-matter into recalling this mystery friend. My mind went blank and Melanie was no help at all. Having stared at him for what felt like an eternity, I felt obliged to reply.

'Hello. I'm fine. How are you?' My blank facial expression, and nervous reply, gave the game away.

'You don't recognise me, do you?'

'I'm sorry, but no.'

'I'm the manager from the Regina Viarum winery in Doade.'

Like switching the light on in a pitch-black room, my brain burst into life. 'Ah yes, of course.'

The three of us let out a short, nervous chuckle in response to our belated recognition.

'Anyway I must go, my wife is waiting for me,' he turned to walk away, 'enjoy the Carnival,' he added as he waved goodbye.

The bars and cafes on the approaches to the college were doing a roaring trade. The smell of strong black coffee, and cigarette smoke, hung in the air. The crowds were already building as we neared our destination. Roadside standing room was at a premium. Spotting a narrow gap in the crowd, we manoeuvred our way to the edge of the kerb and waited patiently. As the sun disappeared over the rooftops of nearby apartments, a slight chill shivered through the expectant crowd.

The cold was soon forgotten as the distant melody of a marching band drifted through the busy streets. We leaned forward and peered down the road. Bright blue lights bounced off windows and reflected in shop fronts as a police car crept its way towards us. Following close behind was an orchestral band booming out Latino-influenced, marching rhythms. A flotilla of four-wheel drive vehicles, hauling colourful floats followed. Every float represented hours of hard work by school children, youth groups, and sporting clubs; each one was individually distinctive.

Their creators wore equally colourful attire and sat proudly riding on their unusual creations. Interspersed with this hotchpotch assembly of mobile art were dancing troops and musical groups with an international flavour – International on the proviso that they were from a Spanish speaking nation.

As the final float passed, the assembled roadside crowd joined the back of the parade. By the time this heaving throng reached our station, it was 50 metres long and occupied the whole road. We waited patiently and tagged on to the back of the carnival followers. I spotted Pepe and his wife Emily, waiting further up the road to join the crowds. I looked across and caught his eye. Unusually for him, he managed to squeeze out a smile followed by his customary nod; Emily smiled back and waved.

By the time we reached the square in front of the college, the dozen or so floats were parked in a line stretching its length. From a small, central platform, the mayor of Monforte announced category winners. These ranged from float design to costume colours, seemingly everyone was a winner. The final prize went to the best overall float and was greeted with an almighty cheer from the massed crowds.

The evening had taught us that Carnival is not an event to stand and enjoy but a celebration to embrace and get involved in. As if to highlight this fact, we spotted Pepe's 15 year old son making his way through the crowd with half a dozen of his mates. They were immaculately dressed: shoulder-length, blonde locks flowed from underneath a red hooded cloak. The theme of their float was the children's story, *Little Red Riding Hood*. Their evening of fun was just beginning, but the announcement of the overall champion was our cue to head home.

By the end of the week, Ricardo had rung again, this time with excellent news.

'The car is registered. You can collect it whenever you want.'

Exactly 110 days after we placed the order, we were finally going to take delivery of our new car.

'We'll be there within the hour,' replied Melanie.

At long last the car was ready to collect. We sped down to the dealership and delightedly took delivery of our gleaming new Megane.

'Are you sure that you don't want to keep the Laguna instead?' joked Ricardo.

'It's not such a bad car,' I said, trying to put a positive spin on the knackered, old wreck.

We couldn't wait to take our gleaming new car for a spin and headed straight off into the Galician countryside. The morning was bright, warm and sunny. By the time we'd driven 10 km, the long wait for our new carriage was resigned to history – nothing more than an amusing tale to recount over dinner with friends.

The good weather continued throughout March and progress at the house was swift. By the end of the month, most of the interior work was finished. Pepe was busy constructing a small outbuilding in the back garden, this would become the laundry room, outside toilet, and a garden storage shed.

The milder spring weather had brought an explosion of new life and colour in Elo's garden. The fruit trees had blossomed, one after the other, creating a magnificent display of nature's palette. The plum was the first to bloom with a sun-burst of pastel pink, next the cherry with a rich, purple-centred blossom, then the pear and peach and finally the virgin-white petals of the apple trees. Even the grapevines were bursting into life. In the front garden, hydrangea buds were fanning into leaf and the two large camellias, either side of the driveway, had begun to bloom: deep crimson on one side and creamy-white the other.

Throughout the area, trees were starting to leaf and winter's dormant bulbs were blooming. Thorny broom blanketed the countryside: its bright-yellow flowers shimmering in the breeze, reflecting the sunlight like a mythical golden fleece. Farmers too were hard at work, tilling the land and sowing their spring crops.

When it comes to working the land, there's a definite farming hierarchy. At the bottom of this perennial ladder is the farmer's wife. In this isolated backwater of Spain, it's often the women who do most of the work. Men have far more important duties to undertake, like tastefully appreciating the progress of their wine.

The next rung up on the ladder is the family donkey. It's not quite as multi-skilled as the former and certainly can't prepare lunch or dinner, but it's stronger, quicker, slightly less temperamental, and much easier to manage.

The heavy weights of this division are a team of oxen. They appear ponderous and docile but are incredibly powerful, ploughing through the land like a warm knife through butter. Keeping these beasts under control, and the furrows straight and parallel, requires a small compliment of workers and is often shared among neighbours.

These mighty beasts signal an end to livestock and the beginning of mechanisation, and what a beginning. Not even Leonardo da Vinci could have imagined the next magnificent machine on the hierarchical ladder. Its main component is a powerful diesel engine. It resembles a small refrigerator tipped on its side and mounted on two wheels: one on either side. The wheels are a similar size to those on a Mini Cooper but have a heavy tractor-like tread.

Extending out from the engine are chopper-style motorcycle handlebars. It's finished off with a flatbed trailer, reminiscent of those seen in old Westerns, coupled to the back. To start this unusual contraption, the farmer winds an old piece of rope, twice around a fly-wheel, and gives an almighty tug.

If he's lucky, the beast fires into life with a cough, a growl and a puff of thick black smoke. With the necessary equipment loaded, the farmer hops on the trailer, engages a gear, and with a jerk and a bump, trundles off to his field. Upon arrival, this ingenious invention comes into its own. The trailer is uncoupled. Out comes a wheel-brace, and off come the wheels. With the assistance of a lump hammer, the wheel axle is knocked through the engine block. Once removed, a whole host of farming implements can be attached, depending on the job in hand.

After this mechanised marvel, things become a bit more sophisticated with the introduction of the miniature tractor. Although it appears toy-like, this is a serious piece of cultivating equipment. It has a proper seat, steering wheel, familiar foot operated pedals for the engine, and hand operated levers for the assorted attachments.

Fractionally ahead of these in the pecking order, are older, full-sized tractors. None of which, would look out of place in a farming museum. The area is littered with museum pieces, still in daily use.

At the pinnacle of this cultivating hierarchy is the latest model John Deere, a true thoroughbred in modern tractor manufacturing and a rare sight indeed.

For all man's ingenuity, the results remain the same, a ploughed field ready for planting.

24

One More Day

With the benefit of improved weather, days merged into weeks and before we knew it March had drifted into April. Our new home in the village of Canabal falls under the administrative centre of Sober council. For the village of Sober, Easter is the most important time in the calendar year. Every year, on the weekend of Palm Sunday, Sober hosts its annual wine fiesta. This major event involves organisation, logistics and management: Three skills not normally associated with the mañana, mañana approach to life in Spain.

When we first heard of the event, we thought someone was having a joke at our expense. How on earth can a wine fiesta be held in a place called sober? Even now, the mere thought of it brings a smile to my face.

Sober is nestled in the heart of the Ribeira Sacra, a small and little known *denominacion de origin* (a wine and food quality standard for a specific geographical area). The most prestigious grape growing area within the Ribeira

Sacra is the *Zona* Amandi. By chance, this area falls within the council boundary of Sober.

The start of the fiesta is heralded by ear-shattering explosions. They were so loud that we could hear them in the garden at Elo's, 8 km away. We had agreed to go to the fiesta at dusk with some friends. They had agreed to drive, in exchange for a bed for the night.

On a normal evening the road to Sober is very quiet, this weekend is the exception. The closer we got to the village, the busier the road became. Cars jostled for roadside parking places and small groups of people weaved in and out of the traffic on their way to the main square.

'There! There's a space,' I blurted, as we approached a small gap in the parked cars.

A few minutes later we'd managed to squeeze in. We climbed out of the car and made our way to the village square. Unlike the wine fiesta in Ferreira, this is a much bigger event. The main square was packed with partygoers and onlookers, all sampling the liquid delights of the region's vines. About 20 booths occupied three sides of the square. Each one housed a different local wine producer, promoting their wines by offering visitors a free taste. On the fourth side of the square, directly in front of the town hall, a temporary stage had been erected: complete with lighting and a serious looking sound system.

The roads leading off the main square were packed with stall holders selling anything from angle-grinders to commemorative personalised earthenware pots. For the youngsters, there were small fairground rides and the compulsory *camas elasticas*. We wandered around, feasting on the sounds and smells, soaking up the atmosphere. Occasionally we would pause at a stall and marvel at the diverse variety of goods and services on offer.

Browsing market stalls is one thing but after half an

hour or so I was keen to get involved in the main event – wine tasting.

'I think it's about time we had a taste. Don't you?' I asked, confident of a positive response.

'That sounds like a good idea,' replied Melanie quickly.

The village square was packed with partygoers and the area immediately in front of each booth was a heaving mass of bodies, all jostling to get served. Most people were sipping from white plastic cups supplied by the wineries. I mingled with the crowd, waiting for an opening at one of the booths. The phrase *puedo probar* (can I try) was bouncing around in my head. Suddenly a gap appeared at the counter in front of me. Without hesitation I darted into the space – here we go.

'*Hola. Puedo probar?*' at least I'd remembered that.

A tall, young man was standing behind the counter holding a bottle of red wine. I felt a bit cheeky, demanding a drink without so much as a please or thank you, but this is the Spanish way and he was happy to oblige.

'*Para cuatro*' (for four) I added quickly.

My newly found linguistic confidence was working well. I handed two cups to Melanie and prised myself free of the thirsty crowd, clutching the other two cups for dear life. We jostled our way to the middle of the square where there was a bit more room.

'Cheers,' I declared, raising my cup in the air.

A good, oak-aged *Mencia* has a very distinctive taste and can be a deliciously refreshing drink. Unfortunately, all the offerings here were very young and not a patch on their older namesakes. Not that we were complaining.

Hanging above each booth was a personalised sign sporting the name of the *bodega*. Over the heads of the crowd, I spotted a familiar name – Adega Algueira. We drank up and headed towards it. As we approached I could see the owner Fernando, busy serving customers. I squeezed my way to the front of the crowd and leant against the counter.

'*Hola, que tal* (Hello, how are you)?' said Fernando, with a cheerful smile.

'I'm very well, how are you?'

Fernando answered with a flurry of prose most of which were lost in the melee, but ended with a question, 'Would you like a taste?'

'Yes please,' I replied.

He pulled a clean cup from a stack at the end of the counter.

'There are four of us,' I added quickly.

Fernando smiled and poured four measures, stopping only when the cups were full. We thanked him for his generosity and moved away to give others a chance to be served. As the night wore on the fiesta became much livelier.

Earlier in the evening, the main stage opposite the booths was the venue for a local potter to demonstrate his skill at the potter's wheel. With the setting sun it became a far more energetic focal point, as an accomplished pop group hammered out their version of the latest hits.

It felt great to be able to soak up the atmosphere, taste the wine, and enjoy the evening's entertainment, in a safe and trouble-free environment. The party was still in full swing when we left, but for us, sundown to sunrise parties are a thing of the past. Twenty years ago we might have been tempted to stick around but not tonight.

Our visits to Canabal became less frequent as the work neared completion. Pepe was convinced that both inside and out would be finished by the end of the month. We were so confident of moving in that we told Elo of our impending departure. She seemed quite sad by the news.

The only stumbling block was the kitchen, or to be more precise the lack of one. We had ordered it back in December but still had seen neither sight nor sound of Jose the kitchen fitter. We weren't overly concerned; he'd agreed to pay our rent if we had to stay at Elo's beyond the end of April. We were confident that this financial penalty would focus his mind and get the job finished on time. We should have known better.

By the end of April, Pepe and his brothers had finished all the inside work as promised. Unfortunately, the work outside the house was taking much longer than they'd expected. That didn't really matter to us: the outside work didn't hinder our plans to move in. Jose managed to do that all on his own. We were sure he wouldn't let us down, particularly given the financial penalties, but once again we hadn't counted on Spanish working practices. We decided to pop down to his showroom and find out what was going on.

Jose had started work on another kitchen for a client who'd been waiting even longer than us. Once he started a job, he wouldn't break off until he had finished. In some small way his attitude reassured us that once he started on ours, nothing would stop him.

'So how soon can you start?' asked Melanie, determined to get a date from him.

'I'll be finished in two weeks and then I'll start on yours straight away,' he replied.

'*Two weeks,*' I exclaimed.

'It could be a little sooner,' he added sheepishly.

We were disappointed, and annoyed, but that didn't change anything.

As things turned out, he finished the other job earlier

than planned and started ours straight after. He felt confident of finishing by the following Friday. With this in mind we set our sights on moving in on the 17th of May. What better birthday present for Melanie than moving into our dream home.

The week leading up to the 17th was hectic. To start with we had two houses to clean. Although everything was brand new at Canabal, dust from the building work meant that the entire house needed scrubbing from top to bottom. As for Elo's, she had trusted us with her marital home without even asking for a security deposit. We were determined to repay that trust by leaving the place as clean and tidy as we'd found it.

Logistics were another major headache. Having made two return trips to England and spent twelve months shopping in Spain, we'd managed to accumulate a mountain of household belongings. Although Canabal is only 8 km from Ferreira, the last thing we wanted was any breakages. All the smaller items were carefully packed into cases. The bulkier ones proved far more tiresome to move: trip after trip with nothing more than a few garden chairs and the odd sunlounger. In between times, we'd arranged to take delivery of a few essential pieces of furniture, a new bed and mattress, and the three piece suite.

After an incredibly busy final day we were both shattered. We'd been up since dawn, ferrying back and forth from Ferreira to Canabal with all our worldly belongings. By the time we'd finished the setting sun was sinking over the distant horizon.

'Let's just go back to Ferreira, get washed and changed and go out for a meal,' said Melanie, as we dumped the last of the packing cases into the back bedroom. 'The bed is still to make up and I've no idea where the clean sheets are,' she added, staring at a mountain of packaging boxes.

'Are you sure?' I asked.

'I'm sure,' she said. 'Anyway, if we don't go now it's going to be too late to go out and we'll both be too tired. Another day isn't going to make any difference,' she added.

It hadn't been much of a birthday for Melanie, toing and froing from Ferreira to Canabal and lugging heavy boxes around; but she was right. I was slightly disappointed that we wouldn't be sleeping in our new home tonight, but Melanie was right: one more day wouldn't make any difference.

THE ~~END~~ *Beginning*

Epilogue

After a good night's sleep we bid farewell to Casa de Elo, and headed for our new home in Canabal: a short drive at the end of a long journey.

On the 18th of May 2003 I turned the key in the lock, pushed open the door, and stepped across the threshold. For the first time since leaving England, I felt at home: comfortable in my new surroundings but perhaps more importantly, comfortable with my adopted country.

By the end of May, Pepe and his brothers had finished the outside work and left us in peace. Melanie and I laboured long and hard in the gardens; as usual, Jazz settled in immediately: wherever we lay our hat, that's her home.

My writing apprenticeship began the following year. Out of the blue, Peter Hinchliffe, former editor of our hometown newspaper *The Huddersfield Examiner*, contacted us. Although retired, he kept his hand in by writing freelance articles and wanted to write an expat piece about our move to Spain; we agreed. During his questioning I happened to mention that I wrote a newsletter: roughly scribbled emails keeping family and friends informed of our progress (or lack of it). Peter asked if I would consider writing for his new online magazine Open Writing. Initially I declined; there were far too many matters that needed my undivided attention. Besides which, keeping family and friends updated is one thing; writing for public viewing is a different matter entirely. After Pepe's departure, I decided to give it a go; it sounded fun, and challenging.

For the next four years I wrote a regular weekly column for Open Writing, and loved every minute of it. My early efforts, under the heading *Spanish Secrets*, were terrible; but I'd caught the bug.

As well as writing, 2004 saw my first attempt at wine making: the elixir of life. Unfortunately, my effort tasted more like the elixir of death. I soon rectified this problem with the acquisition of a pot-bellied still. We might not be able to drink the wine but converting it into Galician moonshine, *aguardiente*, gave us an endless supply of the dreadful stuff.

The plan to buy a second home and rent it out to tourists had been temporarily shelved. Having spoken with Elo about the matter, we began to question the scheme's financial credibility. She had told us that we were only the second guests ever to stay at her house. The first being three nuns who had chosen to visit the monastery in Ferreira for their holiday: rather like a busman's holiday, but for nuns. Elo had been advertising her house with Brittany Ferries for the past five years: three weeks rental income in five years didn't sound like a viable proposition.

However; during the search for our home, we had discovered a potential gap in the local property market. Throughout all our viewings, we had not seen anywhere in the ten to twelve million pesetas price range that could be consider habitable. If we could find a house at a reasonable price, needing only DIY renovation, we could fix it up and sell it on: buy it cheap and sell it cheap. It sounded like a great idea, so the search began. Eventually, we found a house that fitted the bill. We did the work and found a buyer: purchase to sale in eight months.

That winter we holidayed in Lanzarote. Melanie and I flew economy class and Jazz travelled in the hold: baggage class. Her arrival, on the luggage carousel at Arrecife airport, was greeted with a crescendo of *ahhh* from the massed holidaymakers waiting for their cases.

In between buying and selling the second house, an English neighbour (by neighbour I mean a house across the valley, visible through my spotting scope) had tried his hand at property rental and enjoyed a modicum of success. This set us thinking. Perhaps our initial idea to buy a second property and rent it out to tourists wasn't such a bad idea after all. The arrival of a discount airline to the area convinced us that we should give it a go.

After a long and exhaustive search we found the perfect place: a ruined farmhouse with no water, no electricity and no access. The protracted sales process took 13 months, to the day, to complete. This time; however, we were better prepared for the challenges ahead and three years after we first clapped eyes on the place, the phoenix rose. Letting the house proved a great success and bookings far outstripped our expectations.

Life in Galicia is never dull. We entered a house swapping arrangement with an Australian family: exchanging a fortnight in Galcia for five weeks in Oz - great result! On our return we planted a small vineyard at the back of the house. My wine making skills hadn't improved, but it seemed like a good idea at the time.

Year-round, Galicia is beautiful and the changing seasons are a real delight; having said that, our extended trip to Australia had given us a taste for warmer winter weather. We decided to follow the sun and migrate south for the winter. Initially we tried a month in Mijas. The following year we spent three months in Nerja, and for the last two years the same length of time in Elviria: the coastal winter climate in the south of Spain is much kinder to my ageing joints.

In 2011 we adopted, albeit temporarily, another vineyard. The time had come to take viniculture more seriously. We invested in some equipment and most importantly a book, *From Vines to Wines* by Jeff Cox. For the first time in seven years I made wine worth drinking – thanks Jeff.

On the 5th September 2011, Jazz died. She'd been ill for quite a while. We needed to make the most difficult decision any pet owner can make. She had trusted us in life and trusted us in death. Rescued from a centre in Halifax, she'd enjoyed a wonderful life; she'd travelled throughout Europe, flown to Lanzarote, and spent the last 9 years basking in the Spanish sunshine. Carrying her from the back patio to her final resting place in the vineyard is one of the most difficult tasks I have ever undertaken. We vowed never to have another, the pain was too great.

That sentiment lasted four days. The house felt empty, there was nothing to walk around and nothing to step over; the place fell eerily quiet. I swear we both spoke more to the dog than we did to each other. Ten days later we made a new addition to the Briggs family – Slawit.

Like Jazz, Slawit was *abandonado* (abandoned). The similarity ends there. Unbeknown to us, Slawit is a pure bred Podenco Galego. Thought to have been introduced to Spain by the ancient Egyptians, they are bred to hunt rabbits. True to her breeding, she loves nothing more than running off into the scrub in search of her prey. Unfortunately, two years down the line, she still hasn't quite got to grips with the command *COME!*

On the language learning front, Melanie streaked ahead: she chats with the neighbours like a local. I on the other hand have progressed at a rather more sedate pace, *poco y poco* (little by little) as we say here in Spain.

Not in our wildest dreams could we have imagined how rewarding our move to Galicia would be. This book has come to an end, but the story continues – so keep an eye out for the next instalment.

8298011R00192

Printed in Great Britain
by Amazon.co.uk, Ltd.,
Marston Gate.